With the first light of morning came the realization that there would be no emergency extraction because a thick fog covered the ground. Using natural cover, Jacques decided to move his men from their hiding spot in the banana grove in an attempt to find one of the trails they had discovered while patrolling. As they began to move, the NVA suddenly started firing. Jacques's men froze in place, only to discover that the enemy firing was not directed at them, but at the ARVN survivors. Knowing that the enemy still occupied the hilltop above them, Jacques changed the team's direction once again.

"We had moved about three thousand meters away from our hiding place when I finally thought that it was safe to rest. I had just put the team in a tight little 360-degree defense when I heard the sounds of the nearby brush starting to break. I thought to myself, 'This is it. I've done everything I can to get away, but the NVA won't give up. They're not going to take us alive.'"

Also by B. H. Norton
Published by Ivy Books:

FORCE RECON DIARY, 1969

FORCE RECON DIARY, 1970

B. H. Norton

IVY BOOKS • NEW YORK

Ivy Books
Published by Ballantine Books
Copyright © 1992 by B. H. Norton

Library of Congress Catalog Card Number: 91-92408

ISBN 0-8041-0806-4

Manufactured in the United States of America

First Edition: July 1992

ACKNOWLEDGMENTS

My sincere thanks to Mr. Owen A. Lock, Editor in Chief, Del Rey Books, who has always been a straight shooter since the day I started writing.

My special thanks and most grateful appreciation to Lt. Col. Alex Lee, USMC; Lt. Col. C. C. "Bucky" Coffman, USMC; Col. J. J. Holly, USMC; Col. "Chip" Gregson, USMC; Lt. Col. Don Scanlon, USMC; Capt. Mike Hodgins, USMC; Sgt. Maj. M. Jacques, USMC; 1st Sgt. Charles O. "Bud" Fowler III, USMC; Mr. James C. Holzmann; BUC Michael A. Hobbs, USN; and to Mr. Rick Jenkins, Mr. Donald J. Mahkewa, Mr. David Draper, Mr. Mike "The Big M" Wills, Mr. Paul Keaveney, Mr. Wallace J. "Nic" Murray, and Mr. Guillermo "Hi-ho" Silva.

To the memory of these Force Reconnaissance Company Marines: Capt. Norman B. Centers, 1st Lt. Steve Corbett, Gy. Sgt. V. R. Thornburg, S. Sgt. D. E. Ayers, Sgt. R. C. Phleger, Sgt. D. J. Wickander, Cpl. Allen M. Hutchinson, Cpl. Adam Cantu, L. Cpl. Daniel Savage, and L. Cpl. W. M. Clark. They are not forgotten.

To the corporals and sergeants of the United States Marine Corps.

DEDICATION

This book is dedicated to my father, Mr. George H. Norton and to the memory and spirit of my father-in-law, Mr. Steen Borell Goldey.

FOREWORD

Combat—like the fabled elephant described by the nine blind men—is a thing that cannot easily be described. Facing the enemy from an altitude of thirty-five thousand feet is combat, as is the serving of endless hours of flight-deck duty aboard a carrier on Yankee Station. Cannoneers see one kind of war and tankers another. The infantry experience in combat ranges from life in line units shared with hundreds, or even thousands of others, to that experienced by those few in 3d Force Reconnaissance Company, who for the period 1969–70 were alone at the tip of the spear. Major Norton has done a magnificent job of creating for the reader a sense of the time, of the tone and tenor of those who did the intelligence-gathering missions—fifty to eighty miles from the nearest friendly unit. He has captured the intensity without phony bravado; he demonstrates the love of Corps and comrades that pervaded all that we did together, and throughout his narrative, he illustrates the psychological ties that bound the reconnaissance teams together—the total interlocking reliance that kept them alive. As you read, you may even taste the bitter copper in your saliva that comes to those who are in mortal danger of losing their lives to a determined enemy. That taste is the taste of fear, and anyone—I repeat, anyone—who, like Doc Norton, has faced up to that mortal danger, has known fear. There were no fearless Rambo characters in the real world of Force Recon, only young Americans trying hard to stay alive and do their job.

As a matter of interest to the reader, I might note that by 1969 it was clear to everyone, from Lt. Gen. Hermán Nickerson—our general—to the lowest ranking Marine in I Corps, Republic of Vietnam, that the United States of America was not going to stay on in Vietnam to win. In the fall of 1969, the 3d Marine Division left Vietnam for Okinawa as part of the troop reduction, and more and more land became the property of the North Vietnamese. No one should misunderstand and see this narrative as being about a portion of the war fought against the Viet Cong insurgents! The units facing 3d Force Reconnaissance Company were elements of regular North Vietnamese Army forces, often deployed for no other purpose than to track down and kill the recon teams collecting intelligence information in their areas. In many instances, the enemy brought to bear sophisticated Soviet-made equipment—mobile radio direction finders, for example—against the teams, backing that effort up with reconnaissance battalions tasked to find and kill the Marines. Knowing full well at a conscious level that there was no national will to win made every day harder, and as the commanding officer of 3d Force, it was my duty each day to send brave men like HM3 Norton and a host of others like him on missions far into the heart of enemy-controlled territory. All such missions were part of the larger intelligence-gathering plan, but being part of the "big picture" did not do a damn thing to make them any less dangerous. As the troop reductions went on, we found that we were the *only* Marine ground unit in northern I Corps. We were then truly the tip of General Nickerson's spear.

The profession of soldiering is often referred to as the second oldest profession in the world. In concert with practitioners of that well-known older profession, all the competent warriors that I have known share a need to enunciate a certain depth of philosophical thought about that which we are required to do. A small unit like 3d Force Reconnaissance Company can laugh and sing and act the part of a fighting unit, but it cannot perform when under the stress of sustained hard use unless the members share a philosophical oneness that will carry them past any and all adversities. Stories from previous wars are woven into the fabric of being a Marine, but it is the unit philosophy that has been developed through hard work, that comes out when there is not enough food, not enough water, not enough air support, not enough clothing, not enough radio batteries, not enough explosives, and far too many complaints from staff officers in headquarters far from the scene of the fighting. In 3d Force Reconnaissance Company, our philosophy was solidly based on one guiding principle: as the tip of the spear, we were going to be asked to do great things, and you *cannot* do great things unless you are willing to dare *greatly!* Both this book and Major Norton's earlier volume give the reader a clear look at how this philosophy translated to war at the team level. There were fifty thousand plus Marines in Vietnam after the 3d Marine Division left the country—only 142 of them were in Northern I Corps to fight on the ground, and those Marines and Corpsmen went out looking for the North Vietnamese Army in six-man teams.

Finally, I want the reader to understand that the Vietnam War pain will not go away, and it cannot be assuaged—ever. Being forced to walk away from our responsibility to finish, on a winning note, that which was begun for honorable purpose, does that to men! It is a tribute to Major Norton that he has brought across the chasm of twenty years of that pain, a true picture of how it was in that small band of brothers known as 3d Force Reconnaissance Company as we went out to "dare greatly" for our Corps and our country. I read through the volumes, and as the commander who was responsible for the events in Major Norton's story of the young Hospitalman 3d Class Norton and his comrades, I know beforehand who will live and who will die—yet I cry today as I did then for each young American that we lost in that far land, each one a warrior gone to Valhalla.

It was an honor and a privilege to have served with Maj. Bruce H. "Doc" Norton and to write this foreword to his second book. I am proud of Major Norton for reaching back across the years to place his well-written story before the American people who deserve to learn just how superlative their sons and husbands were when challenged to do more than just do their time to get by—when asked "*TO DARE GREATLY.*"

Alex Lee
Lieutenant Colonel United States Marine Corps (Retired)
"Ancient Scout–Six"
Commanding Officer
3d Force Reconnaissance Company, FMF 1969–70

Alpine, California
May 1991

PROLOGUE

IN JULY 1975, I WAS INTRODUCED TO RAY STUBBE when he visited our rifle battalion, wearing the uniform of a United States Navy lieutenant commander in the chaplain corps. Besides wearing several rows of ribbons on his chest and the embroidered gold cross on his sleeves, he wore the gold jump wings, insignia of an advanced Navy parachutist.

Chaplain Stubbe had come to 3d Battalion, 1st Marines, at Camp Pendleton, California, to interview our commanding officer, Col. Alex Lee. The chaplain was writing a historical account on the specialized and Force-level reconnaissance units of the United States Marine Corps, from 1900 to 1974, and Lt. Col. Alex Lee had recently played a major role in that history as the commanding officer of 3d Force Reconnaissance Company in 1969–70.

After interviewing our battalion CO, Ray was pointed in the direction of my platoon's squad bay, and it was there that we began to talk about life in a Force Recon company. Our talk lasted for three days, and by the time that Ray departed, I felt that I had bored him with enough information about my experiences with 3d Force Recon and 1st Force Recon to last him a lifetime. I wished him well and asked him to someday send me a copy of his book whenever it became available.

It was not until 1981 that I finally got to read a draft copy of Ray Stubbe's original, 318-page history. He had submitted it to the director of the Marine Corps's Historical Division, and it had sat there for almost six years!

In July 1989, I received a small, brown package in the mail, and I was quite pleased to find that it contained a signed copy of Ray's book, *Inside Force Recon*. When I finished reading the book, I fired off a fast thank-you note to Ray, who had since retired from active duty, and mentioned to him my surprise at the differences between his original draft and what had been edited into book form. I mentioned that someday I would like to read an account by someone who had actually been in the "bush" with a Force Recon team. To date, no one had attempted this. Ray's response to my note was simple: "Why not write one, yourself? You were there."

I took his challenge on as a new mission.

My first book, *Force Recon Diary, 1969*, covered in detail that period of training from my enlistment in the U.S. Navy, as a hospital corpsman, to my first assignment as a recon team member with 3d Force Reconnaissance Company in Vietnam in 1969.

This second book describes the tour of duty that I experienced upon returning to Vietnam, following my training at the Navy's scuba school and the Army's Airborne school on the island of Okinawa and my reassignment to 1st Force Reconnaissance Company in 1970.

Prior to leaving Vietnam for scuba school, I had spent eight months learning the complexities of reconnaissance patrolling deep inside the territory that was owned and occupied by the North Vietnamese Army (NVA). These areas included the demilitarized zone (DMZ) and that notorious piece of paradise on the Laotian border known as the A Shau Valley.

On 5 February 1970, my team, code-named Snakey, was ambushed less than half an hour after being inserted into the A Shau Valley. Within seconds three Marines were killed and one was severely wounded. Two days earlier, and in the same area, three Marines from another 3d Force recon team had been killed and two members seriously wounded.

The unfortunate deaths and wounding of these courageous young men had a dramatic impact on the Marines of 3d Force Recon Company. The other recon team leaders operating in the A Shau Valley during the time of these two ambushes had listened to the dialogue between the team survivors and their radio-relay site, known as Zulu Relay, and were helpless to assist their fallen buddies. The recon teams wanted revenge and radioed back to our company commander for permission to go hunting "gooks."

Just two days after 3d Force Recon Company conducted memorial services to honor the fallen Marines, I was given orders to the Philippines to attend scuba school. First Lieutenant Singleton, one of our former platoon leaders, and a lance corporal from our communications platoon named Thompson, had also been selected to attend the Navy school at the ship-repair facility in Subic Bay.

We had left 3d Force Reconnaissance Company in Phu Bai, expecting to return to Vietnam three weeks later to patrol against those soldiers of the North Vietnamese Army headed south along the Ho Chi Minh Trail, intending to extract a heavy payback for what they had done.

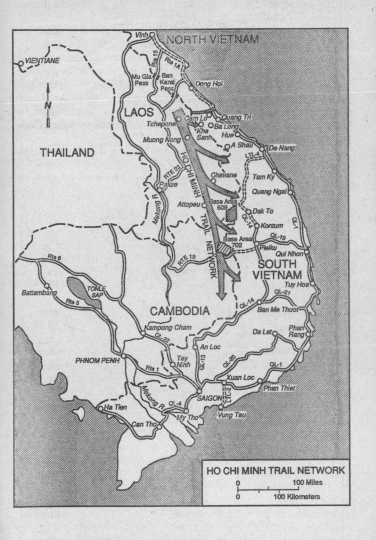

VIENTIANE

Vinh

NORTH VIETNAM

Rte 15

Rte 1A

Mu Gia Pass

Ban Karai Pass

Dong Hoi

N

LAOS

Tchepone

Cam Lo

Quang Tri

THAILAND

Muong Nong

Khe Sanh

Ba Long

Hue

A Shau

De Nang

RTE 23

Pakse

Chavane

Tam Ky

Quang Ngai

Attopeu

Base Area 609

Dak To

Kontum

QL-19

Base Area 702

Pleiku

Qui Nhon

SOUTH VIETNAM

RTE 19

TONLE SAP

Battambang

Rte 5

Rte 6

Tuy Hoa

QL-21

CAMBODIA

Ban Me Thuot

Kampong Cham

QL-22

An Loc

Tay Ninh

QL-13

Da Lat

Phan Rang

QL-20

Phnom Penh

Rte 1

Xuan Loc

QL-1

SAIGON

Phan Thiet

Ha Tien

Mekong R.

QL-4

My Tho

Vung Tau

Can Tho

HO CHI MINH TRAIL NETWORK

0   100 Miles

0   100 Kilometers

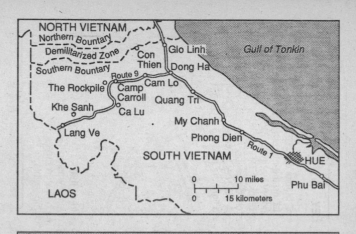

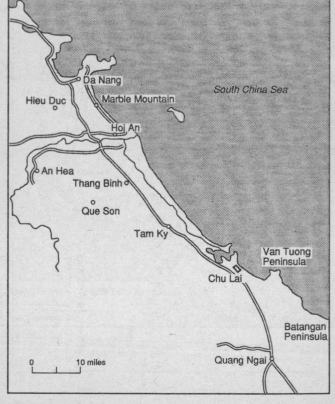

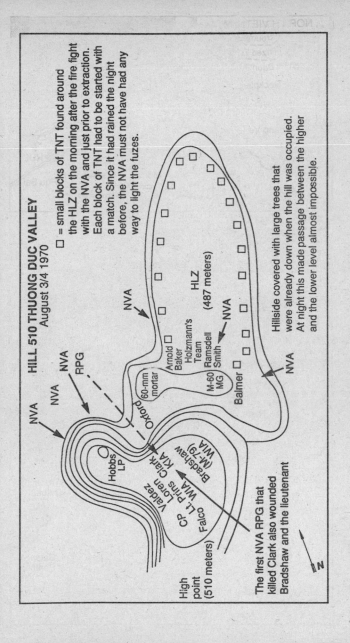

HILL 510 THUONG DUC VALLEY
August 3/4 1970

□ = small blocks of TNT found around the HLZ on the morning after the fire fight with the NVA and just prior to extraction. Each block of TNT had to be started with a match. Since it had rained the night before, the NVA must not have had any way to light the fuzes.

Hillside covered with large trees that were already down when the hill was occupied. At night this made passage between the higher and the lower level almost impossible.

NVA

NVA

NVA
RPG

NVA

NVA

CP OXO

60-mm mortar

Arnold
Baker
Holzmann's
Team
Ramsdell
Smith

M-60 MG

Balmer

HLZ
(487 meters)

Hobbs LP

High point
(510 meters)

Valdez
Loren
Prins Clark
KIA
Bradshaw (M-79)
WIA
Lt.-WIA
Falco

The first NVA RPG that killed Clark also wounded Bradshaw and the lieutenant

N

—— SCUBA SCHOOL ——

WHEN OUR MILITARY AIRLIFT COMMAND (MAC) C-130 finally rolled to a stop on the runway at Cubi Point Naval Air Station, the hydraulic cargo doors opened, and we were directed by the crew chief to grab all of our gear and carry it down the aircraft's loading ramp and move away from the flight line. As our group stepped onto the hard-surface apron of the runway, we were immediately engulfed in a blanket of hot, damp, tropical air that stank from the smells of jet fuel and ripe, raw sewage. As we walked away from the C-130, I wondered aloud why it was that each time I arrived in a new location, my olfactory senses kicked into gear and left me with a memorable first impression based primarily on the location's stink. It certainly didn't require genius for any of us who were new to the P.I. to realize that the Philippines had some serious problems with sanitation.

We threw our seabags into the back of a gray Navy schoolbus that had been requested by our pilot prior to arrival. The short drive down the hill and away from the naval air station took us past the naval ship-repair facility and to the billeting office, for room assignments. Those of us who were enlisted men and assigned to scuba school were marched off toward the barracks, while the staff noncommissioned officers and officers were driven away to somewhat more comfortable living accommodations— they would get to sleep in the comfort of single, air-conditioned rooms, while we "snuffies" would again enjoy all that life had to offer in a forty-man, open squad bay featuring screened windows, steel bunk beds, and a community bathroom. The barracks would be our home for the next three weeks.

Once inside the barracks, we were told that we had five minutes to pick out a rack and to stow away our gear in the nearest wall locker. Once that task was completed, we were told to gather at the far end of the squad bay where one of the scuba-school instructors would conduct an informal welcome-aboard briefing, covering the dos and don'ts aboard the naval base and what we could expect to learn during the next three weeks as "guests" of the United States Navy.

A Navy 1st class petty officer, who was also a 2d class diver, conducted the informal briefing.

"The Navy's scuba school is designed to teach you qualified swimmers the basics of underwater diving, utilizing the self-contained underwater breathing apparatus commonly referred to as scuba gear. You men will also learn the techniques of day and night underwater navigation and open-water survival swimming. Your schooling will last for three weeks, and it will be divided into three phases. Phase one will begin with another complete physical examination and continue with our weeding-out process, built around long, early morning endurance runs, countless laps in an Olympic-size swimming pool, and with several open-water swimming events in the South China Sea.

"Tomorrow, those of you who remain will be introduced to one of our favorite daily exercises, which we use to strengthen your legs and guts—the flutter kick. Last, but certainly not least, you will each be assigned a diving buddy from amongst your fellow classmates. We believe in the buddy system around here. It works and may one day save your life. Once this buddy assignment is made, it will not change. You and your buddy will not allow yourselves to become separated from one another. If you should become separated, you will pay a heavy price. You and your buddy will wear a nine-foot length of hawser line, like a yoke around your necks, to connect you to one another. You will wear this heavy mooring line as a constant reminder not to become separated, and you will wear it until some other inattentive students fail to stay together. Then, the hawser line will be worn by them. As I said, this is a strong reminder to stay together.

"For those of you who manage to get through phase one, phase two will be your introduction to scuba gear. It will begin in the pool, and once you graduate from the pool work, we will enter phase three. This last phase is a period of progressively deeper day and nighttime ocean dives, which will culminate with a graduation dive to a depth of 130 feet.

"On an administrative note, please read the bulletin board that is located for your convenience at the entrance to your barracks. It will answer many of your questions. Pay attention to what is happening around you. I'll look forward to seeing this class to-morrow morning at 0700. Welcome to scuba school.''

We were soon to learn that the Marines and Navy students, whether they were officers or enlisted men, who could not pass the basic but difficult physical tests that followed were quickly returned to their parent commands. A failure to keep up was usually followed by a strongly worded letter from the commanding officer of the ship-repair facility to the students' command, stating that those who failed should not have been sent to the school in the first place. It was not considered by the officers to be "career enhancing" to be dropped from this school.

Because the primary mission of the Force Reconnaissance company is to conduct preassault and distant postassault reconnaissance in support of a landing force, scuba school was considered to be a significant part of the overall training of Force Recon Marines and the corpsmen who would accompany them on such missions. The concept of preassault and postassault ground reconnaissance dictates that training programs develop Force Reconnaissance teams capable of undetected activity on the enemy's ground under conditions which severely limit support from sources outside of the teams themselves. Such undetected activity includes entry into a recon area of operation, movement of the team within the operating area, execution of information collection, submission of timely patrol reports, eventual withdrawal from the operating area, and debriefing and the submission of final reports. Scuba school was one of the unique training programs which furthered the Force commander's ability to obtain information about the activities and resources of an enemy. It was also considered one of the more demanding schools.

Smaller classes of student divers were easier to handle, and the Navy instructors were rumored to use every opportunity to trim the size of the class. This reputation for being overly strict kept everyone on his toes, and the instructors particularly targeted Marines as the subjects of their anger.

In 1970 the U.S. Navy was utilizing state-of-the-art scuba equipment that would be considered antique by today's standards. As new students, we were shown in our earliest classes what was later to be our standard daily equipment. The heavy steel oxygen cylinders, referred to as "twin 72s," were the air tanks that we would use. Our breathing regulators were the double-hose regulator type that would keep us supplied with a flow of compressed oxygen. Mask, snorkel, swim fins, buoyancy vest, leaded weight belt, and K-bar knife finished out the equipment list for each student. Before we graduated to the status of "qualified Navy scuba diver," we would have to demonstrate our abilities as student swimmers and play the game according to the rules and the various personality quirks of our diving instructors.

The scuba school was located on one of the piers at the ship-repair facility and was within easy walking distance of our barracks. The nucleus of the school was a gray Navy diving barge that also served as home to the senior instructors. Each morning we students would leave the barracks and assemble on the street that bordered the pier. From this assembly area we began our training day with a formal morning formation, during which time all the administrative word was passed along and our daily training schedule was covered in detail. Officers, who were scuba-school students, were placed in charge of the training class and were responsible for seeing to the needs of the students. Our class began with thirty students.

During the first week of school, morning formations were immediately followed by a three- or four-mile run that would end, miraculously, at the entrance to the officers' swimming pool. At the pool, our training day continued with endless flutter kicks and countless laps in the pool, all in the name of conditioning. Once the pool work was finished, we were instructed in the proper use of the different types of equipment that we would soon be using in the ocean. Our hours in the pool required only the use of the mask, snorkel, and swim fins, and by the end of the training day we were so exhausted and red-eyed from the high chlorine concentration that a freshwater shower and a good night's rest were the only things we wanted.

Given the physical demands of our training, getting away from the barracks to take in the sights in the town of Olongapo should not have been foremost in anyone's mind, but at the age of twenty, common sense did not always dictate the rules of normalcy; liberty in Olongapo quickly became a "mission" for those of us who had just arrived in the Philippines after six months of reconnaissance patrolling in the jungles of Vietnam. Although liberty call was usually sounded once our training had ended for the day, we found that required reading had to be completed, classroom notes had to be studied, and our squad bay would always have to undergo the routine cleaning and inspection before any plans could be made for liberty call.

The presence of the U.S. Naval base at Subic Bay had brought financial prosperity to the small town of Olongapo in the days following World War II, and by 1970 Olongapo had grown from a sleepy little port to a service town with a reputation ranging somewhere between Heaven and Dodge City, depending upon who was describing it. The unwritten rules had to be learned quickly if the unknowing wanted to survive a night of liberty on the streets or in the bars of Olongapo. The rules were different there!

The first rule that we learned was that there were no rules once anyone left the security of the base and went into town. Olongapo was adjacent to the Naval base, and to get into town, all servicemen had to pass through a security checkpoint that was manned by members of the Navy's shore patrol, Marines, and their Philippine Armed Forces military counterparts. Each serviceman wanting to enter Olongapo was required to show the gate guards his green military identification card before being allowed to leave the base. Large signs were strategically placed along the way that stated the penalty for being caught out in town after midnight, when curfew began for all enlisted men holding the pay grade of E-5 or below, and remained in affect until 5:00 A.M. This was commonly called "Cinderella liberty."

The second unwritten rule was that no one should venture out into the town alone. Very bad things were known to have happened to those individuals who were foolish enough to think that they could beat the streetwise Filipinos at their game of hustling drunken sailors and Marines.

Life in an open squad bay always managed to forge friendships that lasted a long time. The majority of students in our class had come to scuba school from either the Marine's 1st Reconnaissance Battalion or from 3d or 1st Force Recon companies. Also assigned to the class were a number of Navy enlisted students from Seabee units stationed in Vietnam.

The Marines from 3d Force and 1st Force Recon companies immediately grouped themselves into a closely knit clique. They felt that as long as we were in the Philippines, we would go everywhere together, just as we had done in the bush, and by forming this group of streetwise combat veterans our survival was assured; the weakest member was helped by the stronger ones, we would be mutually protected out in town, and our leadership was known and maintained both in the classroom and on the streets of this foreign town. The Marines did this instinctively, taking me in as one of their own, but the Navy personnel never caught on to the idea. While we enjoyed the comfort of safety while on liberty together, the sailors always suffered the consequences of trying to be independent.

The first night that we decided to go into Olongapo to test our buddy system was a learning experience that deserves a detailed description. A lance corporal named Morse, who was assigned to 1st Force Recon Company, had arrived at Subic Bay one week prior to the beginning of the class. Morse had already been out to visit Olongapo, and being a good reconnaissance Marine, he had written down a number of his observations, making himself a good source of preliminary information that he willingly shared with the rest of us. Knowing that there were several of us who wanted to see the sights of Olongapo, and being a very gregarious individual, he offered up his services as our guide. Our first night's liberty group consisted of Lance Corporals Thompson, Morse, and Jackson; two corporals named Grubb and Smith; and me. We gathered around Morse's rack as he began his informative briefing.

"There are some things that you should know before we leave here for Olongapo, and I'll try to tell you as much as I know, based on several nights out in town. If you have any questions, ask me before we leave.

"First, don't wear your watch out in town if you have a twist-a-flex-type watchband. The best trick on the street is for a group of little Filipino kids to walk up and surround you, begging for spare change. All of a sudden one of them will move in close, hit you hard in the nuts with a quick flick of his little brown hand. As you bend over in pain, grabbing your groin, this same kid will pop your cigarettes out of your breast pocket and rip your watch from your wrist with the speed of lightning. The group of kids will then run like hell down the street, screaming bloody murder, and when they split up, you won't know which one to chase.

"The next bit of information that you should know is that from the time you leave the base till you return you are a target for every hooker, pimp, and con artist on the street. They make their living on unsuspecting prey just like you guys. You are going to get ripped off in any deal that you try to make with any Filipino over the age of four. No matter how slick you thought you were back home on the street, you will not get over, here.

"You had better be prepared to lose all of the money that you take with you when you hit Olongapo. There are more opportunities available to separate you from your money than you can imagine. The bar girls have heard every come-on and lie imaginable at least twice. They have the most incredible communications network I have ever seen. Once they see your ID card and know what pay grade you are, they will know how much money you'll draw every two weeks. These girls will pretend not to know any English until you refuse to buy them a drink or try to cheat them— then watch out! Assume that everyone is on the take, don't drink anything that you didn't order, or better yet, have a bar girl taste it first. If she refuses, get out of the club and don't return.

"There is a 'blacks only' section of Olongapo known as the Jungle, and if you are white, you are not welcome there, period. There are also many 'Filipino only' clubs. Stay away from them, because once you're out in town you are looked upon as guests of this country. Ferdinand Marcos likes the U.S. troops because of all the money that we bring into this poor area, but the local police will shoot first and ask questions later. So, if you all still want to go out and see what's on the other side of Shit River, then let's go."

As we walked toward the main gate, we found ourselves being channeled into a growing line of servicemen, all headed in the same direction. At the end of this line stood two Navy SPs, two Marine staff sergeants, and two Filipino MPs checking ID cards and making sure that everyone was dressed in proper liberty attire for the evening. Personal appearance was viewed as an important issue in maintaining good relations between the United States and the Philippines, and no one was allowed to leave the base unless he was sober, clean-shaven, and "squared away."

Once we had passed through the security checkpoint, we began to cross over a two-lane bridge that spanned a filthy and stinking little tributary known as Shit River. Ahead of us some of the sailors and Marines were tossing things into the water below. When we moved up to where they had been standing, we saw half a dozen dugout canoes anchored in the middle of the stream. In each canoe stood several young Filipino boys or girls who called up to the passing pedestrians, "Hey, Joe, you got coins? Throw me coins, Joe. Watch me dive, Joe."

When the men threw pennies and nickels over the side of the bridge, the kids executed perfect dives into the polluted black water and soon emerged, proudly holding high in their hands whatever coins they had found on the muddy bottom.

The young boys in the canoes wore only dark shorts, but the young girls all wore beautifully embroidered white dresses. The thought of these poor little girls having to dive into the stinking waters of Shit River, wearing their finest dresses, for the sake of a few dollars in change was saddening. The young boys thought little of it and could be found in their canoes anchored all night long beneath the bridge in pursuit of money.

Once we had crossed the bridge, our first visual impression of Olongapo was one of filth in motion. The main street was a dirt-surface, two-lane road, with patches of cobblestones scattered about. The damp, tropical air was always thick with the smoke from the exhaust pipes of dozens of worn-out jeepneys, buses, and motorcycles. Trash was piled high on every corner, with papers, liquor bottles, and assorted waste littering the ground.

The first buildings that we came to on the other side of the bridge were the money-exchange houses. In the front of each of these buildings stood heavily armed security guards, no two individuals wearing the same type of uniform. Their weapons ranged from new M-16 rifles to old Thompson submachine guns, shotguns, revolvers, and semiautomatic pistols. Several of the rent-a-cops carried only long, razor-sharp machetes. We, of course, went to town unarmed.

Typically, servicemen would come up to the teller's glass cage to exchange American dollars, watches, rings, and jewelry, or any other personal item that struck the fancy of the exchange owner, for local currency. In early 1970, the exchange rate for one U.S. dollar was six pesos. This rate of exchange fluctuated daily, and better deals could be made on the black market when large amounts of money were involved, but particularly when the ships of the U.S. Navy's 7th Fleet came to visit Subic Bay.

Once we had exchanged our dollars for pesos, we walked along the main street and into the center of the town. The carts of the local vendors lined both sides of the street. Many of these mobile merchants had built charcoal fireboxes onto the tops of their carts, using them to cook thin strips of chicken, pork, and beef that had been marinated in a spicy soy sauce, then skewered with slivers of bamboo. All of the meats looked the same once they had been barbecued and were ready for sale. These snacks were commonly referred to on the street as "monkey meat," and one peso bought four sticks of the customer's choice.

Jewelry, T-shirts, monkeypod wood carvings, and assorted knickknacks were sold alongside the vendors' carts and in the countless shops facing the main street. The majority of the one- and two-story buildings of Olongapo were bars, restaurants, whorehouses, or sleazy hotels that catered to liaisons lasting from half an hour to all night. At fifty cents for an ice-cold bottle of San Miguel, local beer was cheap; the Filipino girls working the clubs were all beautiful; and the latest in Stateside rock-and-roll hits blared into the streets from loudspeakers placed in front of each of the clubs. To any young sailor or soldier witnessing the street scene for the first time, Olongapo was better than a carnival; it was considered nothing short of a dirty version of paradise to any young man from middle America. No matter how Olongapo is described, it was one hell of a fun place for us to be, considering our alternative.

As we followed Lance Corporal Morse down the main street, we could not help but notice that at one particular place the majority of black servicemen turned down one street and divorced themselves from the main flow of human traffic. This was the entrance to the segregated territory known as the Jungle, which Morse had told us about earlier. According to Morse, the Jungle had existed in Olongapo for years; to us it was interesting that the U.S. Navy allowed it to exist at all.

The possibility of finding real trouble existed if we wandered into the Jungle and, considering that scuba school would be difficult enough, we didn't want to complicate our lives by visiting an area where we knew we were not welcome. Our group was capable of getting into enough trouble on its own. Our destination was a club that Morse had visited earlier in the week, Club Oasis. This small club had a good band, cold beer, and according to our guide, "Every one of the twenty bar girls at the Oasis is stunning. They all speak English and know more about scuba school than the Navy." Seeing was believing, so on we walked.

Less than a block from the entrance to Club Oasis was an interesting diversion that was famous in Olongapo, the Crocodile Gardens. The "garden" was a shallow cement pool of dirty green water surrounded by a wrought-iron fence. Living in the small pool were two five-foot-long crocodiles and several large mud turtles. Next to the Crocodile Gardens was a vendor, who just happened to sell live yellow baby ducks. These ducklings could be purchased for a few pesos, and they usually became the main meal for the crocodiles next door. A crocodile's fast attack on an unsuspecting duckling was considered fine entertainment in Olongapo. After watching this event for a few minutes, Lance Corporal Morse must have begun to feel sorry for the plight of the baby ducks tossed into the pool; he approached the vendor and purchased the remaining ducklings in the hopes of saving them from a very short life span. He then handed each of us one of his newly acquired pets, and we walked into the Club Oasis, armed only with down-covered ducklings in our breast pockets. Climbing the stairs to the bar on the second floor, we found an unoccupied booth and ordered a round of San Miguel beer.

When our waitress reappeared with a tray of cold beers, she was accompanied by several of her "unescorted" girlfriends who must have thought we'd come straight from the farm to Olongapo. Our initial conversations were interrupted by the constant chorus of five peeping ducklings, which created quite a sensation among the bar girls. They all wanted to know why the "crazy Maleens" had bought the ducklings and not fed them to the crocs outside. Sensing a golden opportunity to relieve ourselves of the cute but troublesome baby ducks, we presented each of the bar girls with a new pet. It was a smart thing to do because even though some Filipinos had an undeserved reputation for being cruel to their animals, it was the visiting foreign servicemen who helped to perpetuate the need for places like the Crocodile Gardens. Give the public what they want, so to speak. Our small display of humanity endeared us to the girls, and the Club Oasis became our central meeting place for the remainder of the time we were in Subic Bay.

The live bands that played in the clubs of Olongapo were absolute masters of mimicking American music, and even though the lyrics to Creedance Clearwater Revival's latest hit song was sung as "Rollin on de Reeber," no one could complain about the quality of the band. Nearly all of the clubs employed a large number of bar girls, whose sole purpose in life was to sit close to the servicemen, listen patiently to each man's life story, and quietly encourage him to drink, while occasionally insisting that the "date" purchase for them a three-dollar, nonalcoholic bar drink known as "tea" in payment for the companionship. Everybody in Olongapo got what they wanted. When the fleet was in, all the bars made money, and additional girls were brought in from as far away as Manila and Baguio. They profited from a percentage of the evening's take, while the soldiers, sailors, and Marines paid generously for their companionship. They never knew when they would return to Olongapo, and with a war going on, they wanted to make the most out of every minute.

When our group had seen enough of what Olongapo had to offer, we headed back toward the security of the base. By then it was close to midnight, and as we walked along the main street, we could not help but notice the gathering of young sailors and Marines at each of the side entrances to the many clubs. They were drawn like so many moths to the dim lights of the alleys, all waiting to meet with the one bar girl who had promised them more than simple conversation after the clubs closed down for the night. It was to be the same scenario each and every time we went into Olongapo. Each bar girl would promise half a dozen different guys that she would spend the night with "only him," and then she'd quietly slip out into the night through some hidden door and avoid the anxious gathering in the alleyway. It was a learning experience for all of us. The girls wanted no part of just a one-night stand, opting instead for servicemen who were stationed at Subic Bay on tours of duty lasting more than two years. The possibility of their marrying an American was just their best ticket to take them as far away as possible from the filthy streets of Olongapo.

Lance Corporal Morse had proven himself to be a capable and professional guide, wise to the ways of the city and able always to avoid trouble, and at his insistence, we called it a night. As we moved down the street and closer to the entrance of the base, we again joined the great ebb and flow of servicemen, crossing back over the Shit River bridge and walking past the scrutinizing gaze of the shore patrol. We had gone out in town, seen the sights, had fun, and learned more about the ways of the Philippines in a few hours than we had ever thought possible. But more importantly, we had returned to our darkened barracks, all together.

It wasn't too long after our first night out in Olongapo that our class suffered its first casualty. A young, fair-skinned lance corporal assigned to the Marine barracks at Subic Bay had managed to get himself a set of orders for scuba school. He had started out well and had demonstrated that he was a very capable swimmer and physically fit, but his unfortunate weakness was hereditary.

At the end of the first week of school, the class was required to complete a two-mile open-sea endurance swim. Once we emerged from the water at the end of the swim, we were to run in formation all the way back to the barracks, roughly six miles. We waited on the shore for all of the swimmers to finish, and as we waited, several of the Marines happened to find a fresh water spigot. We drank the fresh water to hydrate ourselves before the long run, and while we waited, we washed off the saltwater crust from our bodies. The lance corporal had been one of the last swimmers to enter the water with his diving buddy, and by the time they had made it to shore, they were red from sunburn. Our group was anxious to get on with the run, but the benefit of cool, fresh water and a cleansing off was not accepted by either one of them.

By the time we reached the barracks, the lance corporal was in considerable pain. His delicate skin was bright red, and his thighs had been rubbed raw by the sea salt during the one-hour run in the hot sun. Once inside the barracks, his diving buddy told him that he had a sure cure for his painful sunburn and rash and told him to lean forward and place his hands on an upper bunk bed while he dampened a facecloth with rubbing alcohol to apply to his partner's back. At first the isopropyl alcohol must have soothed his pain, but his partner was too heavy-handed and had soaked the facecloth with alcohol. With the next application, a stream of rubbing alcohol flowed over his raw skin. With a tremendous scream of pain, he raced toward the showers, hoping to rinse the burning alcohol from his body. But in his haste and panic, he grabbed at the wrong faucet and scalded himself with hot water. Jumping back and away from the hot water, he slipped on the wet shower floor, and then hit his head against the wall. The lance corporal was taken away by ambulance to the base Naval hospital. We never saw him again, but heard that he was discharged from the hospital several days later and had rejoined the ranks at the Marine barracks.

There were two dreaded events that occurred during the second week of scuba school, and both had to be successfully mastered by all students in the class. To fail either of them meant immediate dismissal from the school. The first was known as the "ditching-and-donning" event. Each student was required to enter the pool, wearing all of his scuba equipment, swim submerged to the deepest end of the pool, and at a depth of fifteen feet, we were to remove our face mask, snorkel, fins, weight belt, and scuba tanks. Our twin tanks were to be left on the bottom of the pool, and beneath our tanks we were to leave our mask, snorkel, and fins, placing our weight belts over the tanks. Having removed all of our equipment, we were to take one last breath of compressed air, shut off the air-flow valve on the double-hose regulator, and swim to the surface, having successfully ditched our gear. Once on the surface, we were allowed to take one or two breaths of fresh air before diving back down to the bottom of the pool to recover our equipment. It was most important to remember to retain enough air in our lungs so that we would be able to clear the water from the mouthpiece before attempting to breath the compressed oxygen. Once the air valve was turned back to the "on" position, the water in the mouthpiece was purged from the hose with a hard blast of our remaining air, forcing the collected water out of the intake hose so that normal breathing was again possible.

Each diver then quickly replaced his weight belt, helping to keep him on the bottom. The face mask was put on next, and clearing the face mask of all water had to be properly demonstrated to our diving instructor who sat on the bottom, watching, only a few feet away from the student diver. Most of us had experienced no problem in demonstrating this technique, having practiced it in the prescuba class. But one student diver in our class became something of a sensation when he demonstrated to our instructor much more than what was already required.

Corporal Vincent Swederski, who had befriended me eight months earlier when I joined 3d Force Recon Company, had been rewarded for his many months in the bush with orders to scuba school. Ski was due to return home to the States after completing scuba school and was looking forward to being distinguished among Marines as dual qualified (jump and scuba), when he reported in to his next duty station, Quantico, Virginia. Something as insignificant as this little ditch-and-don exercise was not about to stop my buddy, Corporal Swederski.

Ski swam easily to the center of the pool and made his way effortlessly to its deepest end. There on the bottom sat Communications Technician 1st Class Draper, a no-nonsense U.S. Navy diver, who prided himself on making life difficult for every scuba-school student who came to Subic Bay. It was believed that he particularly disliked Marines. He certainly made no effort to conceal his views that diving should be left to the Navy, and only the Navy. He was an early sufferer of the zero-defect mentality, and his reputation for being a demanding teacher was well known throughout scuba school and even extended into the sea stories told by Force Recon Marines returning from Subic Bay. Much to his credit, it was also said that Draper had done several demanding combat tours in Vietnam with various Seal-team units. It was obvious by his demeanor that he had no room in his heart for half-steppers, Navy or Marine.

When it was his turn to demonstrate, Corporal Swederski placed himself about six feet in front of Draper and assumed a kneeling position on the bottom of the pool, quickly removing his face mask and snorkel, and placing them beside him. Then he unhooked his weight belt and placed it beside his mask. He pulled on the quick-release straps of his harness, and once free from the weight of his full tanks, he flipped them off his back and pulled them over his head, placing them on the bottom of the pool, keeping his regulator mouthpiece clenched firmly between his teeth. The very last thing that he had to do was to turn off the air-flow valve at the connection point where the regulator was attached to the manifold of the steel oxygen tanks. But instead of turning off the air-supply valve, Ski had unscrewed the regulator from his tanks! It was obvious that that predicament could spell ruin for Ski. With only a limited amount of air in his lungs, he headed for the surface of the pool.

But Corporal Swederski was not to be denied his chance. Upon surfacing, he took one large gulp of air and quickly returned to solve the problem that he had created fifteen feet below. Ski swam straight down to his scuba equipment and grabbed his lead-weight belt, placing it across the back of his legs, helping to anchor himself to the bottom. He held the disconnected regulator in one hand and lifted his tanks up with his other hand as he tried unsuccessfully to reattach the regulator to the tank's manifold. But he was close to being out of air. If he surfaced, he would be dismissed from scuba school.

Ski did the only thing possible: he swam over to Draper and calmly yanked the mouthpiece from his instructor's face. He took several breaths of much-needed oxygen and then offered the regulator back to the astonished Draper. Returning to his gear, he managed to attach his regulator to his tanks, clear the intake hose, and put all of his equipment back on: "donning" his gear. Then he swam over and took his place, joining the rest of us along the wall of the swimming pool.

Draper signaled to all of us to head for the surface. We assumed that this would be the end of one Cpl. Vincent Swederski, USMC, but once we had gathered at the shallow end of the pool the surprise was on us. Staring at Ski, he asked, "What's your name, jarhead?"

"Corporal Vincent Swederski, sir."

"Corporal Swederski, here, has just demonstrated to me and to you that he is extremely cool under pressure. Well done, Corporal Swederski! Gentlemen, the thing that you must remember, when you are underwater and find yourselves temporarily out of air, is that you will always have a diving partner to depend upon. If you panic, if you bolt for the surface, if you abandon your partner, you will probably kill yourself, and your diving partner as well. If you remember anything from what you have just seen, please remember that when one man had to make a difficult decision, he did it, and he did the right thing. This class is dismissed."

Not all of the students were as cool as Corporal Swederski. The ditching-and-donning exercise reduced our class by half a dozen students, and the following day we were subjected to the second and more difficult event known as the "harassment" dive. The harassment dive was the final weeding-out event that was a favorite of all the scuba-school instructors. The rules were simple: students paired up with their diving partners, entered the pool and started to swim around the outer edges, staying as close to the bottom as possible. Once in, we would be subjected to harassment by our instructors and were not to defend ourselves from them. The instructions were not more specific than that. Each pair of student divers was to help one another correct the situations to which we would be subjected, and anyone who panicked and surfaced during the harassment dive would be eliminated from the school.

My diving partner was named John Terrijo. John was a married father of three who had been accepted in the Navy's newest recruiting program called IPO (Instant Petty Officer). IPOs were recent civilians who possessed an important skill that the Navy needed but either had no school for, or had no time to train men to the specialty skill level the IPOs had achieved in the civilian world. John had been a heavy-equipment operator, who joined the Seabees as a bulldozer operator, 2d class petty officer. The rank and rating normally required three or four years of service, but there was a war going on and, apparently, a need for heavy-equipment operators. John had been in the Navy less than four months and he volunteered for scuba school because the Department of the Navy paid sixty-five dollars per month to scuba divers who were serving in a combat zone.

We began to slowly swim around the pool and watched as other students were "attacked" by the instructors. Face masks were yanked from faces, quick-release straps were pulled, and swim fins were removed. Soon, hands began to search for regulator valves, and my tanks were removed from my back. Within seconds, I found myself buddy breathing with John. He was missing all of his equipment but had managed to hang on to his tanks. They had even stripped him of his bathing suit! We continued to swim around for almost one hour and had no idea how much air had been pumped into our tanks; we *assumed* that they had been filled before the harrassment dive. The chlorine had started to take its toll on our eyes; we couldn't see anything, and by the time we heard that long-awaited sound of metal rapping on the ladders of the pool, signaling us to surface, we were exhausted and temporarily blinded. But we had made it! Six of our fellow students had decided that the struggle wasn't worth their effort and had opted to leave the water. They were gone from scuba school by the end of the next day. What remained before graduation was one week of open-water diving in the South China Sea. Just one long week of night-navigation dives, one week of progressively deeper dives, culminating in our final graduation dive to a depth of more than

130 feet. It also meant only one week of grand and glorious liberty in Olongapo before most of us returned to our units in Vietnam.

On the first day of our last week at scuba school, 1st Lieutenant Singleton met with Lance Corporal Thompson and me and told us of his success with his plans to get the three of us jump qualified while we were still in the Philippines.

Our lieutenant had apparently made some new friends at the Cubi Point officers' club, and during a discussion there he explained to them his desire to become jump qualified. They, in turn, discussed the possibilities of their being able to accommodate him in this request. Several of the naval officers were assigned to UDT (Underwater Demolition Team), and some of the other officers were from one of the Navy's Seal teams. There were also several helicopter pilots present who had routinely jumped these same officers and their men, and they, too, offered their services and expertise to 1st Lieutenant Singleton. Not wasting any time, the lieutenant sent a message to 3d Force Recon Company and requested that permission be granted to extend us five additional days so that we could attend jump school. Permission verification from Maj. Alex Lee, our company commander, came back immediately, via the MAF commander. We would begin our ground-school classes during our last week of scuba school and be able to jump as soon as we finished it.

Our scuba class had been reduced by more than a third of its original number. The steady reduction meant that less time in the water was required for training, so our early morning training dives to thirty, forty, and sixty feet were accomplished with more than half of the day still remaining. So 1st Lieutenant Singleton, Thompson, and I could get from the ship-repair facility to the Navy's flight line at Cubi Point. When we arrived at the Cubi Point operations office, we were met by a Navy lieutenant commander flight surgeon and by one of the Navy's Seal team jump masters. The flight surgeon mentioned that he would not require us to take the lengthy physical examination normally required as a precondition for parachute training after he glanced at our medical records and saw the recent data of our scuba-school physicals. These instructors were also members of the Cubi Point Sport Parachute Club and said that they were familiar with the type of aircraft that we would soon get to use and with the locations of the various drop zones.

Being given permission to become jump qualified was more than any of us had hoped for. The prospect of returning to 3d

Force Recon Company both jump and scuba qualified was wonderful. The new and special qualifications would enable us to participate in types of reconnaissance operations that had been reserved only for Marines (and the *very* few corpsmen) who were qualified and trained to do so. We left our initial meeting at Cubi Point and returned to the ship-repair facility, thrilled with the possibilities and excitement that lay ahead.

Diving classes during these few remaining days were conducted several miles away from the entrance to Subic Bay harbor. The diving conditions were excellent, with clear visibility to at least eighty feet, and as our confidence levels grew, we enjoyed our newfound freedom to dive to sixty feet and stay under for the better part of an hour. During our many dives in that area, we were also rewarded with being able to explore several sunken Japanese landing craft, quiet reminders of World War II that served now as home to large quantities of the delicious lobsters called longosta, or simply referred to as "bugs" by our diving instructors.

We began to sharpen our skills in the fundamentals and complexities of underwater navigation. Each pair of divers was given a plastic board that held an underwater compass and a writing instrument. Before entering the water from the Navy landing craft that took us out of Subic Bay for our dives, we were given a specific distance and various compass azimuths to plot and to follow. To assist those students and instructors assigned as lookouts, or "bubble watchers," a sixty-foot-long line, with an international-orange color balloon, was attached to each diving team's tanks. Our progress and underwater position were always known to the diving instructors leading the dive and to those who remained on board the landing craft. Strong, changing currents; bottom formations; the passing of Filipino fishing boats that always seemed to manage to get within our designated diving area; and fatigue were all factors that contributed to the difficulties of being able to maintain a true heading. We reasoned that if it was difficult to master underwater navigation in crystal-clear water at a depth of sixty feet, what must it be like to navigate at night? Hadn't our instructors told us that nighttime was when the "big feeders" appeared? We would find out shortly.

As our small landing craft moved slowly past Grande Island, near the entrance of Subic Bay, we watched the always spectacular sight of the sun setting into the South China Sea. We were filled with anticipation about swimming in total darkness at a depth of sixty feet, to cover a course of several nautical miles, with the small luminous dial of our compass our sole navigational aid.

The experience of our first night dive was memorable. The clarity of the warm water and a bright half-moon aided subsurface visibility as we began our descent to forty feet. We passed through the band of light into progressively greater darkness, and by the time we leveled off at sixty feet, it was impossible to see anything at a distance greater than two feet. There was a great sense of comfort in having my diving partner close beside me. We knew from past diving experiences that our exposure to this new type of unnatural environment would cause us to use more air than normal. Descending into total darkness is certain to make anyone breathe much faster than normal, but we moved on with growing confidence. The sea life that we encountered was nothing more than schools of small fish, the occasional jellyfish, and small biting microorganisms known as sea mites. We finished our first night-navigation dive on time, and all of us with empty tanks. As we motored back toward the pier, we listened to each other share stories of our experiences on the dive.

We passed the next several days with more open-sea dives, to eighty feet during the day, and with more night-navigation dives designed to increase our level of confidence. All that remained by the end of the week was for our last graduation dive that would take us to the depth of 130 feet. It, too, was another grand experience. The water pressure that a diver experiences during descent increases at a rate of 14.7 pounds per square inch (one atmosphere) for every thirty-three feet of downward travel. At 130 thirty feet, we would feel more than 230 pounds of pressure on our bodies. The face masks would be pushed so hard against our faces that deep oval grooves would remain for hours after the dive.

The total amount of time that we would spend on the bottom was less than six minutes, which normally would not require a decompression stop during our ascent, but as a safety precaution we were scheduled to make two stops along the way to the surface. The exact locations of the stops would be clearly marked on the safety line that led from the diving barge to an anchored point on the floor of the ocean. The graduation dive subjected us to one last experience that we had read about but had not been prepared for—temperature change. The surface-water temperature ranged close to seventy degrees, and was always comfortable, but at 130 feet beneath the surface, the water felt ice-cold. This was another learning experience—air consumption increased quickly. This was definitely not the place to make some simple mistake that could be better handled in the pool or at a depth of thirty feet. It was now quite clear why the weeding-out process was so critical to our diving instructors during the first week of scuba school.

When our group of divers finally reached the 130 foot mark, the instructors checked each student to make sure that everything was going as planned. Our six-minute stay seemed to drag on for hours before we received the signal to begin our ascent. As John and I made our way toward the brighter light at the surface, we knew that it was over. He signaled to me with thumbs-up, and his great broad smile almost caused his mouthpiece to fall away from his face. Our feelings at the moment of success were shared by all of us once we hit the surface. Amid the great shouts of "aarruuug-gaarrr," we helped one another as we loaded our tanks aboard the diving barge for the last time.

We had done it. We had finally completed the Navy's scuba-school course. The day's training schedule called for the afternoon to be set aside for the administrative paperwork that would produce the orders necessary to return most of the class members to Vietnam. The next morning we attended a small graduation ceremony and received our graduation certificates as qualified scuba divers. Following graduation, Thompson and I moved our gear out of the scuba-school barracks and relocated ourselves in an old, transient barracks while awaiting the word from 1st Lieutenant Singleton as to when we would begin parachute training. Our wait was not long. We were told to meet the lieutenant at noon in a snack bar near the ship-repair facility. From there we would travel by taxi to Cubi Point to begin parachute training.

PARACHUTE TRAINING
—— AT SUBIC BAY ——

WE BEGAN OUR TRAINING BY LEARNING TO EXECUTE
the parachute landing fall, or PLF, which is the basic landing
technique that is taught to all military parachutists. It is designed
to lessen the shock of impact when the parachutist first comes in
contact with the earth. PLF drills are practiced over and over again
until the correct body position becomes instinctive. The first hours
of our preparation for parachute training consisted of performing
countless PLFs. We stood on a wood-framed red platform that was
built to simulate the outer door of an aircraft. This "door" was
eight feet above a large, sawdust landing pit, and as we stood in
the door, we were given the command to "go." Before landing in
the sawdust, we would quickly assume the proper prelanding position: legs together, knees slightly bent, head facing forward,
arms extended above our heads. When we exited the "aircraft,"
always jumping off with left foot first, we would hit the ground,
roll to the right or left side, make the proper contact with the sides
of our bodies (ankles, knees, and then butt), and then roll over
onto our backs. In this manner the shock of landing is supposed to
be absorbed through the legs, up to the knees. As the jumper
twists over onto his back he is able to turn and face the canopy of
his parachute. Then, standing upright, each jumper pulls in on his
risers and attempts to collapse the canopy. (All military jumpers
were taught never to land standing upright. Failure to obey this
rule usually resulted in penalty push-ups after the jump.)

By the time we had completed twenty or more of these PLFs,
all to the perfect satisfaction of our Navy jumpmaster, we began
to exit our mock aircraft door backward onto the sawdust landing
pit. The jumpmaster wanted us to "experience every possible type
of landing that we might encounter." Backward?

By midafternoon we were exhausted, but we felt much more

confident for having learned the intricacies of a proper landing, whether it was forward or backward. When we finished our PLF class, we returned to the paraloft for a very detailed briefing and familiarization class on the type of parachute that we would use, the use of our reserve parachute, and the type of aircraft that would take us to the drop zone. At that point, Lance Corporal Thompson asked the jumpmaster when we would make our first jump. "We will all meet here tomorrow, at 0730, for our prejump brief. We'll be airborne by 0800. If there are no other questions, gentlemen, I'll see you here tomorrow."

We checked in at the paraloft at 0700 the following morning and were outfitted with the standard military T-10 main parachute and reserve, and then we walked over to the operations office for our jump-zone brief.

"The drop zone that we will use today is located approximately twenty-five miles northeast of Subic Bay, and thirty-five miles east of Manila. This is a large zone next to an old abandoned military airstrip that the Japanese built during their occupation of the Philippines in World War II. We have a ground security team located at the airstrip, with a safety vehicle provided for your transportation back here to Cubi Point. The weather looks good for the next several days, with some ground winds coming out of the north, but nothing that would exceed five to ten knots. Today, we will be using a prop-driven, twin-engine cargo plane that will be able to accommodate eight jumpers. If there are no questions, please get into your parachute harnesses for a riggers' check, and we'll get on board."

The parachute harness was easy enough to get into, but once on, the shoulder and leg straps had to be tightened down to such a degree they kept us bent over and very uncomfortable. The idea was that once the main canopy was fully deployed, the harness would be pulled skyward and become much more of a pleasure to wear. Four members of one of the Seal team detachments, Lieutenant Singleton, Lance Corporal Thompson, our jumpmaster, and I made up the two, four-man sticks that would jump out onto the drop zone known as "Costa Laos." As our rigger made his final inspection of each man's harness, main, and reserve parachutes, we were given a number to indicate the sequence in which we would exit the aircraft. For some unknown reason, I was given number one.

When our aircraft, a twin-prop S2F, taxied over to where our small group of jumpers had assembled, we climbed on board in reverse order. It was exciting to think that I would be the first one to jump. But that feeling changed dramatically when the jump-master told me that I would be used as the "wind dummy." As such, I would serve to alert the jumpmaster and the other, more experienced jumpers to any changes in wind conditions above the drop zone.

"Doc, you're bigger than most of these other guys, so we always use the bigger guys as our wind dummies. Once we get to jump altitude, I'll bring you back with me, and we'll open up the back hatch. As I'm sure you noticed, this aircraft doesn't have a real door to stand in, so on the signal to go, just tuck your head forward and roll out. It may look like you'll hit the tail, but don't worry about it, no one has hit it yet."

The jumpmaster went forward to talk with the pilot and left us to think about what we had gotten ourselves into. It would be half an hour before we were over the drop zone.

Like every person who has somehow convinced himself that it would be manly and exciting to throw himself out of a perfectly good airplane at an altitude of three thousand feet, I had begun to have second thoughts once the door was shut and our airplane began to taxi down the runway. I looked at the faces of the other jumpers and noticed that each man was staring at someone else. Perhaps we were all looking for the reassurance that none of us was crazy—just a little concerned. There was simply no way that we were going to return to Cubi Point sitting in this same S2F.

At first my thoughts turned toward my former recon team leader, Cpl. Ted Bishop. He had been jump qualified and had really loved it. Our platoon guide, Sgt. Arthur Garcia, had worn not only the gold jump wings of an advanced parachutist but also wore the silver combat jump wings of the Vietnamese Army. They had managed to overcome their initial fear, hadn't they? Those of us who had yet to wear these gold wings of distinction held these Marines in high regard. Could it be so difficult to jump when the order was given?

As I watched the seconds tick by on my Zodiac watch, I did what most new jumpers always do, but would never confess: I talked to God. I told Him that I was grateful to Him for allowing me to live this long. I knew that only with His divine help had I been able to cheat death on several occasions, and I gave Him full credit for that. I then thanked Him for sparing my life each time that I had gone out to patrol against the North Vietnamese. I told Him that I wanted to continue to live, even if it was only to return to Vietnam to avenge the deaths of six close friends. Finally, I confessed to Him that all I wanted was to survive this first jump, and perhaps later we could renegotiate my pledges of fidelity. Someone yelling in my right ear brought me back to reality.

"Listen up! In two minutes we will be over the drop zone. Doc, come back here with me, and I'll hook you up once we get the rear hatch opened. After the doc jumps we'll circle to check on his descent before we put out the rest of you. Just keep seated till I call you back here."

The small hatch had two handles inboard to unlock the door from inside the plane. The jumpmaster unlocked the handles and stowed the door in the back of the plane, then signaled me to come to where he stood. I could feel the warm air as I approached the door, then stood with my hands on top of my helmet so that he could conduct his final check of my gear. He fastened the static-line hook to a steel ring that was bolted to the floor of the plane, then took up several feet of slack static line in his hand.

"I'm going to give you a fast pull when you exit the plane. You won't have to wait long before you have a full canopy. Now, get yourself into the door, and when I say 'go,' roll out!"

The seconds seemed to hang as I waited for that one word which would send me headfirst out of the plane. The jumpmaster's hand went up, and then came the command: "Go!"

As soon as I heard it, I leaned forward and cast my fate—not into the hands of God, but into the hands of the unknown man who had rigged my parachute. I certainly didn't worry about hitting the plane's tail. If you can't see it, it isn't there.

I heard the sounds of my parachute ripping away from the pack as it began to deploy. Then I felt a tremendous jolt as the parachute canopy opened and immediately stopped my forty-three-feet-per-second drop to a gliding forward motion of just about five miles per hour.

I could see our aircraft begin to turn and gain altitude as the pilot and jumpmaster watched my descent and prepared the remaining jumpers to follow suit. The view above the lush Philippine jungle was now spectacular. I had survived the first half of the jump.

It was easy to see the outline of the old airfield as I drifted downward. I could see several people and two vehicles parked beside the runway. I practiced making complete turns to my left and my right, as I had been instructed to do in ground school. There were no sounds other than the distant hum of the aircraft's engines and the sound of the wind under my canopy. I was able to watch the other jumpers as they exited the plane high above me.

We had been told to aim at the drop zone (DZ) by keeping it

between our feet during descent. As I dropped below tree-top level, I remembered not to concentrate on the ground below but to watch the horizon. This would help eliminate the effect known as "ground rush" and prevent me from bracing myself against contact with the ground. It sounded easy, but the experience was a different story.

As I passed between the tops of the closest trees, I wanted to make sure that I was going to land in an unobstructed area. There was no sense in impaling myself on bamboo stakes or landing on any rocks if I could avoid it. We had been told to turn into the wind before landing to help slow the descent. As I looked down, the ground appeared to be rushing up to meet me, and I braced for the impact.

I hit the ground with a perfect two point landing: feet to face. My initial impact knocked the wind out of me. It took several seconds before I could stand up. I was concerned with collapsing my canopy to avoid being dragged across the open ground of the DZ. The area where I landed was level, and it afforded me the opportunity to look up and watch the other jumpers as they prepared for landing.

My elation of having just survived this first jump was not to be denied. I was soon joined by 1st Lieutenant Singleton and Lance Corporal Thompson. We congratulated each other over and over again. We were convinced that we had cheated death and lived to tell about it.

As we rode back toward Subic Bay, we were told by our jumpmaster that we would be able to make two jumps into the same area the following day from a Marine CH-46 helicopter. Our goal was to complete the required five static-line jumps. We celebrated our first jump in the all-ranks club on Grande Island and prepared ourselves for what would be required the following day.

The advanced parachutists who had gone along with us knew that our second jump was going to be considerably different from our first attempt. The thrill of jumping was still alive, but the question "Why?" remained to be answered.

The CH-46 is easily capable of carrying a dozen jumpers, but when we assembled at the Naval air station the following morning, there were only five of us who would be ready to go up. As we flew away from Subic Bay, the realization that we would not be able to simply roll out of the helicopter began to set in. We would get the word to go from the assistant jumpmaster, positioned at the rear ramp of the helicopter. The jumpmaster would spot the DZ and give his assistant the signal. This time I would be the last to go. The honor of being wind dummy went to the lieutenant.

As we approached the DZ, the assistant jumpmaster gave us the command to "stand up," and we went through our last equipment check. The pilot positioned the helicopter on a course that would take us over the old airfield. We moved toward the rear ramp. Our altitude was slightly over thirty-five hundred feet, and we were traveling at approximately ninety knots.

When the command "go" was shouted out by the assistant jumpmaster, the lieutenant stepped off on his left foot and disappeared below the CH-46. The helicopter then banked to the left, and we could see the canopy of the first chute as Singleton drifted toward earth. Once we returned to our original heading, Lance Corporal Thompson and I would jump together.

It took only several minutes to get ourselves back into position, and again the seconds seemed to last for an eternity before we heard the command to "move forward." I watched as the assistant jumpmaster slapped Thompson on the leg and yelled, "Go." I followed right behind Thompson and stepped off into empty space.

We were supposed to count to four thousand, using the one-thousand-and-one, one-thousand-and-two system, so that by the time one thousand and four rolled around, we would be experiencing the opening of our T-10 main parachute. I watched Thompson's main deploy and then lost sight of him. My chute quickly deployed, but something wasn't right. I could feel my head being bent forward and realized that my risers had become twisted behind my neck. I kicked my legs as though riding an imaginary bicycle to untwist myself. It obviously looked pretty funny to Thompson, who was laughing hilariously as we descended together. This time, I wanted to be able to make my landing without having the wind knocked out of my lungs. As I kept the view of the DZ between my feet, I prepared myself for landing. This second jump was indeed better than the first one. The DZ came up to meet me, and my landing was fine.

Thompson and I had come down less than one hundred yards apart, next to the old runway. Within a few minutes, we had rolled up our chutes and joined the lieutenant, waiting for the CH-46 to land. Some of the Filipinos who lived nearby came running over to the DZ and were kind enough to bring along several bottles of Coke, which they shared with us.

After the CH-46 touched down, we stowed our used chutes and prepared ourselves for the last jump of the day. This jump altitude would be twenty-eight hundred feet, and our drop speed was one hundred knots. All five of us would be exiting in a single-file formation, commonly referred to as a stick. Our stick was led by Lance Corporal Thompson, giving each of us the opportunity to stand first in the door. We experienced no problems on this third jump, other than the emotional highs and lows of psyching ourselves up. The exit was smooth; there was no hesitation on anyone's part, and this time we were much more confident of our ability to pick up the DZ, make several midair turns, and actually enjoy ourselves as we descended. The CH-46 landed soon after we did and took us back to Subic Bay. We would make our fourth and fifth jumps from a Marine CH-53 the next morning.

The Marine CH-53, commonly referred to as a "Jolly Green Giant," was fueled and ready to go by the time we arrived at the flight line, carrying our gear. We had assembled a total number of six jumpers, including one flight surgeon who had been a member of the Cubi Point skydiving club. Our drop zone was to be the same old Japanese airfield near Costa Laos. We would be able to complete both of our planned jumps and return to Subic Bay by midafternoon.

After we had become airborne, our Navy jumpmaster came to the rear of the helicopter and told us that we could expect to encounter some gusting winds over the drop zone. He said that he would usually cancel any military jumps if the ground winds were expected to exceed twenty knots, but he felt that there would be little chance of the winds increasing to that speed within the next hour, and so we headed on to the drop zone.

The prearranged order of our stick had me going out first as the wind dummy, followed by Thompson, Singleton, and the two Navy jumpers. As we took our first pass over the DZ, it was impossible to tell if there were any gusting winds at ground level. The DZ personnel had popped a yellow smoke grenade so the pilot of the CH-53 could get a visual sighting of the DZ. The yellow smoke appeared to be thick, indicating little ground wind. We began a slow turn to the right to pick up the compass heading for the drop, and the commands came to "stand up," "hook up," and "stand in the door." I assumed my position on the edge of the wide cargo ramp and waited for the command to go. I felt a slap on the leg, heard the word, and threw down my static assist line, clutched my reserve chute, shouted "Airborne!" and jumped.

Just as before, the short count to 1004 was an eternity, but that now familiar jolt of my harness and the reassuring sound of my nylon canopy ripping open above my head served notice that I had a "full blossom" and could enjoy the trip down to the DZ. It was a bad assumption.

The sound of the wind passing through my canopy and risers began to increase, and I began to sway beneath the parachute. I turned to the left, trying to get myself into the wind instead of being driven forward by it. The oscillations became greater the closer that I got to the DZ. By the time I was one hundred feet above the DZ, I was moving back and forth like the pendulum of a clock. In an attempt to stabilize myself, I pulled down on both sets of my risers, planning to release them just before hitting the ground. But one last gust of wind pushed heavily against my canopy, and as it swung down, I went up. The last thing that I remember was seeing the ground rush up to meet me.

I hit the ground so hard that the football-style helmet that I was wearing broke in half on impact. Unconscious, I was dragged along the ground into a recently cut cane field. My parachute snagged itself on the cane stubble and stopped me from further injury. When I awoke, I was in the back of the CH-53 helicopter, headed for the hospital at Clark Air Base. I was told that I had been unconscious for half an hour.

As we flew toward Clark Air Base, I experienced one of the more interesting phenomena of human physiology, known as "projectile vomiting." The force of impact that I had suffered had created enough pressure on my head to induce this sensation. I could puke with great accuracy to a distance of at least eight feet, with the spasms occurring every few minutes.

The CH-53 landed on a medevac pad next to the hospital, and I was quickly taken by stretcher to the emergency room. Thanks to the CH-53 pilot and the flight surgeon, the Clark hospital emergency room had been contacted, and my current condition had been radioed to the receiving staff. After the preliminaries of my vital signs were checked out, I was X-rayed and placed on the "head ward" of the hospital. My blood pressure had registered at 185 over 100. My head felt as though someone had used it as a bass drum, using hammers for drumsticks. When my X rays were read by the doctor, I was told the unsurprising news that I had suffered a traumatic concussion to my "gourd," and unless the swelling went down soon, the medical staff was considering drilling a series of holes around the skull to relieve the increasing pressure. This was not exactly the sort of news I wanted to hear. In the meantime, there were several large slivers of sugarcane embedded in my back and legs, needing removal. This debridement procedure did not concern me as much as did the thought of having some masked Air Force surgeon apply a Black & Decker drill bit to my forehead. Fortunately, the medication that I was given did work to relieve the pressure in my cranium, and the drilling was scrubbed. I was required to remain on the neurological ward at Clark Air Base hospital for a week of observation.

During the week that I was at Clark, I was visited once by Lieutenant Singleton and Lance Corporal Thompson. They were leaving the Philippines, en route to Vietnam, and had brought my gear with them from Subic Bay. It was the last time that I would see either of them, and I suddenly found myself wondering how I was to get back to Phu Bai and my platoon at 3d Force Reconnaissance Company.

When I was given the green light to be discharged from the hospital, the Marine Corps liaison representative produced a set of orders that transferred me from the Clark Air Base hospital to Okinawa for further processing back to Vietnam. I was more than a little anxious to leave.

——— OKINAWA ———

AFTER OUR C-141 STARLIFTER CARGO JET LANDED AT the Kadena Air Base, it taxied to a stop in an area that was close to the main administrative processing center, making it easy to find the transportation that would take me to the 3d Marine Division headquarters at Camp Hansen. There I would find the division surgeon's office and wait to be processed with a new set of orders, taking me back to duty with 3d Force Recon Company in Vietnam.

The bus ride up the eastern side of the island to Camp Hansen took less than an hour, and as our bus passed through the camp's first gate, it was readily apparent that the war in Vietnam was still on, as the nonstop business of processing newly arrived Marines and corpsmen continued. Small groups of Marines could be seen marching to and from the different areas of the camp. The processing still required three or four days. Life in this staging camp was comprised of four distinct activities: processing, assignment to working parties, eating, and sleeping. None of the four events was particularly enjoyable, and the only positive thing was that they served to burn up the long hours of waiting.

When I arrived at the office of the division surgeon, I placed my orders and medical records on the countertop and waited for one of the administrative clerks to assist me in checking in. I was approached by a Navy hospitalman apprentice, who was one of several corpsmen working for the administrative section. He read through my orders and medical records, looked up and smiled.

"Hi there. It looks here like you're headed back to Vietnam after a short vacation in the Philippines. That parachuting stuff must have really been a bitch. I don't think I'd ever want to do that kind of duty!"

"Well, it wasn't exactly a vacation. If you looked at the last part of that medical record, you'd see that the only relaxing that I got to do was a week on a head ward at Clark Air Base hospital. I barely escaped having my skull drilled on by the Air Force."

"The way that I see it is that anyone crazy enough to jump out of a perfectly good airplane should have his head examined."

Disgusted at having to look at, and listen to, this lisping clown, I asked, "How long do you think I'll be here before I can rejoin my unit in Vietnam?"

"You're just one of a million waiting to get a seat out of here. What's the rush? The war may be over by the time you get slated, and I'm sure you wouldn't want to be the last doc to die with the Marines, would you?"

"Listen, why don't you just start processing my orders, get me on a flight manifest, and point me in the direction of someone who can answer a few simple questions? Can you do that?"

My comments got the immediate attention of one of the 1st class corpsmen who was seated behind a green metal desk. He came over to the counter and stood beside the clerk. He wore the gold jump wings of an advanced parachutist above his left breast pocket.

"Sorry about him. His act has a way of irritating people. What can I do for you?"

"My name is Norton, and I've just come from the Philippines. I went to scuba school there and did some parachute training out of Cubi Point with the Navy. My last jump got me a week in the hospital at Clark. All I want to know is how soon it will be before I can get on a flight that will take me to Da Nang so that I can rejoin my company?"

"Well, the clerk was right about one thing. There are a lot of people waiting to go. I think that I might be able to do you a favor while you're waiting for your flight. This morning the chief told me that we had received a request for medical support at the Army's jump school down at Camp Zukeran. Would you be interested in helping me out down there, or have you decided not to pursue a career in jumping out of airplanes? They wanted some trained medical support to be available around their drop zone. You'd be doing us a favor, and you'd get to spend three or four days with the Army instead of sitting on your butt around here."

"I'll go, and I appreciate you asking me to help. Is it okay if I check back here at the end of each day to see if there's any word on my flight?"

"Yeah, sure. I may be able to work things out so that we can even make a few jumps while we're down at Zukeran. I'll make sure that you don't go and get yourself killed here before you go back to Vietnam. That would be too ironic for the chief to handle. In the meantime I'll take care of getting your orders and flight date. The transient barracks for our corpsmen is out that door and two buildings down on the left side of the street. There are only four other docs billeted there who are waiting to go in country. One is waiting to go back to the States. Be here at 0600 tomorrow for your ride to Camp Zukeran, Norton, and good luck."

The transient barracks was the same building that I had stayed in nine months earlier, and nothing about it had changed. For each occupant there was one metal-framed bunk bed, one wall locker, and a common head. I threw my seabag beside one of the lower racks, and was in the process of unsorting my gear when I heard a familiar voice.

"Well, no shit, look who's here on Okinawa!"

I looked up to see the round and smiling face of HM3 Mike Barry. Barry had been a ward corpsman with me at the Newport Naval hospital, and now he was on his way home after his overseas tour. He was the first person from home that I had met in nearly nine months. Knowing Mike's great sense of humor, my immediate thought was that life in the transient's barracks would not be so dull after all. Then I found out that he was leaving Okinawa the following day. But there would still be time enough for us to go to the enlisted club and rekindle old memories of the good times that we had shared at the hospital and on liberty. We spent the evening swapping lies, telling war stories, and drinking beer until we closed the club. The next morning I was up early enough to say good-bye to a very hung over Mike Barry, and I was ready to meet the van that took me and the 1st class corpsman, Bliss, down the coast to Camp Zukeran, and the Army's jump school.

The U.S. Army's Airborne School at Camp Zukeran was a place of constant activity. Soldiers could be seen moving from place to place, vehicles were in constant motion throughout the camp, and student jumpers were utilizing the training towers when we arrived. The camp had a musical quality to it. Whenever the Airborne students moved from one place to another, their pace was at a constant double time. Their jump boots beat out a steady rhythm that was accompanied only by the sound of deep voices

singing the various running chants as they moved. The chant that
no Airborne student failed to learn began:

> C-130 rollin' down the strip,
> Airborne daddy gonna take a little trip.
> Stand up, hook up, shuffle to the door,
> Jump right out and count to four.
> If my 'chute don't blossom wide,
> I've got another one by my side.
> If that 'chute don't blossom round,
> I'll be the first one on the ground.
> If I die in a combat zone,
> Just box me up and send me home.
> Pin those wings upon my chest,
> And tell my mom I did my best.
> Airborne, all the way,
> Airborne, every day.

There were many variations to this one theme, but this was
the basic song that carried men to and from classrooms, formations, PT sessions, and into aircraft. It was a motivation chant
that bonded student companies in a common cause, and it
worked.

I followed Bliss into the office of one of the senior enlisted
Army medical representatives at the school, a master sergeant
named Moljeski, who was also a master parachutist. After he and
Bliss exchanged greetings, the master sergeant invited us to sit
down and offered us a cup of black coffee.

Bliss explained that we would be available for several days of
additional duty at Camp Zukeran and then told the master sergeant
how I had arrived at Camp Hansen from the Philippines and
related the story of my hospitalization via parachute operations.

The master sergeant said that he had an instant cure for anyone
who had had their confidence shaken in a bad jump, and without
a moment of hesitation, he picked up his telephone, dialed away,
and told the person at the other end of the line to add one more
name to the afternoon's jump manifest, then spelled out my last
name.

"Doc, have you got any problems with that? I talked with the
operations chief, and he and I are old friends. You can jump with
one of the student companies this afternoon."

"No, sir, I don't have any problems with that. What type of
aircraft will we be jumping from?"

"This afternoon's jump is scheduled to be from a C-130, and if you haven't jumped one, then you're in for a pleasant experience. I'll tell you all about it while we're driving over to the DZ. Let's get the hell out of here. That first stick will be on the ground in less than an hour, and we need to be there."

As we left Camp Zukeran and rode toward the drop zone, the Army master sergeant began to recount his experience and thoughts about parachute operations.

"There have been a hell of a lot of changes made since I first joined the Army back in 1948. I was a straight-leg infantryman and wanted something just a little more exciting than digging fighting holes and wearing out the leather soles of my boots walking post, so I volunteered. I came from a poor Polish neighborhood near Pittsburgh, and I wanted to be a part of something special. Being a paratrooper was just the ticket. It was really special back then. Men like Gavin and Ridgeway had made world history being with the paratroopers in Europe.

"The selection process was a lot different then, too. No one under the age of eighteen was allowed to go Airborne, and no one older than thirty-two could join, either. No one could wear glasses, and 20/40 vision was the minimum requirement. If you weighed more than 185 pounds you'd be sent back to your command. Rules were strictly enforced. They didn't care if you were Eleanor Roosevelt's kid, if you walked through the door at 186 pounds, you were told to hit the bricks.

"We were really conscious of accidents and injuries. The rate of injuries had a direct link to the purse strings. If you had few injuries, the money to train was made available. But if someone was hurt badly, or killed, in a jump, there was a fast change of command and investigations galore.

"The training has gotten a lot better," said Moljeski. "We still use the thirty-four-foot tower to start out our 'cherry jumpers,' and then we move them over to the 250-foot tower for four controlled drops. That is the real gut check. After that, we figure that they're ready to hit the silk, and we move them to the flight line at Kadena for five jumps. The days of the DC-3 and C-47s are over. The C-117 was my favorite bird to jump while I was at Fort Benning, but now the CH-46, C-130 Hercules, and C-141 are all we use here—outside of some C-47 Chinook helicopter jumps and the occasional Huey hot-dog stuff for Special Forces dog-and-pony shows.

"The way we were taught was that jumping was only a small part of the game. The real business began once we got on the ground. It's no different today. Sure the aircraft have changed a lot. Christ, we're even making jumps from C-141 Starlifters at 160 knots. But that just allows us to get there faster. But, I can't deny that I still get that thrill every time I suit up. It is always unforgettable.''

Bliss and I spent that morning standing beside one of the Army's great characters. He was a true believer, and he continued on with his litany of Airborne history as we watched stick after stick of student jumpers landing on or near the drop zone.

All around the drop zone the Army Airborne instructors, called "black hats" because of their black, drill-instructor-type covers, shouted up instructions to the descending parachutists over battery-powered bullhorns. The drop zone was on the western side of the island and was part of an old runway still within the confines of the air base. The powerful bullhorns could make the instructors' voices heard over the noise of aircraft passing over.

"You there! Turn into the wind! Turn left! Bend those knees— now turn, turn! That's right! Watch where you're headed. You there! Don't be looking down here at me. Into the wind, not with it!''

After the jump had been completed, we followed the student company back to Camp Zukeran and listened as orders were given to the student company. They were told to be seated in bleachers at 1330 for the afternoon's jump briefing, then sent off to eat lunch. Following the briefing, they would draw their gear and be ready for the transportation that would take them to Kadena. This time, I would not be going along for the ride, but for the jump!

"All right, knock off the chatter and listen up. This will be your fourth jump. This morning's jump went well, with the exception of several individuals who wanted to practice stand-up landings. Once again, gentlemen, we do not do stand-up landings. Is that clear?''

One hundred voices responded in unison, "Yes, sir!''

"Now, let's get on to the business at hand, this afternoon's jump brief.''

The information that was standard for a daytime parachute jump had been written out in paragraph format on a large blackboard. The date, time of execution, name of the drop zone, conditions within the zone, weather conditions for the next twenty-four hours, radio frequencies, wind direction, altitude, and type of aircraft gave all student jumpers the information that they would need. In fact, there was usually more information presented than was really required. The purpose of the brief was to ensure that the logistical requirements had all been met and that nothing had been forgotten.

The company of student jumpers that I now sat with had been through the physical conditioning known as "ground week," and had been thoroughly schooled in the basics of exiting aircraft and safe landing procedures. The second week of training, known as "tower week," had prepared them for landings in water, through trees, and for dealing with electrical wires. All that remained in this third week of training, appropriately named "jump week," was to complete the fourth and fifth jumps, and to graduate from Airborne school.

"The last part of this brief is to cover the emergency procedures for a towed jumper. If the jumper, in his attempt to exit the aircraft, has not broken away from his static line, then he is assumed to be a towed jumper. He will signal the jumpmaster that he is conscious by placing both of his hands on top of his helmet. The jumpmaster will then notify the pilot who will attempt to gain altitude. The jumpmaster will attempt to break the static-line connection, so that the towed jumper will then separate from the aircraft. Once freed, the jumper will immediately deploy his reserve parachute and land accordingly. In the event that the towed jumper is unconscious, he will be unable to signal to the jumpmaster. The jumpmaster will notify the pilot, and after gaining altitude, the jumpmaster may elect to reach the unconscious jumper by lowering himself down the static line to cut the jumper free, or he may elect to try to retrieve the unconscious jumper back into the aircraft. The last course of action considered is to land with the towed jumper. In the event of using the landing option, the runway will be foamed to protect the unconscious jumper. Are there any questions?"

After listening to such an extraordinary briefing dealing with emergency procedures, there were bound to be some interesting questions. And given the character of most of these men, black humor was the order of the day.

"Sir, do you think that a towed jumper will stand a good chance of surviving a landing on a concrete runway at 130 miles per hour, or do you think that he would choke to death first from ingesting the foam before he would be scraped to death?"

"Sir, what would happen to the unconscious towed jumper if the jumpmaster hasn't quite reached him and the static line separates from the aircraft?"

"Sir, is the towed jumper supposed to wait for the plane to gain altitude before he signals to the jumpmaster that he is okay?"

These rapid-fire questions were more than the briefing instructor could handle.

"Look, you wise guys, none of this kind of stuff has happened as long as I've been here, and I don't expect it to start now. The captain said to read everything on the brief sheet, and that is exactly what I'm doing. If you end up as a hung jumper, you will either live or die. If you live, you can tell me all about your new experience. If you die, then you obviously didn't pay attention to my safety brief. Now, get off your asses and get into those trucks. This concludes today's brief."

Doc Bliss and Master Sergeant Moljeski met me to say goodbye next to one of the trucks. They said that the next time they would see me would be at the drop zone. Within an hour, I was fully suited up in a new parachute harness and helmet and waiting to board the Lockheed C-130. I was in the third of four sticks of jumpers who boarded the aircraft, and within minutes the engines came alive, and we taxied down the runway for takeoff. Our jump altitude was set for thirteen hundred feet, much closer to Mother Earth than I had experienced in the Philippines. It did not take our C-130 long to be in position. As the rear side door opened to expose the ground below, the jumpmaster began his ritual of barking short commands.

"Get ready!" were the first words that filled the plane.

"Stand up and hook up!" brought all four sticks to a standing position, reaching for the retainer cable that would connect each man's static line to the aircraft. As each man went through the drill of last-minute equipment checks, the fateful words were heard throughout the aircraft: "Stand in the door!"

The moment that I had been waiting for was now at hand. I was comfortable being in the third stick, as it enabled me to watch the way the first two sticks exited the C-130. This would be no cakewalk out the back door of a CH-53. The last jumper in each stick was trained to push his people forward. There was no time given for hesitation or second thoughts. The stick would exit almost as one, so that everyone would land in the same zone and at the same time.

The command "Go" put people in motion. The first stick of jumpers ran past me toward the exit door. The second stick began to follow in trace, but their momentum was suddenly stopped when one student froze at the door.

The technique used to exit the C-130 requires the jumper to

place his hands on the outside of the door and simply throw himself forward and away from the aircraft. To go out the door halfheartedly allows the blast of outside air to turn a timid jumper inboard and slam him facefirst against the side of the plane. The unusual sound of someone being slammed down the outside of the airplane instantly produced looks of disbelief within the plane.

Once the frightened jumper was gone, great shouts of laughter could be heard from those remaining to go. My stick began to get caught up in the momentum of the movement, and we began to shuffle toward the door. The sight of men stepping out in the roar of the engines caused a rush of adrenaline to wash over me, and within seconds, I found my hands on the outside of the C-130, trying to jump on top of the man in front of me. My entire concentration was fixed on him, and it kept my mind from wandering back to my last episode of parachuting. Once this moment had passed, I would be free from the memory of past events.

I don't remember counting out loud to reach the point of 1004 when I would have to grab for the D-ring of my reserve chute. That familiar ripping sound of my parachute deploying and the sudden shock of the nylon harness tightening between my legs let me know immediately that I had a good canopy over my head. The sky was mine, and I could enjoy the ride down to the drop zone.

I turned sharply to the right, trying to get my bearings centered on where I could land. There were dozens of parachutes in the sky around me, and the sound of voices coming through the bullhorns on the ground could be heard by all of us. Exiting at thirteen hundred feet did not give us much time for hanging in the air, and the time was rapidly approaching to get into a good landing position. The drop zone was flat, and the ground was soft, but I wanted to make sure that I would not repeat my last experience. I had enough time left to turn into the wind, "milk" my risers down, and prepare for an easy landing. As soon as I felt I was within twenty feet of the ground, I let go of the toggles and executed a good PLF. There was no gut-wrenching slam into the ground, and I recovered into a standing position, looking at Doc Bliss and Master Sergeant Moljeski.

"Not too bad for a cherry jumper. Any problems with this jump?" Moljeski asked.

"No, sir, it worked out okay. One guy froze in the door for a couple of seconds and kissed the side of the plane on the way out, but other than that there were no hang-ups. There's a lot to be said for the Army's method of moving people out of an aircraft as fast as these guys do it. It's a lot different from the style I was using in the Philippines.''

With my parachute stuffed into its carrying bag, we walked back toward the center of the large drop zone.

This was one memorable moment of great relief for me. Knowing that I had just completed my fifth jump, I could look forward to getting my gold wings once I returned to 3d Force Recon Company. I would need to complete five additional jumps to be considered an ''advanced'' parachutist. The jump-qualified Marines of Force Recon did not consider those individuals who wore the Army's ''lead wings'' to be on an equal scale. In fact, those Marines who were assigned to Force Recon and were not jump qualified were simply referred to, in disgust, as being ''legs.''

Doc Bliss and Master Sergeant Moljeski had shown me the way to regain my lost confidence. They said that they, too, had each experienced the same kind of moment, when fear of the unknown had taken over, but it was easy to regain lost confidence as long as the desire to do so was there. I was able to participate two days later in one more memorable jump on the island of Okinawa.

The Air Force had a number of squadrons of C-141 Starlifter cargo jets based at Kadena, and periodically they were utilized for parachute operations with the Army. The last jump for the student company that I had been with the day before was a scheduled night jump. The night jump was considered to be the most difficult of the five required jumps because of the obvious visual restrictions and the *feeling* of the jump. The various sounds of the aircraft engines, the constant smell of jet fuel that lay heavy in the air, and the jarring impact of the opening of the parachute are no different than a daytime jump. But the unusual sensation of stepping out in the black void of darkness provides the added dimension of the unknown. The first-time night jump is an attention getter of the first order.

Our C-141 left the Kadena runway shortly after 2200 on the moonlit night of our jump. I was in the last of the four sticks of ten jumpers aboard, and there was very little talking between any of us. When the command to ''get ready'' was given, the reaction inside the plane was automatic. The dim, red-colored interior lights of the huge cargo bay made the effect that much more sensational as the loud whining noises of hydraulic motors alerted us to the cargo doors opening. This sound was quickly replaced by the screaming pitch of the aircraft's jet engines, and the feeling of warm, wet, outside air filled the interior of the plane. The command to "stand up and hook up" started us in motion, and the long-awaited command to "go" quickly followed.

A shield had been placed behind the inboard jet engine to protect us from the tremendous blast of the jet engine, but it really did little good when the airspeed at the time of exiting was close to 160 miles per hour! The opening of the parachute in total darkness seems to take forever.

I experienced no problems during my exit from the C-141. Our stick had no delays, and the entire movement ran smoothly to the door. It was what happened outside the aircraft that made the difference. Trying to picture where I was in relation to the drop zone was difficult. I knew that I had a good canopy. I could feel it, and when I turned to get a 360-degree view of the surrounding area, I had no trouble. The night sky was full of voices of the other jumpers as they talked back and forth to one another, trying to figure out how high up they were. We knew from our briefing that our jump altitude was eighteen hundred feet, and it was easy to time the descent time to the ground. It was simply the fact there was so little light to guide on that made the jump so scary. No one wanted to be caught off guard as the ground below rushed up to greet each of us. Fortunately, being in the fourth stick gave me and my fellow jumpers enough time above to hear the grunts and groans of those below us as they met with the surface of the drop zone. That was the best way of judging how soon we would be amongst them. A dog kennel was located close to the drop zone, and the additional sounds of barking dogs gave us their position and a place to avoid.

Once on the ground, it was only a matter of a few minutes before we had accounted for the members of the stick. There had been no injuries suffered by any of the students. What had been considered a difficult situation was now a great memory, and I felt confident that I could stand in the door without my knees knocking.

After spending these four days on Okinawa, I was finally scheduled for a flight that took me back to Vietnam. I thanked Doc Bliss and Master Sergeant Moljeski for all of their help and guidance in allowing me to make the two jumps. It had made a great difference.

Carrying just my half-filled seabag, I stood, once again, in the long line to board an American Airlines jetliner that was taking more than one hundred Marines and corpsmen into Vietnam. The thought of rejoining 3d Force Recon Company had given me a great deal to think about, and unlike those men who were experiencing the utter loneliness of this flight, for the first time, my mind was full of anticipation of seeing my closest friends once more.

— BACK IN COUNTRY —

I HAVE SAID MANY TIMES IN THE PAST THAT THE SINgle most lonely event I remember was that first flight taking me from the island of Okinawa into the country of Vietnam. I could recall the feelings of uncertainty and of being alone. I knew no one on the plane, and I thought that it was best to just keep quiet and think about what I had gotten myself into. Now that I was about to return to Vietnam with another group of strangers, those same thoughts and feelings returned.

The announcement was made for us to board the plane, and the mood of the passengers changed instantly.

These same men, strangers to me, and perhaps to one another, who had only moments earlier been laughing and joking with one another as they waited in line to board the plane, now sat very much alone in an aircraft that was filled to capacity. All of the talking that could be heard above a whisper went dead still the moment our jet's wheels lifted off the runway at Kadena Air Base.

The eyes of many of these men were fixed in a reflective stare as they searched their minds for the answers to so many lingering and unanswerable questions: Have I prepared my family for this long period of separation? Am I really prepared for what is about to happen to me? Did I pay close attention to what was being taught to me during those many hours and days of training prior to this flight? Will I be around 365 days from now to be on a flight home, or will I be returned to the United States in a flag-draped casket? What if there are no pieces to bring home?

Age, rank, branch of service, race, and religion made no real difference. These common thoughts affected everyone. The experience was probably more difficult for those men who were going into Vietnam for their second or third tour of duty. I can only liken it to a person who is about to dive from a great height into a pool of water. Standing on the diving board was like waiting on Okinawa; the flight over was the dive, and hitting the water was landing in Da Nang.

As we headed west, I thought that there would be plenty of time for me to organize my thoughts in preparation for my return to 3d Force Recon Company. It had been less than a month since I had left Phu Bai for the Philippines, but being away from the daily routine of life in the reconnaissance company had allowed me the luxury of putting aside thoughts about what was important in a combat environment. I could only imagine what new areas the company may have been assigned to patrol, and since I had not been in communication with anyone in 3d Force, I could only hope that there had been no other casualties or deaths since I had left. It was reassuring and very comforting to know that I, unlike the majority of the men on this flight, was going back to a unit that I was familiar with, and that I would be reunited with trusted and well-trained Marines. I felt sorry for those who were experiencing the great sensation of the unknown for the first time, and I secretly hoped that they would fare as well as I had.

When we began our final approach into Da Nang, the pilot's voice came over the intercom speaker. He told us what the weather conditions were on the ground and asked us all to get off the aircraft in a "quick but orderly manner," and then he wished us all "good luck." Immediately, there began to be heard the audible mumblings that Marines are famous for in making reference to the fact that at least this pilot would get to leave on the same plane that brought him into Vietnam. "Good luck" be damned!

Our movement from the plane to the processing hangar was as orderly as had been requested, and once my eyes had adjusted to the reduced light inside the building, I could make out those huge and familiar red signs that hung high above the administrative clerks' counter: WELCOME TO VIETNAM 1ST MARINE DIVISION HERE, FORCE LOGISTICS COMMAND HERE, STAFF NCO'S AND OFFICERS HERE, and ALL OTHERS HERE. I headed toward the all-others line, knowing that I was a member of the 3d Marine Division, whether there was a sign for me to stand before or not.

I wondered why the powers that be had made it more confusing by removing the old 3d Marine Division sign from the ceiling. That question was soon addressed by a staff sergeant, who sat behind the counter.

"Where are you headed to, Doc?"

"I'm assigned to 3d Force Recon Company which is located at Phu Bai. I've just come back in country after being in scuba school and jump school. Do you think that you can help me get out of here and up to Phu Bai?''

"Sure, Doc, that'll be easy, and you won't have to go up to Phu Bai to find your company.''

"Why not? They were there when I left.''

"'Cause I've got a good friend over at 1st Recon Battalion, and I know from having just come from the division headquarters that 3d Force Recon is colocated with 1st Recon Battalion, over near 1st Medical Battalion.''

"How can I get from here to there?''

"Just wait here for an hour or so. I have to make another admin run over to the division CP at noontime, and I can give you a lift.''

As we rode in the jeep from the Da Nang airport toward the 1st Marine Division's headquarters, I asked the staff sergeant why the 3d Marine Division sign had been removed from the ceiling of the hangar.

"The 3d Marine Division started to pull out of I Corps in October, and it wasn't too many weeks later before we were told to yank the sign down. If incoming people still had orders to report to the 3d Marine Division, we rerouted them into the 1st Marines. I'm starting to get the feeling that the war may be winding down. When you listen to those guys who've gotten here for the first time, they start talking about not wanting to be the last guy killed before the war ends. I hadn't heard new guys talking like that last year. Maybe they know something that we don't.''

The jeep ride to the division CP took less than half an hour, and it was my first opportunity to see Da Nang from the view afforded by an open jeep. The roads around Da Nang were a flurry of activity as military vehicles, commercial trucks, and motorcycles all tried to jockey for position. Our pace was a constant stop-and-go action, as handcarts pulled by very old men, and huge brown-black water buffalo herded by small boys, interrupted the traffic pattern.

I squinted to see through the glaring silver sheen caused by the sun's brilliant reflection off the hundreds of little rice paddies, which covered the flat ground around Da Nang. Only the sporadic rise of the earthen dikes that bordered the paddies broke this mirrorlike effect.

As the wind changed direction, the heavy stink of night soil coming from the rice fields filled my senses. It was that familiar foul stench of Vietnam, quickly returning to remind me where I was.

As we got closer to our destination, my mood began to change from apprehension to great anticipation in being reunited with old friends. The voice of the staff sergeant brought me back to reality.

"Okay, Doc, this is where you get off. First Recon Battalion is straight up that road, and 3d Force Recon Company is on the other side of their mess hall. Good luck."

The jeep roared out of sight, and I walked on toward the big, red, circular sign that read 3D FORCE RECONNAISSANCE COMPANY, III MAF.

I went into the green hootch marked S-1, and reported to S. Sgt. Frank Schemmel, the company administrative chief.

"Welcome home, Doctor, we've been waiting for you."

"Sorry to have been away for so long. I liked the Philippines so much that I tried to stay there, but they wouldn't have me."

"Lieutenant Morris is in the back. He said that when you showed up, he wanted to talk to you, so don't disappear on me. There's a lot to tell you."

"Well, no shit, Doc, where the hell have you been?" the lieutenant asked. "Singleton and Thompson came back here a couple of weeks ago and said that you had tried to kill yourself jumping out of Navy airplanes. You don't look any worse than you ever did. Welcome back!"

I spent the better part of the next hour relating stories about my scuba diving, parachuting, and liberty experience to the company adjutant and admin chief, who were kind enough to sit and listen. When I was finished, it was their turn, and they shared their story about what had happened to 3d Force Recon since I had left the company in early February.

Staff Sergeant Schemmel began, "There are only twenty-five of us left as part of a cadre force."

"Where did everyone go?"

"Major Lee was sent down to the 7th Marines, and they are down by LZ Ross. Captain Hisler went back to the States with orders to Quantico, Virginia. Lieutenant Robinson went to Quantico, too. Lieutenant Brown said he was going to get out when he got back to Camp Pendleton. First Sergeant Henderson went back to duty at Treasure Island. I feel sorry for those hippies in San Francisco when he shows up. He must have taken twenty other Marines with him when the orders came down from the division G-2 section."

"So, who's left?"

"Lieutenant Coffman is our new commanding officer, and Lieutenant Hodge is still here, too. But that's it for the officers. The only staff NCOs left are me and Staff Sergeant Tapp. The rest have either gone back to the States, or over to 1st Force Recon Company, depending on how much time they had left to do when 3d Force was placed in cadre.''

"Why did they do this?"

"To tell ya the truth, I don't really know. There were lots of rumors floating around. We heard 'em all. The war is nearly over. The Army was taking over our AO [area of operation]. The ARVNs were going to push into the A Shau Valley and run the NVA out. You name it, we heard it back at Phu Bai. The one person who can tell you more about it than anybody is Lieutenant Coffman. He's over in the operations hootch and I know that he wanted to see you when you returned. You'd better get over there, Doc, and let him know you're home.''

Lt. "Bucky" Coffman, formerly the operations and training officer of 3d Force Recon Company, was sitting on the back steps of the S-3 hootch when I walked in to see him. Clad only in his tiger-striped shorts, dog tags, and jungle boots, he was busy attacking a bowl of vanilla ice cream, and for the first time since I had met him, he appeared to me a very tired man. On all other occasions, Lieutenant Coffman was nothing short of a ball of fire. His enthusiasm, eagerness, and spirit had always been a well of inspiration to the Marines of the company, but it was clear in seeing him now that something had happened to change that spirit.

He turned around to see me approaching, and a broad smile started to spread over his face.

"Well, no shit, Doctor! What took you so long in getting back home? I figured that you had gone over the hill to the P.I. and fallen for the charms of one of those little brown-skinned virgins of Olongapo.''

"It seems like I've been gone a lot longer than a month, sir. Lieutenant Morris told me to come over here and check in to let you know that I was back. Sir, what has happened to all of the men who were in the company? This place looks like a ghost town.''

"Sit down, Doc, and I'll tell you what has happened since you left us.

"General Nickerson was due to rotate back to the States, and when that happened, his protection as our 'godfather' went away, too. He used his reconnaissance assets the way that they were designed to be used, but other people in very high places don't have his great wisdom. Once the way was cleared for III MAF to leave I Corps, the new powers that be decided to shut down 3d

Force Recon Company and let 1st Recon Battalion and 1st Force Recon Company finally earn their pay.''

"Hadn't they been earning their pay all along?''

"The team members had, but there are too many political game players who have gotten themselves in our business. It's too complicated to explain right now. Just realize that we still have a job to do for as long as we're here. You'll probably be back in the bush in a couple of days. How does that sound?''

"That's okay with me, but I'd like to take a look around and see who's still here. Can you tell me who has gone back to the States?''

"Major Lee is still here in I Corps, and he's working for Lt. Col. Charlie Cooper as his operations officer. Captain Hisler went back to see his wife and kids, and he's got orders for Quantico, Virginia. He left a letter for me to give to you. It's with your gear. The 1st Sergeant, Gunny Collins, Gunny Hamilton, and Gunny Bilodeau, all went back to the States. Staff Sergeant Williams is over at 1st Force Recon Company, and Staff Sergeant Tapp is still here. The corpsmen who were here when you left, Hansen, Montgomery, and Goodard, have all been reassigned. We wanted to keep you with the company, but the division surgeon's office knows that there is need for a jump-and-scuba-qualified corpsman over at 1st Force. We can keep you here for a little while to help in training some Korean Recon Marines from the 2d ROK Brigade. But sooner or later, you're going to end up over at 1st Force. You'll find McVey, Draper, Sexton, Gable, and Mahkewa all waiting for you there. I'll talk to their XO, Captain Centers, and let him know what we plan to do with you. That's it for right now, Doc. Have you got any questions?''

"No, sir. I just want to find a hootch, locate my old mail, and then get my gear squared away.''

"All of your personal gear stayed right where it was. When we got the word to move from Phu Bai down here to Da Nang, we boxed, labeled, and banded it, and put it all in our new supply hootch.''

In jest he added, "If you can find that worthless corporal, Sonny Cannon, he'll know exactly where it's located. He was one of the guys on Staff Sergeant Tate's working party who had to load and unload all of that crap. It's the first time that he's worked since he's been here. Go find Sonny, and I'll talk with you later. Dismissed.''

When I left the operations hootch, I headed toward the sign that read 1ST PLATOON AREA, hoping that I would find Corporal Cannon in one of the hootches. Sonny Cannon had been the team leader of Team Eversharp, one of the recon teams from the 1st

Platoon, for nearly a year. He had come to 3d Force Reconnaissance Company from 5th Force Recon at Camp Lejeune, and he called Darlington, South Carolina, home. He had earned a fine reputation as a team leader, and he was known to be as good as his word. Sonny also had a keen sense of humor, and that was a common bond between the two of us. We had become very good friends, and I was looking forward to seeing him again.

While looking for Sonny, I encountered Lance Corporal Kirkindall, who welcomed me back and told me that I would find Sonny asleep in his rack. Not wanting to miss a golden opportunity for having some fun, I quietly entered the hootch and crept up next to the unsuspecting form of the corporal. He had fallen asleep with his boots and utility trousers on, still wearing his sunglasses. The mosquito netting which hung down and around his rack had not been placed in a position to protect him, and next to his head, on an ammunition-box nightstand, was his shaving kit. Seeing the can of shaving cream, standing upright in his leather kit so close to his head, gave me the idea to pull off an old squad-bay practical joke that we had learned in boot camp.

When the command "attention on deck" is given, all personnel are trained to immediately snap to the position of attention. This instantaneous response to orders is so well instilled in Marines that they behave automatically. Knowing that Corporal Cannon would be awakened by my shouted command, it was not enough just to watch him try and leap out of bed from a sound sleep and attempt to stand at the position of attention. There had to be more to it to make this gag worthy of screwing with the likes of Sonny Cannon.

I removed the can of shaving cream from his kit and squirted a sizable dab of the thick, white cream into the palm of my hand. I then silently applied equal amounts of shaving cream to each lens of his shades. When he opened his eyes, he would first be blind. I unlaced his left boot and tied the lace to the outer rail of his steel-framed bed.

Several recon Marines from the 1st Platoon had seen me enter their hootch, and wanting to witness the practical joke on their teammate, they managed to keep quiet as I went about my business. They had even gathered several other Marines from outside of their hooch and invited them inside to share in the experience. With half a dozen Marines standing around the sleeping Corporal, I knelt down beside him and shouted, "Attention on deck!" The results were nothing less than perfect.

The shout of the command so close to his ear caused a tiny "eyes-open" switch to be turned on inside of Cannon's brain, and the second switch to "get off your ass and onto your feet" was instantly blown when the "eyes-open" process met with total darkness. Sonny's body was trying desperately to keep up with what his brain had been trained to do, but shaving cream and a hamstrung boot caused a malfunction. His body was set in motion to execute standing at attention on one leg and in total darkness. It was hilarious.

Cannon's arms shot out straight as his hands tried to grab at the invisible enemy. His right leg felt gingerly for the floor, and when his boot met with the plywood flooring, he tried to stand up, wrapping himself tightly in his mosquito netting. He looked like some poor black insect with bulging white eyes, helplessly ensnared in a great, green spider's web.

"Norton, you rotten som' bitch! I know you is behind this shit."

My dark-skinned, human-fly buddy had sensed my masterful hand in his misery, and now I knew that I could never turn my back on this corporal for even one isolated moment. Cannon was looking up at us from the floor as we backed out of the hootch; his shouted curse was aimed squarely at me.

"Payback is a medevac, you no-good, rotten, squid son of a bitch! When you left us at Phu Bai I never thought that I would see you again. Now you've come back, and the only thing you brought back to me is trouble. You will pay for this!"

Ten minutes later I returned to Sonny's hootch, hoping it was a safe area to approach. There was Corporal Cannon still lying in his rack.

"What do you want, Doctor? I knew when I heard that you'd returned to the company that you'd want something from me."

"Lieutenant Coffman said that you'd know where my gear was stashed in the supply hootch. What I want is for you to get off your butt and point me in the direction of my footlockers. Do you think you can handle that?"

"If it will get you out of here and away from me for the rest of the afternoon, then I will agree to help the helpless. Let's go."

Not long after Sonny had left, 1st Lieutenant Coffman came into my new hootch, and sitting on my rack, he lit up a Salem cigarette.

"Doc, I want to ask you a straight question, and I expect a straight answer."

"Sure, sir. What's on your mind?"

"How did all of you guys get along at scuba school? What I'm really getting at is you're one of the few guys who has left the company for the outside world and returned. Are things really different out there?"

"I guess not, sir. I didn't see any big changes. Why?"

"Well, I know that you and Cannon are tight, and something happened just after we came south to Da Nang, and I want to know if we've been out in the bush too long, or if things have taken a turn for the worse."

"What happened?"

"Just after we came to 1st Recon Battalion, I just happened to be walking behind Cannon, on the way to the mess hall. Three black Marines approached him, and when they got close, one of them says, "Hey, Bro', give me some power," and holds out his fist for Sonny to start doing that knuckle-knockin' shit. Sonny, God bless 'im, squares this shithead PFC away, and says, 'First of all, I ain't your bro', and second of all, the power I got is right fuckin' here,' and points to his corporal chevrons on his collar. Then he punches the first PFC in the mouth, kicks the second one in the gut, and watches as the number three guy hauls ass out of the area. I was just trying to figure out if this is what we can expect around here, or if this is the way it's gonna be in the future."

"Lieutenant, if what I saw in the P.I. is any indication of what's been happening since we've been gone from the World, then you'd better prepare yourself for a big shock. Sonny Cannon is one of a kind, but there are some real problems ahead for all of us."

"Thanks, Doc, I was just wonderin' if that was an isolated incident, or if I should prepare myself for more of the same from these half-steppers in the rear."

Shaking his head in disbelief, 1st Lieutenant Coffman snuffed out his smoke and walked out of the hootch.

Having gotten Cannon to help me drag my three wooden foot-lockers from the supply shed over to my new hootch, I spent the remainder of the afternoon reacquainting myself with my equipment and some treasures gathered during my past nine months in Vietnam. There would be plenty of time to find old friends later, but this was important to me.

Inside the first footlocker, I found most of my 782 gear. Anything that was leather—my boots, .45 holster, and K-bar sheath—was now covered with fine green and gray mold caused by the dampness and humidity that was Vietnam. I had packed my other essentials in my rucksack, but anything that was metal that had been left unprotected was lightly rusted. My Unit-1 emergency medical bag had been left undisturbed, but I would need to replace several bottles of medication that I had left inside of it.

The three sets of well-worn camouflage utilities that I had planned to save for my return hadn't made out too much better. I had given them to the local laundry woman at Phu Bai and watched her process them. She had washed them in her cleanest dirty stream, smoke-dried them over a water-buffalo-chip fire, ironed them, and then neatly placed them inside of a clear plastic bag. That was nearly two months ago. The mildewed smell of these ''clean'' utilities was, again, very familiar. All of the men in 3d Force smelled the same way, which was another common bond.

My second footlocker contained two clean blankets, two clean poncho liners, a pillow, one sleeping shirt, and several boxes. One was full of photographs that I had taken while patrolling on the DMZ and in the A Shau Valley. The other contained letters that I had received from my parents, sisters, and friends since my arrival in Vietnam. I had arranged them all in chronological order according to the month they were received and by their date stamp. I set that box aside to remind myself to reread all of those letters during the night.

The third footlocker was the most valuable, as it contained North Vietnamese uniform items: one set of NVA camouflage utilities, one homemade leather belt, one green pith helmet, one metal canteen, a homemade plastic wallet, some NVA paper money, and half a dozen North Vietnamese stamps. The leather belt was a source of many arguments within my team. Because it had six holes in it, I argued that we must be winning the war since the enemy was apparently getting less to eat, and waist sizes were obviously shrinking. Naturally, Keaveney and Bishop thought that with the NVA hiding in Laos for so long, they had started out from Hanoi skinny and had now gained weight, hiding in their underground sanctuaries along the borders of South Vietnam.

In the bottom of the footlocker, wrapped in a green woolen blanket, were two well-oiled AK-47 rifles. Having acquired a good number of these automatic weapons from past encounters with the North Vietnamese Army, and knowing that we were not allowed to bring them back to the States as war souvenirs, we used them as trading stock with the Seabees and other service units stationed nearby in Phu Bai. One of our company gunnery sergeants, William ''Rip'' Collins, was famous for trading off captured AK-47s for the supplies that the company needed but, for one reason or another, could not obtain through the normal, but sometimes lengthy, supply channels. None of the Marines ever objected to giving up one of these weapons if the company could benefit from it, but the gunny took a great deal of ribbing from the men in the company. It was often hinted around the company area that if he really wanted to get an AK-47, he should run the bush with one of the recon teams and get his own trading stock. Pallets of plywood, rolls of communication wire, cases of C rations, and pallets of warm beer would always show up soon after a recon team's contact with the North Vietnamese Army. The value of AK-47s to the intelligence people was minimal, but their value to those who could not come by them easily made them choice items for trading.

After spending the remainder of that afternoon cleaning, oiling, and preparing all of my 782 gear, I felt ready to resume life in the field. I would find out soon enough what team required the services of a corpsman, but now I wanted to read those letters that had been sent to me and held, awaiting my return, and reread the letters that I had received from my parents, sisters, and friends. I wanted to study the pictures that I had taken of our team Snakey while the team members were still alive. I thought that it wouldn't take very long for me to get back into the groove of life within the company and to rekindle my desire to resume patrolling against the soldiers of the North Vietnamese Army. I wanted to feel comfortable by reassuring myself that I could remember all of what was required of a team member. That opportunity would present itself sooner than I had ever anticipated.

I opened my green notebook. I had carried this notebook with me since my very first mission into the DMZ, and the pages revealed my thoughts and fears. I had written down quotations from books I had read, quotations that related to my present life. The first quotation was a reminder to come back alive, given to me by Robert Browning, and shared with all of my teammates from time to time. It was simple but eloquent:

> Grow old along with me,
> the best is yet to be,
> the last of life for
> which the first was made

Next came several pages of the names and addresses of family and friends that I would write to on a regular basis. After the address portion were a number of pages of notes from our training classes, entitled "patrol seismic intrusion devices," "ambushes," and "harbor sights." The pages that followed contained information that I had recorded during the twenty-two missions I had experienced with 3d Force. Memories came rushing back to me as

I reread each entry. I came to a page that was titled "thoughts for letters," and read:

There are some things which cannot be learned quickly, and time, which is all we have, must be paid heavily for their acquiring. They are the very simplest things, and because it takes a man's life to know them, the little new that each man gets from life is very costly and the only heritage he has to leave.

This was followed by:

We sing songs silently to ourselves and think about their meaning more than others do, because we know how swiftly death can come. We have seen it, and we have caused it. We live two lives here. One in the rear area, and one as the cunning animal-man in the bush. I will never forget these long, long nights of waiting for the sound of death to approach, yet only hearing the crash of the sun's rays break through the jungle. Thank God the night is so short.

For luck you carried a horse chestnut and a rabbit's foot in your right pocket. The fur had been worn off the rabbit's foot long ago, and the bones and the sinews were polished by the wear. The claws scratched the lining of your pocket, and you knew luck was still there.

After these pages of quotes came more sobering memories of past missions. The different radio frequencies that we had used, the names, blood types, and service numbers of each team member on the mission, and the map locations of where we had been inserted and extracted had all been recorded.

My letter reading was interrupted when S. Sgt. Byron Tapp came into the hootch. He had brought the mail that I had missed since leaving the company and handed me a small stack of letters. The top letter was from Captain Hisler, but before I could get it opened, Staff Sergeant Tapp stopped me.

"Doc, Lieutenant Coffman said he wants to see you in the ops hootch. It sounds to me like you've been tapped to help the teams train some of those Republic of Korea (ROK) Marines. You could be back in the bush in a couple of days, and that sure as hell beats sitting around here."

THIRD FORCE RECON IN
——— CADRE ———

WHEN I LEFT 3D FORCE RECON COMPANY IN FEBRU-
ary 1970, the company headquarters was physically located beside
the southern edge of the military airstrip at Phu Bai, forty miles
north of the city of Da Nang. I had assumed that when I returned
from scuba school, the company would still be at Phu Bai and that
I would resume my position as a team member, patrolling along
the Laotian border, looking for the North Vietnamese Army. The
seemingly small number of casualties that we had suffered in the
A Shau Valley during early February had a significant impact on
limiting the company's ability to keep highly experienced reconnaissance teams in the field. The permanent loss of just one well-
trained Force Recon Marine had far-reaching effects on each team,
platoon, and on the company. Having lost nine Marines in such a
short period of time made the job of keeping experienced teams in
the field that much more difficult. For these reasons, and because
of tactical and political decisions made in very high places, it was
decided that 3d Force Recon Company would be reduced in size
from its original strength of 142 officers and men, to a cadre that
now numbered less than thirty Marines and one corpsman. Our
area of operation (AO) had been given over to the Army's XXIV
Corps, and we had seen the last of the A Shau Valley.

Third Force Recon Company, or what remained of it, was now
colocated within the defensive perimeter wire of the 1st Marine
Division's 1st Reconnaissance Battalion. Our four platoons had
been reduced to one large thirty-man platoon, and the majority of
officers and men who had been with the company in February had
either been reassigned throughout the 1st Marine Division or had
returned home to the United States. What remained of 3d Force
Recon were those Marines who had extended their tours of duty

earlier in the year and those who would be needed to rebuild and reorganize the company in the states.

Although the 3d Force Reconnaissance Company sign was still proudly displayed in front of the operations hootch, proclaiming our existence, the company was an entirely different organization from the one I had left. The pride and spirit of our company still remained, but we had been reduced from a courageous and viable fighting force to a platoon of Force Recon Marines looking for a mission.

The new living arrangements between the Marines of 1st Recon Battalion and the Marines of 3d Force Recon Company had created some minor problems within the compound. Discussions at the battalion enlisted-men's club, fueled by large egos and too many beers, as to who were the better Marines had resulted in a number of serious fistfights. Professional pride, loyalty, and unit integrity were taken very seriously by these Marines. The Marines from 3d Force Recon were viewed as having invaded the turf of 1st Recon Battalion, and once territory had been taken by a Marine he usually fought to keep it, even from his fellow Marines.

When 3d Force Recon had received the order to stand down at Phu Bai, logistical wheels were quickly put into motion. The relocation of the company had been made in a series of helicopter lifts and one truck convoy, bringing all the Marines of the company and all of the company's equipment to Da Nang. Lt. Dave "Brother" Brown, our company supply officer, and S. Sgt. Jim Tate, the S-4 ops chief, had done another masterful job at relocating the company. Remembering our company relocation in October, from Quang Tri to Phu Bai, it had been no small feat to tear down the entire company, relocate, and then rebuild, still keeping our recon teams operating in the field. The experience gained in having done this once before paid off when the call had come to move to Da Nang.

The movement of individual Marines was never a problem, but having to inventory everything in the company, including the medical supplies, armory, scuba locker, parachute loft, and all administrative records within four days was a major accomplishment. Knowing that the company was to be placed in a cadre status made the job no easier, and the spirit of the moment had been documented in an article that appeared in a March 1970 issue of *Stars & Stripes* newspaper:

WHEN A "GOOD OUTFIT" GETS AXED
DA NANG, VIETNAM—The lieutenant colonel that the

young Marines threw into the South China Sea—fully clothed with a briefing to deliver in half an hour—was a 1st Marine Division intelligence officer who stopped down by the beach to watch the party.

The short, balding, barrel-chested Marine major who stood on the shore—already soaked from an earlier dunking—laughed like a madman at the colonel. The major was the commanding officer of the men who had dumped the colonel. They were having a party because they've all been put out of work, and while everyone was laughing, no one seemed happy.

The outfit was a small one, the 3d Marine Amphibious Force Recon Co., and was widely considered to be the best in the business. Their business was six-man patrols along the Demilitarized Zone and the Laotian border. Lately they had been counting truck convoys in the A Shau Valley, fifty-five miles west of here.

The major, Alex Lee, is said to have written the book for the Marines on the subject. Book writers, these Marines say, don't make lots of friends.

When they were operating, the company answered to III MAF commander, LtGen. Herman Nickerson. If they needed something they went to him and asked for it, they said. Often, they say, they got it.

One of the things they asked for and got was helicopter support from the Army. That, they say, embarrassed and angered many Marine staff officers who wanted them to use less numerous and less adaptable Marine air assets.

Nickerson is gone, and now the recon company is being reworked into a small training unit. Many of these men, who at peak strength numbered about 150, are being farmed out to other units. Lee, the muscular recon expert, is now an assistant supply officer for the 1st Marine Division. Some of his men are being sent to other recon units, such as the 1st Marine Division recon elements. About 40 of the company are going to train Vietnamese recon teams. They are through patrolling.

The reason for the gloom-tinged, colonel-soaking beach party was simple—these men, by and large, want to do nothing more than what they have been doing; going out walking through the woods looking for the enemy. For some the adjustment to less dangerous garrison-like living will be hard.

"I have one man," said 1st Lt. David Harrison, an officer

with the company, "who was promoted to sergeant because of the way he handled himself in firefights. He's a great recon team leader, but he doesn't know the first thing about being a sergeant in the rear. I reckon his stripes will get a little heavy. I imagine he'll get busted."

The adjustment to shiny boots; starched, regulation uniforms; and sedate, peaceful clubs may be harder for these men than the adjustment from civilian life to boot camp. Many, such as the young sergeant, want to become mercenaries.

"I know that the war is slowing down, and that's part of the reason we are being put out of business," says Harrison. "But it was a really good outfit, a great outfit, and I'm sorry to see these guys out of jobs."

The newspaper article was on the mark, almost. Major Lee had only been temporarily assigned to the 1st Marine Division's supply section while awaiting orders to become the battalion operations officer (S-3) for the 1st Battalion, 7th Marine Regiment. His interest and influence on 3d Force Recon Company still remained very strong, and he was responsible for getting the jobs that all of us wanted.

In not missing any opportunity to get Force Recon Marines away from the rear area and into the field where they belonged, 1st Lt. Bucky Coffman, now the commanding officer of 3d Force Reconnaissance Company, had been presented with a unique training opportunity for those few recon teams that remained intact and were still a part of the cadre company.

They were assigned to teach the art of reconnaissance patrolling to a company of Korean Marines, who were assigned to operate in the area known as the Que Son Mountains. This reconnaissance training program idea was well received by the Marines of the company and the Koreans. The Republic of Korea (ROK) Marines, "Blue Dragon," 2d Brigade commanding general, ironically named Lee, had specifically requested the use of 3d Force Recon Marines to assist in teaching the complexities of reconnaissance patrolling, artillery and close air support, and rubber boat (IBS) training to his ROK Marines. The Korean Marine company was situated on a beach south of the village of An Hoa, with a detachment of supporting U.S. Marines from 1st Naval Gunfire Liaison Company (ANGLICO), and with another detachment of Navy Seabees billeted close by. The Seabees had set up one mess hall to service the needs of the ANGLICO unit, and the Korean

Marines were grateful for being invited to use the new facilities, which were considered much better than that to which they were accustomed.

First Lieutenant Coffman, tasked with ensuring that the ROK Marines' training was as realistic as possible, had added his personal touch to the program. The Korean Marines were immediately introduced to our methods of reconnaissance training, which included map reading, radio communications tips, patrol orders and types of reports used in the field, camouflage and movement, patrol rehearsals, and physical conditioning. Once they had demonstrated their abilities at the recon indoctrination program (RIP), they were sent to the field to conduct reconnaissance patrols against the Viet Cong and those elements of the North Vietnamese Army that were moving through the Que Son Mountains.

The Korean Marines had a well-known reputation as aggressive and well-disciplined in the field. Reportedly, they took no prisoners and prided themselves on body counts as their proof of relentless patrolling against the enemy. They, too, utilized six-man teams for their reconnaissance patrols, but Lieutenant Coffman had insisted that selected Force Recon team members would accompany these "new" Korean recon teams on their first patrols. The presence of a Force Recon Marine ensured several things. First, the presence of an "honest broker" could evaluate the new team objectively. But more importantly, having a Force Recon Marine as a member of the patrol would ensure that radio communications to U.S. artillery units and subsequent requests for close air support would be understood. It was easy for us to quickly read information from a formatted reporting card, requesting emergency helicopter medical evacuations and fire-support requests, but it was a different story when an excited Korean came up on the net asking for help. Initially the emergency radio request might not be believed, and if the request was considered legitimate, it could be given a lower priority, with emergency requests of any kind going to our own units first.

The reconnaissance training had been going on for several weeks when I returned to 3d Force Recon. It was no surprise when Staff Sergeant Tapp came into the hootch looking for Corporal Cannon and me.

"Lieutenant Coffman wants you to be ready to go with him to An Hoa, first thing tomorrow morning. You, Cannon, Wills, and the lieutenant are going down there to pick up 'Grape' Vineyard, and then you're gonna attend some party that the ROKs have planned to honor the lieutenant."

The news that we were going to fly down to An Hoa and retrieve Sergeant Vineyard was particularly good to hear. It was Vineyard who had been indirectly mentioned in the *Stars and Stripes* newspaper article as having been promoted because he was good at handling firefights. It was also Sergeant Vineyard who had been selected as the first team leader to go into the bush with the ROK Marines when they finished their schooling and began patrolling.

Grape Vineyard had been the team leader of one of 3d Force Recon's most notable teams, code named Tinny. In early December 1969, Team Tinny had been inserted at dawn by an Army helicopter onto a hilltop in the A Shau Valley that was later determined to be a North Vietnamese Army battalion's command-and-control bunker complex. As soon as their Huey had momentarily set its landing skids down, the LZ went "hot," with NVA soldiers attempting to destroy the helicopter. Vineyard's team jumped from the Huey and began to neutralize the enemy ground fire. The Army Huey took off for safer skies, and Vineyard, facing a potentially deadly situation, maneuvered his team away from the area, requesting only an emergency resupply of ammunition while awaiting Marine close air support to destroy the NVA bunker complex. Vineyard's team remained hidden in the area for several days and continued to deliver the fires of close air support onto the unsuspecting NVA. For this and subsequent actions, Corporal Grape Vineyard was meritoriously promoted to the rank of sergeant, and was considered by every man in 3d Force Recon Company to be "one cool dude" under fire.

As we flew south to An Hoa, 1st Lieutenant Coffman provided us with a history of the coastal area below. This was the lieutenant's third tour of duty, and he had covered more ground on foot and in the air than any officer we knew, with the possible exception of Major Lee. His ability to remember particular areas and the gradual changes in the complexion of the war from his infantryman's perspective was sharp. He told us, in great detail, how earlier in the Vietnam War, the Marines would patrol near the villages of An Hoa and Chu Lai, with reconnaissance teams consisting of more than fifteen men, and how they had to constantly change their tactics to catch the Viet Cong. We also knew that the results of his many experiences during his three tours of duty were now evident in the successes that 3d Force Recon had achieved on the DMZ and in the A Shau Valley.

As our Marine Huey made its approach into the ROK Marine compound, we could see a small gathering of Marines waving up toward us. In the center of the group stood a camouflage-painted, blond-haired, and bespectacled figure of a Marine, with arms folded across his chest. There was no mistaking the physical characteristics of Grape Vineyard, even at an altitude of one hundred feet. By the time our skids touched down, Lieutenant Coffman was out of the Huey and headed into the crowd, straight toward Vineyard.

"Grape, you worthless excuse for a sergeant of Marines, it looks like you have been to the forest and seen the tiger."

Before Vineyard could reply, the lieutenant had engulfed him in a smothering bear hug. This unmilitarylike gesture certainly took the Korean Marines by surprise, but it was nothing more than business as usual for Lieutenant Coffman to display these fatherly signs of great affection toward those Marines he admired. Vineyard was one of his favorites.

Looking at us over the lieutenant's shoulder, Vineyard laughed.

"I see that you have brought the doctor of death along with you, sir. What happened? Did he wear out his welcome in the Philippines? Or did he just get homesick for life in the bush?"

"I brought Doc along with Cannon and Wills as my guests to the party. But first I want to go to the ops hootch and hear your debriefing from the recon patrol that you brought in yesterday."

As Sergeant Vineyard and 1st Lieutenant Coffman walked off together, the rest of our group moved on toward the ocean, where the makings of a day-long beach party had already begun. A volleyball game and a softball game were both in progress when we arrived, but we had already been given a mission that was not part of either sports event. We had been told to bring along several sets of masks, snorkels, and swim fins that we were to use in harvesting a dozen bushels of huge clams from a sandbar located off the beach. The water of the South China Sea was crystal clear, and it was easy for us to find the clams. When the news of our clam-diving success reached the sailors from the Seabee unit, they immediately joined the party, bringing with them several huge cooking pots, some blocks of chilled butter, and a case of dehydrated shrimp. We had the makings of a New England clambake. Our seafood contributions to the beach party made a great hit with the Korean Marines, and they, in turn, insisted that we sample several different types of kimchee that they had brought with them into Vietnam. If they were challenged to suck raw clams from the half shell, covered with hot sauce, we had to display the same type of courage in eating their concoctions of pickled cabbage and hot Korean peppers, which had been fermented in garlic juice. For some of us, the hot and heavily spiced kimchee tasted like food from hell. Others couldn't get enough of it.

Within the two hours it took for our clam harvesting to be completed, 1st Lieutenant Coffman and Sergeant Vineyard had completed the patrol debriefing and had joined us at the beach. And for the first time in several weeks, Vineyard was able to enjoy himself, and began to talk to us about his experience tagging along with the Korean Marine recon patrol in the Que Son Mountains.

"These Korean Marines have a well-deserved reputation for being hard and disciplined, but after spending four days in the bush and watching their first recon patrol, I sure have seen some unusual things," he said.

"On the second day out, we found a heavily used trail network, and their team leader, a young ROK sergeant, wanted to move in closer to monitor the trail and see just who was using it. On the third day, we had maneuvered into a good, concealed, position that was about thirty yards off the trail and twenty yards above it. We set up a string of four sensors and monitored the movement on the trail all night long. At 0545 the sensor started to beep, and we watched as four NVA approached, moving in from the west. The ROK team leader then decided on his own to snatch one of the NVA. He shot the first two and wounded one, but their tail-end charlie turned and ran back down the trail, with the ROK sergeant right on his heels. He tackled the gook and then ran him back to us at gunpoint. When his assistant patrol leader saw the NVA prisoner, he requested an emergency helicopter extraction. It happened so fast that there was no way to stop it, and that's how we got out of the Que Sons.

"As soon as we got back here to An Hoa, we had a debriefing session. The ROK intelligence officer wanted to know all the details concerning the prisoner snatch, and the sergeant wanted to skirt the part about him chasing the NVA down the trail, but it finally came out. That Korean S-2 officer was so damn mad he actually kicked the sergeant out of the hootch and then commenced to beat the shit out of him in front of his own team. These guys don't fool around when it comes to strict discipline in the field.

"Last night I told Lieutenant Coffman what had happened, and that's why he came down here. He knows that we didn't teach them to pull stupid stunts like that and just wanted to make sure that everything was square between us. Their sergeant is gone now, and they use his name only as a bad example."

The story of the overzealous ROK Marine sergeant was not too

surprising. The Korean Marines did have that reputation for aggressive action, but when aggressiveness in the bush overrode
common sense, it usually cost someone his life. In this instance,
it was only fortunate that there had been no other NVA soldiers
walking on the trail at the time the sergeant decided to spring his
one-man ambush. It could have cost that team, including Sergeant
Vineyard, their lives. The decision to quickly rid the company of
an idiot was well made and served notice that free thinkers would
not be tolerated in the bush.

The Marine Huey that had taken us to An Hoa returned at 1400
to take us back to Da Nang. Sergeant Vineyard was more than
happy to return to the company area and wasted no time in retell-
ing his story to the Marines of 3d Force, wanting the lesson only
to be learned and never repeated.

—— NEW CAMMIES ——

JUST TWO DAYS AFTER MY TRIP TO AN HOA, I WAS given notice to get my gear packed for three days in the field. Instinctively, I assumed that I had been assigned to one of the recon teams in 3d Force, with a new mission, but I was surprised to learn that 1st Reconnaissance Battalion had requested the services of one recon-trained hospital corpsman. I was told to report to the 1st Recon Battalion's operations hootch for additional details. A Marine 1st lieutenant named Gregson was waiting inside the operations hootch when I reported in. His manner was friendly and direct, and after being asked if I wanted some coffee, I felt at ease asking the lieutenant some questions.

"Doc, just drop your gear over there and sit down. We're waiting for one platoon to show up, and then we're gonna fly you all out to an observation post for a couple of days in the Que Son Mountains. Most of the battalion's corpsmen are in the field, and your name came up in a meeting as a possible solution to our problem."

"What kind of mission is this going to be, sir?"

"I would be lying if I told you that it was a recon mission, Doc. This is going to be another dog-and-pony show. A senior Marine general is coming in country, and he wants to see what life is like in the field. Our people are going to go out and ensure that the area is safe before we bring him out to the bush."

First Lieutenant Gregson had given me straight scoop, but I thought it was unusual that a Marine general officer would come from the relative safety of Washington D.C. just to look at a piece of territory in the Que Sons. But we had learned from our experience with Generals Nickerson and Walt that senior officers could do just about anything they wanted. Ours was not to reason why. . . .

By midmorning, Marines from 1st Reconnaissance Battalion's Charlie Company had assembled at the helipad, and we were briefed by the platoon leader, 1st Lt. Mike Hodgins, as to our assigned mission. We would fly by helicopter to a mountaintop designated on our maps as Hill 840 and conduct a series of security patrols around the mountain, making it a safe area for the visiting general. Those Marines who would not be assigned to specific patrols would be required to dig fighting holes, fill up sandbags, and square the area away in preparation for the visit. The visiting general was scheduled to arrive in three days.

The flight out to the Que Son Mountains was uneventful, but our insertion onto the top of Hill 840 left a lot to be desired. Our CH-46 Sea Knight required considerably more landing area than the usual Huey, and the top of this particular hill was so small that a "tailgate insertion" was decided on as the best method for putting us on the ground. This method of helicopter insertion required that our pilot lower the tailgate of his CH-46 and then slowly move his hovering helicopter next to the peak of the hill. He then backed up his helicopter so that his tailgate would literally touch the mountaintop and provide us with a level ground exit out of his bird. It was a complicated procedure requiring tremendous concentration on the part of the pilot and his observing crew chief, but this particular pilot made it seem easy. Our group of thirteen Marines and one corpsman exited the CH-46 quickly and found ourselves overlooking a beautiful, long green valley bordered by the Que Son Mountains.

The priority of work to be done had been established before leaving Da Nang, and those Marines who had been assigned to patrol the base of the hill moved down and away from the landing zone after it was considered secure. The remainder of our group started to dig in and establish a defensive perimeter along the hilltop and wait for the second CH-46 to bring in the rest of the platoon. One 60mm mortar had been brought along to be used for illumination and defensive purposes. The largest crew-served weapons system was one M-60 machine gun that had been borrowed from the battalion armory.

First Lieutenant Hodgins was considered to be bush smart, having already completed a six-month tour with the grunts before coming to the reconnaissance battalion. He knew where he wanted his mortar tube set up and where his one machine gun would probably do the most good. We hadn't been given a large area of ground to hold, with the entire hilltop measuring no more than one hundred yards long and thirty yards wide. But with the arrival of the second CH-46 had come several cases of hand grenades and several dozen claymore mines, all to be used for our small defensive perimeter. If the North Vietnamese enemy wanted to get to us, they would face a continuous uphill battle for our position.

The remainder of our first day on top of Hill 840 was spent digging out a defensive trench line and a long set of stairs, and filling hundreds of sandbags for the construction of several small bunkers used to protect our radio communications equipment. Our work went on uninterrupted until dusk, when the word was passed to take a break and eat chow. We did this in small two- and three-man groups, so that at no time would we all be caught eating. The lieutenant wanted listening outposts established and had defensive firing cards prepared by his noncommissioned officers. We were then briefed as to where the hand grenades and claymore mine detonators were located, just in case we were visited and probed by the enemy. Then assignments were made as to who had radio watch during the night.

Our only visitor during our first night on Hill 840 was the Vietnamese god of rain, and he must have liked what he saw because he didn't leave. The downpour started near midnight, and continued relentlessly until the steel gray light of dawn grew brighter in the eastern sky. The downpour caused a good part of the new trench line to collapse, and other sections were flooded. Those sandbags that had not been filled the day before would now be filled with mud. Our work continued under constant rain throughout the next day.

By late in the afternoon of the second day, we thought that the bad weather would be reason enough for the "heavies" in the rear to reconsider the scheduled visit of the general. But it was not to be. We worked on, continuing to improve the OP, at the cost of nearly every Marine on the hill suffering immersion foot and cracked and blistered hands. The combination of rainwater and abrasions from clay soil had quickly taken its toll.

By nightfall of our second day, the general mood on Hill 840 had grown ugly. These Marines were certainly used to suffering from the many conditions that the weather of Vietnam had to offer, but sitting on a hilltop in heavy rain was not a part of being a reconnaissance Marine, and the novelty was wearing thin.

The word from the rear was that the visiting general had taken the opposite approach to our thinking. Rather than pass on the opportunity to visit recon Marines sitting on a hill in a downpour, the general, or his planning staff, reasoned that the troops would admire a general officer who braved the hazards of nature just to come out and visit them. They should have asked us what we thought.

Our second night on top of the hill passed without incident, and no enemy sightings were reported by the two recon teams below our position. But the heavy rain continued to pour down, and adding insult to injury, every Marine's uniform was ruined, ripped apart at both knees from the many hours spent kneeling to fill sandbags and improve the hasty trench line. We looked pitiful.

The third day, the day of the general's scheduled visit, brought a brilliant sunrise, and the promise of clear skies and warmer temperatures. By 0800 the word was passed that a Huey was inbound, tasked with the mission to resupply our position with fresh radio batteries, hot coffee, and soup. By 0900, we had a visual sighting of the lone Huey, and by 0910 the pilot had landed on the west side of our position. A small working party of Marines had been detailed to off-load the supplies, enabling the Huey to take off quickly and avoid becoming a target of opportunity to the NVA. To our amazement, the Huey pilot kept his position, and a Marine gunnery sergeant walked away from the Huey and up the hill toward Lieutenant Hodgins.

"Sir, my name is Gunnery Sergeant Kelly, from the division G-4 [supply] section. I was sent out here with the resupply bird to find out the correct uniform and boot sizes of all of your men. The heavies in the rear want to make sure that you and your people present a good image to the general when he gets here. I'm here to make sure that happens. Do you think you can get me a list of their uniform and boot sizes? My orders are to return here with new cammies and boots for all of you, just as fast as we can make turnaround time from here to Da Nang."

First Lieutenant Hodgins had no trouble in simply looking over the number of Marines who had been assigned to Hill 840, and within five minutes the Marine gunny from division supply had departed for Da Nang, promising to return with our new clean and dry cammies.

Turning to his radio operator the lieutenant mused, "I wonder why those stupid bastards in the rear just didn't ask us for the number and sizes of uniforms over the radio? It would have saved that pilot and the poor gunny a trip, and not let every NVA and his VC brother know that we are still here."

The old gunny from division supply returned within several hours, as promised, and realizing that our precarious terrain had provided him with a captive audience, he simply threw the huge bundle of green camouflage utilities and a large cardboard box of jungle boots down from the hovering Huey to the Marines on our little LZ. The bundle of utilities and the box of boots were soon broken open, and our new uniforms were handed out according to size.

The Marine general's visit was scheduled for 1400, and with the majority of work in constructing the OP nearly finished, we prepared for his arrival. Our radio operator had stayed glued to his radio handset, ready to pass any and all information to the lieutenant, when the call came in saying that our ''guest'' was on the way.

In the distance we could see a flight of Marine F-4 Phantom jets tasked with providing us a fast response to any ground fire, should it occur. Following the Phantom, two Marine light observation helicopters and four Cobra gunships came into view, also tasked with providing close air support. Whoever this general officer was, he would be very well protected while visiting the Que Son Mountains. Finally the word came from our lieutenant that the general would be at our ''pos'' in ten minutes and that the Marines were to take up positions around the OP perimeter. The two recon teams who had remained near the base of Hill 840 still reported that they had made no visual sightings of any enemy activity during the last three days. After the teams reported that the LZ was secure and that Marine Air was on station, the general's Huey proceeded in to our LZ.

As the Marine Huey settled in our small LZ, six officers, all wearing starched and pressed cammies, came to the top of the OP. The general spoke to several of the Marines who stood close by, and then was handed a pair of 7x50 binoculars to aid him in viewing the landscape below. As several members of his party pointed out certain key terrain features for him to focus on, others kept looking at their watches, hoping that their visit to our OP would not be any longer than necessary. The visit lasted less then ten minutes. The general pressed some more flesh, and within two minutes, he and his party of straphangers were reduced to being a dot in the sky. Three days of backbreaking work in the rain for a ten-minute visit, and not more than a few words spoken to the Marines who had risked their lives to afford six officers a view of the Que Son Mountains.

The Marines exchanged looks, though not much was said until the lieutenant's radio operator called out that another chopper was less than ten minutes out.

That news sent rumors flying.

"Maybe it's a good deal, sir. Maybe the general liked what he saw and is sending hot chow out to us."

"Maybe it's a CH-46, and they've decided to come back and take us off of this damn hill."

The dot on the horizon grew larger as the lone helicopter came on, and soon the Huey was landing on our LZ. All eyes were riveted on the one person to emerge from the left side of the Huey. It was the old gunny from division supply.

"Lieutenant, that short visit was real special for the general, and we really appreciate all that you and your men have done out here to make it good."

The long pause after the gunny's opening comments meant that there was more to come.

"Sir, I've come back out here to collect up those new cammies. They were just a loan, you understand. We didn't want no general to think that we weren't takin' care of our Marines in the field. Do you think that you could get your guys to kind of speed it up? I don't want to be here any longer than it takes, you understand? You can even keep the boots."

The word was passed for us to take off our new cammies and put back on our old, stinking, ripped, and wet ones. As we filed by the drop-off point, the silent looks of anger, hatred, and absolute disbelief were aimed squarely at the old gunny, but he just couldn't look any of us in the eye.

"Just doin' my job, Marines. 'Preciate it. Thanks a lot."

I guess the last laugh was on the old gunny, for even though none of us had left the hilltop during the time that the general was visiting, we could not account for every set of the new cammies that had been issued earlier that day. The gunny didn't push it, because he didn't want to stay any longer than necessary.

As the gunny's Huey flew back toward Da Nang, 1st Lieutenant Hodgins's radio operator sighed.

"You know, sir, I heard that damn general make the comment that nothin' was too good for the troops. He must have been a man of his word, 'cause that's what we just got, nothin'."

We remained on Hill 840 until we were joined by the two recon teams, who had spent three days moving around the base of the hill. The next day, we collected our claymore mines, filled in our trench line, and took down our communications equipment. We returned to Da Nang the following afternoon, proudly wearing our dirty, ripped, green badges of courage and our new boots.

We had thought that the treatment we had received in the name of the dog-and-pony show was pretty poor until we learned about what had happened to two other Marines from 1st Recon Battalion who had been tasked with demonstrating rappelling techniques to the same visiting general.

First Lieutenant Peter Gray and Corporal Evans were two members of a recon team given the job of conducting the rappelling demonstration. But in the overzealous attempt to impress the visiting general officer, new rappelling line was obtained so that the image of new, clean, and serviceable equipment would be presented.

When the CH-46 flew into the training area for a practice demonstration, the new rappelling line was thrown out of the hovering helicopter. Normally a ten-pound weight would be attached to the end of the line to help smooth it out and to help anchor it to the ground. Several Marine ground guides would be positioned to assist the rappelling Marines. For whatever reason, this wasn't done for the practice demonstration.

Lieutenant Gray was the first Marine to rappel, and when he finally got to the ground, a number of kinks had formed on the new line and in front of his snap link, preventing him from quickly disconnecting himself from the rappelling line. To further complicate the situation, as he was trying to remove the kinks, Corporal Evans began his descent from the hovering helicopter and stopped himself just a few feet above the lieutenant. The CH-46 crew chief, seeing what looked like both Marines on the ground, gave the all-clear signal to the pilot, and the CH-46 changed from hovering to a forward motion, but it did not gain any altitude. With the lieutenant and the corporal struggling frantically to remove themselves from the rappelling line, both Marines, to the horror of those people observing, were dragged into several strands of defensive-perimeter ''razor wire,'' and were, literally, ripped to pieces. Corporal Evans died in the wire, and the lieutenant lived long enough to be medically evacuated to the Naval hospital at Yokosuka, Japan, where he succumbed to his injuries shortly after being admitted to the hospital.

The story is a tragic incident to relate. Overzealousness, shortcuts, and poor planning had created a training accident that could certainly have been prevented. There is no such thing as a training accident.

1ST FORCE RECONNAISSANCE COMPANY

IN LATE MARCH 1970, I SAID MY FINAL GOOD-BYES TO those few Marines of 3d Force Recon Company who were fortunate enough to have remained with the company and who now waited for their return to the United States for future assignments or discharge from the active duty ranks of the Corps. Knowing that I would probably not see most of these men again in my lifetime, I expressed my feelings of gratitude to those particular individuals who had been patient with me, to those who had taught me the finer skills of survival in the bush, and to those Marines who had protected me many times not only by their demonstrated coolness under fire but also by their ability to always think things out.

First Lieutenant Morris and S. Sgt. Frank Schemmel gave me a lift in their jeep from 3d Force Recon Company to the opposite side of the city of Da Nang and into the compound of 1st Force Reconnaissance Company. Always the professional, the lieutenant had wanted to check, from time to time, on those Marines from 3d Force Recon who had been newly joined on the morning-report roster of 1st Force Reconnaissance Company. Using "unfinished administrative work and undelivered mail" as their reasons to visit 1st Force Recon, our company adjutant and admin chief wasted little time in getting into the company area.

The entrance to the 1st Force Recon company compound was marked with a huge red circular sign that was positioned between two stone-and-concrete pillars. In the center of the sign was a carved pathfinder's torch, the symbol of the early reconnaissance Marines of the fifties, and at the center of this torch was a gold-colored parachute canopy framed with crossed rubber boat paddles. Inscribed on the outer edges of the sign were the words 1ST FORCE RECONNAISSANCE COMPANY FMF PAC (Fleet Marine Force Pacific).

Standing directly behind the company sign was a huge red and white water tower, which provided fresh water to the camp, served as a great visual mark to enemy mortarmen, and was used as an expedient drying rack for wet parachutes.

Many times I had listened to the remarks that were made by both the officers and noncommissioned officers of 3d Force Recon Company in comparing the reputation and professionalism of our company to that of 1st Force Reconnaissance Company, but I had no way to compare these two organizations. If their observations and comments were critical and unflattering—and more often than not they were—then I could not help but approach this new assignment with misgivings.

"Okay, Doc, this is the end of the road. I hope that you will remember the things that we taught you. I'd be willing to bet that maybe you and some of the other Marines from 3d Force will bring a breath of fresh air to this company. After we leave here, Staff Sergeant Schemmel and I will stay at 1st Recon Battalion for only a little while longer. If there is anything that we can do to help, just ask. If you need any help from the 'boss,' you'll find him with the 7th Marines. Good luck, and thanks for all your help."

With my last formal ties to 3d Force Reconnaissance Company now severed, I walked, with my orders in hand, toward a green hootch with an S-1 admin sign nailed to the door.

Behind the plywood counter stood a tall, thin, blond sergeant with a hawklike face. As I stared at him, waiting to gain his attention, his stern expression changed, and a broad smile spread across his face as he offered his handshake.

"My name is Sergeant Scanlon. What can I do for you, Doc?"

"My name is Norton, Sergeant Scanlon, and I'm checking into this company."

"Well, Doc Norton, we had heard from your old command that you were on the way over to us from 3d Force. Welcome aboard. We are short of corpsmen, and as you might have guessed, we are really short of corpsmen who are dual qualified. We can use your help. Staff Sergeant Vanner is our admin chief. He's inside talking with Captain Centers, our company XO. When he gets back, we'll assign you to one of the platoons. In the meantime, I'll call down to our company sick bay, and get our senior corpsman, Doc Palmer, to come up here to meet you and start checking you in. You should know some of the 3d Force guys who joined us last month. I'm sure that they'll be anxious to see you again. Just have a seat and make yourself at home."

After I had handed all of my military records over to Sergeant Scanlon, I waited in the admin hootch for the arrival of the senior corpsman. Within a few minutes, the door opened, and a staff sergeant walked over to where I was seated.

"You must be the new corpsman. My name is S. Sgt. C. B. Lynch, and I'm one of the jumpmasters in the company. I heard that you would be coming over here from 3d Force, and tomorrow I will have the distinct honor of throwing your ass out of a CH-46 helicopter. We have three jumps scheduled for tomorrow morning at Red Beach and I'll look forward to seeing you there. Just thought that I'd come in and introduce myself to you, Doc."

Staff Sergeant Lynch vanished as quickly as he had appeared, leaving me with a great deal to think about in a short period of time. I wondered just how many more surprises I would experience as I sat around waiting for Doc Palmer. The answer was soon to come as the door opened once again.

"Good morning, HM3 Norton. Welcome aboard. My name is Palmer, and I'm the senior corpsman here at 1st Force. Just call me 'Doc.' We've been waiting for you to get here. Come along with me, and we'll walk over to the company sick-bay hootch, and I'll fill you in on what this company is all about and introduce you to some of the company along the way."

As we walked away from the admin hootch, Doc Palmer told me about the physical layout of the company area.

"We share this compound with an Army motor-transport company. They don't have anything to do with us, and we really don't bother them. Their soldiers control the gates in and out of the camp, but there is a long line of pine trees that separates our area from theirs. I never thought that I'd find pine trees growing in Vietnam, but you can see them for yourself."

"How many corpsmen are in the company, Doc?"

"We have four, now that you're here. One is on an R & R in Hawaii, and will be back next week. The other one is over at NSA, and should be back here this afternoon. I've been here for the last four months, and it's a great place."

"How often do we get to the bush?"

"Well, that's a good question. The operational tempo has been very slow lately. When the guys from 3d Force began to check in here a couple of weeks ago, we were really surprised to hear how much time you guys had spent in the bush. Most of the patrols that we have been conducting have been run close to Da Nang. There have been a couple of patrols that we routinely run along the beach, south of Da Nang, but those are also used as training patrols for the new guys. How many patrols have you been on, Norton?''

"When I left 3d Force I had been on twenty-two recon patrols. I was qualified as an assistant team leader, and later on as a team leader, too.''

"Jesus, I don't think that we have any Marine in this company with twenty-two recon patrols, let alone a corpsman—unless they'd be on their second or third tour. They must have really used you guys up at Phu Bai.''

"It wasn't a case of 'using us up.' General Nickerson wanted us in the bush to learn what the NVA were up to on the DMZ and in the A Shau Valley, and that's the reason why we went out on back-to-back patrols. Everybody in the company was in the bush.''

"You may find things move at a little slower pace than what you were used to in 3d Force.''

"Well, Doc, I haven't been in the bush in weeks, and if the opportunity comes up, that's where I want to be. Do you think that I can get away from life in the rear any time soon?''

"I don't see why not. The teams that we have go out are always short of corpsmen, and your experience will come in handy.''

As we walked toward the company sick-bay hootch, we passed a small building that was surrounded by a fence topped with triple strands of razor-sharp concertina wire. Several large flood lights were positioned around the outside of the building.

"What do they keep inside of the building that requires all of that security?''

"You wouldn't believe it if I told you. That Army motor company has a small armory inside that hootch, and they use VC POWs to clean their dirty weapons.''

"No kidding? I wondered what happened to those people after they had been debriefed. So, they end up here, cleaning the Army's dirty rifles?''

"Every couple of days, four Army soldiers escort half a dozen VC POWs over here, and then they supervise the cleaning of Army rifles, machine guns, and truck parts.''

As we walked past the fence line of the armory, the bright midmorning sunlight was reflected off a piece of silver metal protruding from the sandy soil, and I stopped to pick it up.

"I don't think that the Army is doing such a good job of supervising their POW working party. Take a look.''

The piece of metal was a firing pin from an M-60 machine gun. "Those POWs must laugh themselves to sleep at night, knowing that they can put an M-60 out of action without firing a shot. There's probably a lot more than one of these buried in the dirt. I think that I'll keep this one with me until the day I run into the Army POW escorts and then give them a little souvenir.''

I spent the better part of the morning with Doc Palmer showing me around the small company area that was now my new home. The mess hall, enlisted club, and company sick bay were all located within two hundred yards of one another, and the entire company area could be easily traversed on foot within ten minutes. When he was satisfied that I knew my way around the camp, he walked with me back to the company admin hootch, where Staff Sergeant Vanner and Sergeant Scanlon were waiting.

"Doc, you have been assigned to the 2d Platoon. Staff Sergeant Martin is on his way up here to meet you and help you get checked in. The company area is so small that you should be able to get your gear and be settled in before evening chow. The S-3 operations chief, Staff Sergeant Lynch, passed the word for all jumpers to assemble outside of the S-3 hootch at 1630 for the brief on tomorrow morning's jump.

"Here's your check-in sheet. Just bring it back here to me when you've finished.''

After being dismissed from the admin hootch, I waited outside with Doc Palmer for the arrival of Staff Sergeant Martin, the senior enlisted Marine of 2d Platoon. Within a few minutes, I watched as a tall, gaunt, hard-looking Marine Corps version of Ichabod Crane walked steadily toward us. His small, dark eyes were set deep within his head, and when he opened his mouth to speak, a slow southern drawl of derisive epithets escaped through prominent gaps between his discolored teeth.

"Doc, ma' name is Staff Sar'ent Martin, and I'm yo' new platoon sar'ent. You can now say ga'-bye to Doc Palmer, here, grab yo' shit, and falla me down ta the platoon area. I'll show ya were ya'll will be livin' an' introduce ya to life in the 2d Platoon.''

Staff Sergeant Martin led, and I followed. Along the way, he asked me where I had been before arriving at 1st Force and asked if I had spent much time in the bush. When I told him that I had been with 3d Force, he stopped and said, "There are six Marines in this company who come here from 3d Force. Y'all think you know every goddamn thing about patrollin'. Are you like them?''

"Staff Sergeant Martin, in 3d Force Recon I got along really well with my team members, the Marines in the platoon, and with my platoon sergeant. He taught me a great deal, but he didn't prejudge me. Are you like him?''

"I see yo' point, Doc. No offense.''

"Staff Sergeant Martin, the Marines from 3d Force who were reassigned here to 1st Force had no choice about it. I did. I wanted to come here. All that we had ever heard about 1st Force Recon Company was that you only patrolled along the beaches and spent more time getting out of missions than into them. I don't know jackshit about you, this platoon, or 1st Force Recon Company. I do know about the bush, and I also know how to work on someone who's been hurt. That's why I'm here. I do hope that you and I will get along."

The staff sergeant smiled his wicked smile, and said, "We will."

We stopped in front of a small green plywood hootch, and Staff Sergeant Martin pointed to the front door.

"Take any rack that's empty, Doc. I'll be back in a couple of minutes with my notebook. I need to get some information from you for the platoon commander."

My new hootch was empty, but signs of life showed me that at least two Marines also shared these living accommodations with me, and sooner or later they would return. As I busied myself unpacking my seabag and storing the gear that I had been able to keep from 3d Force, Staff Sergeant Martin returned with his notebook.

"Are y'all settled in here, Doc? I figured that it wouldn't take ya too long to unpack yo' shit, so give it a rest now and answer me some questions 'bout yo'self."

He first asked me about my military background; when I joined up, why, and what I wanted to do after my tour was over. He was interested in my tour with 3d Force Recon, and asked about my duties as a recon-team member, number of missions, and other cross-training qualifications. I answered all of his questions honestly, and by the time that we had finished, Staff Sergeant Martin had a much better understanding of me, and I of him. I knew that he wanted to be sure that his new platoon corpsman was not going to be the liability that most new guys tended to be. I assured him that I was confident in myself. He ended our conversation by telling me about the other Marines in the platoon. I would get to meet all of them, and the platoon commander, later, when they returned from an all-day training class. As he rose, and started out the door, he turned around, and said, "You can find your old friends from 3d Force over in the 4th Platoon area. But make sure that you're back here in time to go to the S-3's jump brief at 1630.''

I hadn't seen one familiar face since arriving at 1st Force Recon, and this opportunity to move around the company area would allow me to finish checking in at all the various places required on my check-in sheet and to discover where the old 3d Force Recon Marines were hiding.

It didn't take long before I was able to find Cpl. David Draper and his running mate, L. Cpl. Rich Gable. Both of these Marines had been in 3d Force during the time that I was with the company, and as I began to talk with Corporal Draper, Gable ran over to the hootch next door, and brought back corporals Pat McVey and "Stinky" Mahkewa.

Corporal McVey was the first to speak.

"Where the hell have you been for the last month, Doc? We were told by Captain Hisler and Lieutenant Coffman that you had been assigned to join 1st Force Recon with us while you were still at scuba school in the Philippines, but when you didn't show up, we thought that you had joined some other company.''

"I just checked in this morning. I've been assigned to the 2d Platoon and just finished talking with the platoon sergeant. Do you guys know Staff Sergeant Martin?''

"Yeah, we've met him already. He was a drill instructor at Parris Island. This is his first tour with Force Recon, but he's already done one tour here with the grunts a couple of years ago, and he's got a real good reputation around here.''

"He might, but it doesn't sound like you guys do.''

"And what's that supposed to mean?''

"I hadn't been here five minutes before he began telling me that the 3d Force guys who came here come on as know-it-alls. He doesn't like that. You must have made a really great impression on this place when you showed up.''

"This place isn't run like 3d Force, that's for sure. They train differently than we did, and they use officers as team leaders.''

"Have any of you been to the bush, yet?''

"No. Their teams are fairly tight, and they haven't used any of us yet. But there is a new area that we've heard about called the Yellow Brick Road, and it sounds like we'll all be going out to visit it soon.''

Corporal McVey, who was jump qualified, reminded me of the time and suggested that we not be late for the jump briefing due to begin within a few minutes. I told Draper, Gable, and Mahkewa that I would meet them after the briefing, and we could continue our reunion and our discussion about life in 1st Force Recon Company.

As Corporal McVey and I walked toward the S-3 hootch, I told him that it had been several weeks since I was in a parachute harness on Okinawa, and I still had some misgivings about the following day's parachute operations. In an attempt to assure me that I had little to worry about, Corporal McVey laughed.

"Well, there's one bright side to the whole deal. First Force has jumps scheduled several times a month. The CO, Major Bond, loves to jump, and he has made arrangements for us to use CH-46s, and Hueys. We always go to a place called 'Camp Viking' at Red Beach and jump out over the water. Shit, Doc, if you die here, at least you'll be amongst your friends."

With Corporal McVey's philosophical outlook on my short-term mortality still running through my mind, we arrived outside of the S-3 shop and joined in the ranks of those other jump-qualified Marines, who were seated and ready for Staff Sergeant Lynch to begin his brief. .

— THE OV-10 BRONCO —

"TOMORROW MORNING THOSE OF YOU JUMP-qualified members of 1st Force Recon Company will have the unique opportunity to conduct several low-level parachute jumps from the OV-10 Bronco. And, this afternoon, we have with us, as our guest, 1st Lieutenant Davis, from the Marine VMO Squadron, here in Da Nang, to give us a brief on the mission, employment, and capabilities of the OV-10 Bronco. Lieutenant Davis."

"Thank you, Staff Sergeant Lynch. I really appreciate this opportunity to come over here today and talk with you Force Recon Marines about the OV-10 Bronco. We have enjoyed a very close working relationship with you Marines, and my operations officer and your company executive officer, Captain Centers, felt that the more we know about one another's capabilities, the better combat team we'll have.

"I've been in country for a little more than eight months, and have worked in direct support of both Marine infantry and Force Recon operations. I can tell you from my personal experiences that the more familiar you are with what we and our Broncos can do, the better off we'll be. So sit back, listen to my short brief, take notes, and then we'll talk about tomorrow's jump over Red Beach. Just hold your questions until the end of the information brief, and I'll take you guys on one at a time."

The lieutenant's friendly and relaxed manner immediately put our group at ease, and he settled into his brief.

"By definition, the mission of our VMO, or Marine Observation Squadron, is to conduct operations in support of the Fleet Marine Force. Our squadrons are equipped with ten OV-10 Broncos per squadron, and currently we have two of them in country. The OV-10 Bronco is a relatively new member to the Marine Corps's aviation family, taking its first flight on August 6, 1967.

The Bronco is a twin-engine, fixed-wing aircraft, with a combat radius of about 250 miles. It has a crew of two, seated in tandem on ejection seats. It has dual controls, a cargo compartment aft of the rear seat, and a rear loading door at the end of the fuselage pod. It can carry a load of thirty-two hundred pounds or five paratroops or two stretcher patients with one attendant. Our maximum air speed is 281 miles per hour.

"Our primary mission is similar to yours: visual observation of the enemy and the area he operates in. As I said, the Bronco has a crew of two: the pilot and an aerial observer. The aerial observer is a ground officer, specially trained in aerial observation and the use of supporting arms, to include artillery, Naval gunfire, and air strikes. We even have the capability of using hand-held cameras and can drop our developed photographs to Marines on the ground. Our on-board communications equipment allows us to be in contact with both ground and other aviation units at the same time.

"Our ordnance load is limited to Zuni rockets, which we use primarily to mark enemy targets. We have two M-60C machine guns on board for our own protection and for fire suppression. Our other limitations are really based on the skill level of the pilot and aerial observer, terrain and weather, and the use of enemy camouflage and concealment. So, you can see the missions and limitations of Force Recon and VMP parallel one another very closely. Now that you know about what we can and cannot do, I want to get to the reason why I'm here, parachute operations from the OV-10."

With that announcement came a thunderous "Arrrruugggahh" from all of the Marines who would participate in the OV-10 jump.

"The OV-10 Bronco has another unique capability. We can accommodate a maximum of five parachutists in the rear of our aircraft and drop you gentlemen on target by executing a routine 'pop-up' maneuver over the drop zone. The way that this is done is by removing the rear cargo door and rigging the interior of the cargo compartment with a static line for your hook-up point. The five designated jumpers are loaded into the Bronco, similar to the way that five guys would sit on a bobsled. When the pilot and aerial observer have located the drop zone, the pilot signals the jumpers with a two-light system. The red light will be the preparatory signal to stand by to jump, and this signal will be followed by the green-light signal to jump. The OV-10 pilot pulls back sharply on the stick, the nose of the aircraft angles up, and it's 'bombs away' as the five jumpers exit the aircraft, one behind the next.''

At the conclusion of the lieutenant's brief, Staff Sergeant Lynch circulated a manifest sheet for all of us to sign. This training jump was supposed to be a great deal different than what most of us had experienced when jumping from helicopters or other types of fixed-wing aircraft, and it was in preparation for a six-hundred-foot jump scheduled for a later date.

The few questions that were asked of the lieutenant were answered to everyone's satisfaction, and Staff Sergeant Brown took over and conducted the more technical portion of the jump brief. This included map coordinates, radio frequencies, the physical description of the drop zone, obstacles in and around the zone, wind direction and velocity, how the drop zone would be marked, friendly positions, enemy positions, and the direction cleared to return fire. The last two portions of the drop-zone brief were always included as a matter of course, but since this was only a training jump, there was no enemy position or firing of weapons expected.

We were told to be ready to get on the trucks that would take us to the airfield at 0500. The remainder of the day was ours to prepare mentally for the coming event. When we were dismissed from the briefing, Corporal McVey slapped me on the back.

"See, what did I tell ya, Doc? Piece a' cake! We don't even have to shuffle to the door on this jump. We'll fall from the sky like a bomb.''

"McVey, I've already fallen from the sky like a bomb once. The trip down was fine, but the detonation part was another story. It cost me a week in the hospital. But as long as the wind velocity is low, this will be a lot of fun.''

I said I had to get back over to see Staff Sergeant Martin. He had said that the platoon commander wanted to see me after I had checked in and was dismissed from this brief.

"When the lieutenant is finished with me, I'll come back over to see you and Draper and Stinky. I want you to tell me some more about 1st Force Recon Company. I haven't even been here one day, and I'm supposed to jump tomorrow. Is the pace always like this?''

"If the company doesn't have any training scheduled for the day, then the platoons always do. Lately, it seems that that's all we've been doing—training. I think that it's about to change. I'll talk to you later, Doc.''

I knocked on the door to Staff Sergeant Martin's hootch, and my rapping was answered by the command to "enter." Inside, seated on his rack, was Staff Sergeant Martin, in the company of several other Marine staff sergeants. They were all centered around a footlocker playing cards.

"How did yo' jump brief go, Doc? I hear that y'all will be jumpin' from an OV-10 Bronco tomorrow mornin'. That is somethin' I've always wanted to do, and I'm slated to go to Okinawa fo' jump school on the next quota assignment."

"The brief was good, and I ran into several Marines I knew in 3d Force. You told me to come back after the briefing so that the platoon commander could talk to me. Is this a good time, or do you want me to come back later?"

"No, this is a fine time, right now, Doc. Lieutenant Blotz is in his hootch, and I'm sure that he'll want to talk to you now. Wait right here, and I'll tell him that yo' here. I'll be right back. Just keep yo' eye on these so-called 'friends' o' mine, so's they don't magically improve their hands while I'm gone."

With the return of my platoon sergeant, I was told to report to 1st Lieutenant Blotz, the leader of the 2d Platoon. I knocked three times on the outside wooden slats of his hootch, and waited for the standard reply to enter. Hearing the one-word command, I removed my cover, opened the door, walked several strides inside, and centered myself directly in front of the small green field desk that the lieutenant was seated behind.

"Sir, HM3 Norton reporting to the platoon commander, as ordered."

Standing at the position of attention, with my head and eyes focused directly ahead, I knew that the lieutenant was giving me the visual once-over before he would allow me to stand at ease or to sit down. The camouflage uniform that I had put on was clean and pressed, my boots had been spit shined prior to my arrival, and I had even shaved to make sure that this first impression would be a good one.

"Stand at ease, Doc, and have a seat."

When I sat down, the lieutenant stood up.

"My name is Lieutenant Blotz, and I want to welcome you to the 2d Platoon. Staff Sergeant Martin brought your service record book over here earlier today, and after going through it, I'm pleased to have you in this organization. It's not every day that we have a dual-qualified corpsman come into a Force Recon company. I'm sure that we can use your expertise around here. We have twenty-three Marines, and one Kit Carson scout in the platoon, and most of them, with the exception of the KCs, have not had a great deal of experience in the bush. I know from our intelligence briefings that 3d Force did a great deal of patrolling on the DMZ and in the A Shau Valley, and that kind of hands-on experience will help in the teaching and training of the Marines in this platoon. The word is out that we'll be sent out on a number of patrols starting this week. After we return from tomorrow's jump, we'll talk some more about where we're going and what your responsibilities will be in this platoon. That's it for now. I'll see you tomorrow morning. You're dismissed."

I stood up, did an about face, left the lieutenant's hootch, and returned to tell Staff Sergeant Martin that I had been dismissed from the lieutenant's short interview, with an invitation to talk with him again after the jump.

My platoon sergeant said that he, too, had nothing additional for me to do and suggested that I take advantage of his good mood and "get the hell out of the area."

Not having to be told twice to do this, I quickly found my way to corporals Draper, Gable and Mahkewa. They were playing "back-alley bridge" in Corporal McVey's hootch.

"How did your interview go with Lieutenant Blotz?" asked McVey. "Is he a trip, or what? I met him when he was a staff sergeant, back at Camp Lejeune. He still has a real problem about being so short. Did he pull that stupid trick of his, and make you sit down while he stood up?"

"Yeah, he did. I wondered what that was all about."

"Well, don't feel too bad about it, 'cause everyone who has ever had to report in to him has gone through that same stupid bullshit."

McVey was wise to the ways of the world, and he had proved himself to be a valuable source of intelligence not only to me but to other Marines who sometimes could not see the forest for the trees. That was the fun of living life in the squad bay. What was blatantly obvious to some of us was camouflaged to others. Corporal McVey had a certain way of looking at things, often humorous, often morbid, but he was usually right in his observations of how and why things worked the way they did.

Addressing his fellow card players, Corporal McVey suddenly announced that the game was over.

"Draper, you and Gable and Stinky will now excuse us. You are only straight-leg Force Recon Marines. It's a shame that you are not in the elite inner circles of those of us magnificent individuals, us chosen few, who are allowed to throw ourselves from the safety of aircraft to the earth below. Norton and I must mentally prepare ourselves for the demands of tomorrow's exercise. Be gone now and return tomorrow, when you will be permitted to listen in awe, as we recount our stories of incredible greatness and daring to you miserable *legs*."

Looks of disbelief crossed the faces of Draper, Gable, and Mahkewa.

"Why is it," asked Lance Corporal Mahkewa, "that we are always buds until they announce a parachute jump or a scuba dive? As soon as the word goes out that only those certain people can participate, you guys start to treat the rest of us like we have a bad disease."

"Stinky, this is one of those situations that separates those who can, from those who only want to. To be amongst the 'golden chosen few,' advanced parachutists, is a great and glorious honor. And besides, we get paid fifty-five dollars a month for risking our lives. More importantly, we need someone we can trust back in the rear, like you three guys, to mail our gear home if we get killed in the jump. Now, don't you feel better?"

McVey's change from contemptuous corporal to old friend was easier for Draper, Gable, and Mahkewa to deal with.

"You know, Corporal McVey, the only time that you become a complete asshole is when you use words that the rest of us can't understand. I'd remember that the next time I ask someone to mail my shit home if I were you. You can never tell where it might end up."

"You're right, Stinky. I'll ask someone else next time."

"Come on, Doc, I'll walk with you back over to your hootch. By the time I get back here, you three lance coolies had better have returned this place to its original condition of squalor."

We left Corporal McVey's hootch listening to Mahkewa ask Draper and Gable, "What is squalor, anyway?"

"I'll get myself in the same stick as you tomorrow, Doc, and you won't have to worry if you're still spooked about jumping."

"The way that OV-10 pilot made it sound is a lot different from walking out the back end of a CH-46 or throwing yourself out the door of a C-130."

"Yeah, it doesn't sound too bad, the only problem is that no one from this company has jumped an OV-10 before."

"That's really reassuring to know, McVey."

"I'll meet you tomorrow morning in front of my hootch, Doc. Don't eat any breakfast tomorrow morning. We always try to have the truck drivers make a stop at the FLC [Force Logistics Command] bakery before we jump. Their bakery is famous. They have fresh-baked bread and all sorts of doughnuts and cold milk, just for the asking. We'll get something to eat over there. I'll see ya' in the morning, Doc.''

At 0500, I met up with McVey, and we boarded the "six-by" truck which would take all of the enlisted Marines to the military airstrip in Da Nang. The company commander, Major Bond; Captain Centers, the company executive officer; and our new company 1st sergeant, 1st Sergeant Jacques, went ahead of us in the CO's jeep. As promised by Corporal McVey, and through some prearranged manipulation, our truck driver did pull into the Force Logistics Command area. He stopped directly in front of the FLC bakery. As soon as the truck stopped, Staff Sergeant Lynch hopped out of the front cab and yelled, "All right, any of you hungry Devil Dogs who want to fill up on ice-cold milk and warm doughnuts have got ten minutes to grab and growl! Be back on this truck and ready to go in ten minutes. We ain't got all day.''

It was as good as promised. Inside the bakery were several dispensers of cold chocolate and white milk and baskets of doughnuts, all for free. The bakery's reputation had made it a meeting place for dozens of servicemen from the various branches and units in and around Da Nang.

With paper bags filled with doughnuts, we climbed back aboard the big diesel truck and continued to motor on to the airfield. There was not much talking going on among the Marines scheduled to make the morning's jump. It always seemed to be that way. Inner thoughts were not shared, even with the closest of friends.

"Okay, everybody, listen up! Get all of those chutes off the truck, stack 'em right over here, and then line up according to how your names are read off of my jump manifest. Major Bond, Captain Centers, 1st Sergeant Jacques, and Lieutenant Robnick are in stick number one. Gunny Fowler, Sergeant Williams, Corporal McVey, and Doc Norton are stick number two. Staff Sergeant Brown, Corporal Smith, Corporal Morgan, and Sergeant Ledford are in stick number three. Lance Corporal Burke, Corporal Davis, Sergeant Christopher, and Corporal Stevens are in stick number four. Get your gear on and stand by for your final rigger's check.''

Gunnery Sergeant Fowler, the communications chief for 1st Force Recon, led the way toward our OV-10, and waiting by the rear cargo door, he inspected each of us again to make sure that our harnesses, buckles, and chin straps were all securely fastened before we started to load ourselves into the cramped cargo compartment of the Bronco. Being the last name called out for our stick, I was the first one into the compartment. Once I had positioned myself as comfortably as possible, Corporal McVey followed, as did Sergeant Williams and Gunny Fowler. By the time the four of us were seated, Gunny Fowler's position left him sitting on the very edge of the cargo door opening, with both of his legs dangling out of the door. We were seated facing backward, and our view was interrupted by the rear stabilizing bar that connected the twin tails of the OV-10. It looked close enough to touch.

To be heard over the roar of the Bronco's engines as it taxied for takeoff, I shouted into McVey's ear and asked him if he thought that it was possible to touch the stabilizer bar when we jumped. Cocking his head back in a half twist, he yelled, "That's why we're here. That stabilizer has a habit of cutting jumpers in half. They want us to test this new design to make sure it's safe."

I wasn't sure if McVey was kidding me or not, until my complete silence made him start to laugh.

"Don't sweat it. No one has been able to touch the stabilizer. All you have to worry about is getting hit in the face with our three assist bags when you jump."

This time I knew that McVey was not kidding. Each parachute was designed so that the assist bag would remain attached to the hook-up line inside the OV-10. Only the first jumper, Gunny Fowler, would not have to avoid the flapping nylon bags that each successive jumper would see as he exited the OV-10.

The short flight time that was required for us to gain an altitude of one thousand feet meant that we would be over our drop zone at Red Beach within just a few minutes of takeoff. We were in the second OV-10 and would be given the signal to go after the first stick of jumpers was safely on the ground. While we waited, we circled over the South China Sea, waiting for the radio signal that would give our pilot the go-ahead to make his approach and pop-up over the DZ. The sharp banking of our OV-10 signaled the four of us that the pilot had been cleared to begin his run.

The signaling of the bright red light started that great adrenaline rush through everyone in the OV-10. Since we had no means of positive communication with either the pilot or the aerial observer, we had no way of knowing just how long it would take before the red light was turned off and the green light would glow. Still, we continued to fly on our level course, staring at the jump light and waiting.

The OV-10 and the little green light acted in unison. As quickly as that light bulb lit up, the plane changed attitude from level to what felt like a fifty-degree climb, and Gunny Fowler disappeared, with the shout "Airborne!" The rest of us moved forward without hesitation to follow Gunny Fowler out of the back of the climbing OV-10. The steep degree of the Bronco's climb would have made hesitation all but impossible anyway. The primary objective of this jump was for all of us to practice landing together. Within seconds, Williams and McVey had inched themselves forward and vanished below, and now it was my turn to do the same.

Just as Corporal McVey had predicted, it was a piece a' cake. The parachute assist bags were blown far to the right side of the Bronco's tail, and the sensation of falling was not as frightening as I had experienced in the previous jumps that I had made, running out of the back door of the CH-46 or CH-53 helicopters.

Once I had checked to ensure that I had a good open canopy above me, I maneuvered myself into a position close to McVey and Gunny Fowler, but the gunny and I were larger than Corporal McVey, and we went past him on our way to the DZ. I could see that Sergeant Williams had "slipped" about one hundred yards away from us, when suddenly I began to hear the gunny start to swear out a stream of curses directed at the corporal above him.

The reason for the gunny's great unhappiness was that Corporal McVey was vomiting up all the milk and doughnuts that he had been so eager to devour only half an hour earlier, and it was raining down on the gunny.

Gunny Fowler and I hit the sandy area of the drop zone and recovered our parachutes, rolled them up, and returned them to the center of the drop zone. I then went over to find Corporal McVey to see just how sick he was.

"Hey, McVey. It was just like you said."

McVey groaned.

"I'm sick, and now Gunny Fowler will be after my ass forever!"

"No, McVey, you are lucky. Your streams of puke missed him, and that's probably the only reason that he's not over here pounding you into the ground. Do you feel any better?"

"Yeah, sure, sure. It's like I told you, Doc, this parachuting stuff is a piece a' cake."

"It's a good thing that your stomach is empty, McVey, we still have two more jumps to make this morning."

The three training jumps that were made from the OV-10's were in preparation for low-level parachute insertions by Force Recon teams, planned for the months ahead. They were viewed, by those who participated, as probably the best method of team insertion because of the speed of the OV-10. It was much faster than a helicopter. And the OV-10 was more fun to jump from than the other types of aircraft we used for parachute operations.

UNUSUAL EVENTS IN THE CLUB

SEVERAL EVENTS OCCURRED IN THE SERVICE CLUBS of 1st Force Reconnaissance Company during the 1969–70 period that, to me, were quite significant. The officers and staff noncommissioned officers shared a very small club at one end of the camp, while the enlisted Marines and corpsmen in the grades of E-5 (sergeant) and below shared a club with the soldiers of one U.S. Army motor transportation company, which was billeted nearby. The Marine sergeants and corporals had a small partitioned area where they gathered, while the rest of the club belonged to the men in the pay grades of E-3 and below. Our enlisted club contained a dozen tables and numerous chairs, one jukebox with the latest assortment of hit songs, and the club management provided cold beer or sodas at twenty-five cents per can, along with hot dogs, popcorn, and assorted snacks. No hard liquor was sold in the enlisted men's club. It wasn't much of a place to look at, but it served its purpose as a central gathering place to relax.

Several times a week, movies were shown inside the club, usually to a small audience. Our neighbors in the Army had built an outdoor theater for the motor-T company soldiers, which was open to us as long as we behaved ourselves and did nothing to interrupt the movies. Usually, peace was maintained between the two services within the club. But unfortunately, several Marines from 1st Force Reconnaissance Company and a few soldiers had been involved with several significant incidents during the past year which had resulted in military investigations, courts-martial, and even death.

On the night of June 21, 1969, someone went into the company S-3 (operations) hootch and removed from a desk drawer one High Standard, .22 caliber, semiautomatic pistol equipped with a permanently attached silencer. Although considered to be a unique piece of gear, the pistol was in serious need of repair, requiring a new slide-return spring. In its present condition, the pistol could only be fired in a single-shot mode. It also required the shooter to manually push the slide forward into a locked position before it could be fired.

One month after this pistol had vanished from the ops hootch, it magically surfaced in the possession of Marine Cpl. Robert E. Stockham, a less than sterling member of 1st Force Reconnaissance Company. Corporal Stockham shared a hootch in close proximity to another Marine named L. Cpl. Ronald B. Prohaska, and being unable to keep his mouth shut about his newly acquired weapon, Stockham told Prohaska that he had it hidden in their hootch.

Sgt. James W. Killen also lived in the same hootch, and while Stockham and Prohaska happened to be fooling around with the stolen pistol, Killen walked in on them and saw what they had. More fascinated with the pistol than the fact that it was hot, "Pappy" Killen joined in with the two Marines as they talked about how neat it was to be in possession of this unique weapon. Their excited conversation even went so far as to discuss the ease of "waxing someone" by using a silenced weapon. Before leaving the hootch Sergeant Killen told Stockham and Prohaska that he wanted to use the pistol to shoot some of the feral dogs that were living on the outskirts of the company area. Realizing that the sergeant was now in with them by not immediately reporting his discovery of the stolen weapon, Corporal Stockham told him that he could use the silenced weapon whenever he wanted. But little did Sergeant Killen know how potentially dangerous their agreement was to be until the evening of 20 July, when two seemingly unrelated events collided, with deadly results.

Within the 1st Force Recon Company area, Sergeant Killen's nickname was Pappy because he looked older than all of his peers. It was Pappy's usual routine to visit that section of the enlisted men's club that catered to sergeants and corporals and drink beer with his friends until either running out of money and friends or until the club closed down for the night. By 2100 hours this particular evening, Sergeant Killen was in his cups, after having drunk eleven or twelve beers. He staggered from the club, and returned to his hootch to sleep off his drunkenness. Ironically, this was the same night that the Australian musical group, Sweethearts on Parade, was scheduled to perform inside the 1st Force Reconnaissance Company's staff and officers' club as part of a USO tour.

This little club had been packed tight since 1900 hours, with most of the company's officers and staff noncommissioned officers, including the company commander, Maj. Roger E. Simmons, present. They all had arrived early, hoping to get a table close enough to allow a good look at Miss Catherine Anne Warnes, a stunning blond "round eye" and the rock group's lead singer. At 2100, the band was just finishing one of their songs when Miss Warnes stepped back from the stage microphone, suddenly clutched her heart, and fell to the floor, dead. The warning shouts of "sniper" rang out from inside the club. Some Marines took cover behind their chairs and hid, while others ran from the club toward their hootches to get their weapons and search for the sniper.

No more shots were fired into the club, and a hasty search of the company area provided no clues as to who had fired or the location of the shooter. It was not until daylight that a thorough search of the area was conducted. By then the autopsy of the dead girl revealed some important information to investigators. Miss Warnes had been initially hit in her left side by a .22 caliber bullet, which traveled across her chest and pierced her aorta, exiting her right side, and killing her instantly. The round was fired from behind a jeep that was parked no less than thirty-five yards from the side of the staff and officers' club, having cut through a screen window before striking Miss Warnes.

At first there was some speculation that the commanding officer of 1st Force Recon was the intended victim of the sniper because a straight line could be drawn from where the CO sat to where Miss Warnes was standing in relation to the sniper's firing position. But Major Simmons did not believe that this was the case. ("Was Girl's Killer Gunning for Maj?" read one headline.) Persistent investigators continued on with the case and narrowed down a list of suspects that had initially included Sergeant Killen, Corporal Stockham, and Lance Corporal Prohaska.

After obtaining enough preliminary evidence against Sergeant Killen, in the form of physical evidence and damaging statements from both Stockham and Prohaska, a general court-martial was convened to decide the fate of the Marine sergeant. On 29 October 1969, the court members found Sergeant Killen guilty of unpremeditated murder, and he was sentenced to twenty years confinement at hard labor, loss of pay and allowances, reduction to the rank of private, and a dishonorable discharge. Fortunately for Sergeant Killen, an alert defense attorney saved him from having to spend twenty years at hard labor.

The day after the trial, Killen's lawyer heard the trial counsel mention the fact that both Stockham and Prohaska had been offered grants of immunity in return for their testimony against Sergeant Killen, although these immunity grants had not been required. This was the very first mention that such a deal had been agreed to, and Killen's Marine attorney knew that if a witness testifies under a grant of immunity, the members of the court (the jury) must be advised of that fact so that they may evaluate the credibility of the testimony. In the mistaken belief that they enjoyed full immunity from prosecution, they implicated Sergeant Killen.

Because Stockman and Prohaska were the best of friends and had admitted that they had lied to investigators during the preliminary investigation to avoid incriminating themselves, these grants of immunity took on even greater importance. During the trial, Killen had admitted having the silenced pistol in his possession, but said that he had returned the weapon to Stockham. He also testified that he had returned from the club after drinking nearly half a case of beer.

Prohaska, on the other hand, testified that after Killen had returned to the hootch and that during the time that the camp was still searching for the presumed enemy sniper, he had asked Killen, "Why in the hell did you do something like that?"

Killen reportedly replied, "She was just winged." Then, Prohaska asked Killen where the pistol was, to which he replied, "It's taken care of."

Those two statements were the only evidence that had linked Killen to the murder. He did testify that he had handled the weapon earlier, on the day of the shooting, and that he had been intoxicated, but he denied any knowledge of the killing. A motive for the murder of Miss Warnes was never established.

The wheels of military justice can turn slowly, and it was not until a year and a half later that the Navy Court of Military Review, in a unanimous opinion, held that, unquestionably, the testimony of Stockham and Prohaska was induced, in part at least, by offers of immunity. A rehearing of the case was authorized, and in mid-1971, after the 1st Marine Division had returned to Camp Pendleton, California, the commanding general was advised that "Because it had been nearly two years since the death of Miss Warnes, any rehearing would be time-consuming and expensive. . . . Physical evidence and vital witnesses are scattered across the United States . . . however, due to the serious nature of the charges it is recommended that a retrial be ordered."[1]

Sergeant Killen was retried, found not guilty, and was immediately released from confinement. His pay and allowances were returned and his reduction to private was vacated, as was his dishonorable discharge. He had served two years and nine days confinement for the murder of Miss Warnes. But the mystery still remains as to who killed her.

Another tragic event which centered around our enlisted club occurred in February 1970. Two soldiers from the nearby Army motor transportation company had become romantically involved with one of the Vietnamese waitresses who worked serving drinks in the club. Jealous of the other soldier's efforts, one of the soldiers decided that he would eliminate his competition by "fragging" his buddy. One night, he waited outside the club, and when he saw his fellow soldier start to leave the club, he simply rolled a fragmentation grenade down the sandy slope next to the club, and waited as the grenade detonated directly in front of the plywood door. What the soldier had failed to see, after he had taken cover behind the protective slope, was that his intended victim did not exit the club but turned around at the last second, permitting two other American soldiers to pass by him and into the kill zone of the hand grenade. The grenade went off as expected, killing one innocent soldier and seriously wounding another. The day that I joined 1st Force Reconnaissance Company, Doc Palmer showed me the exact spot in front of the club where the exploding hand grenade had cratered a small section of the concrete sidewalk. His observation was interesting.

"The Viet Cong and the NVA must really laugh at the stupidity of the American servicemen. Here, three Army soldiers all leave Vietnam as losers. One gets medevaced back to the States, one goes back to serve a long prison sentence, and the third gets sent home in a casket to his family. The enemy didn't even have to fire a single round to get rid of those three Army soldiers. I guess we are our own worst enemy."

But events in our club were not always so serious. The day that we returned from one OV-10 jump, those of us who had participated decided to meet in the enlisted club to celebrate having "cheated death" earlier in the day. I sat at a table with Gable,

[1] Solis, Lt. Col. J. D., USMC (Ret.) "1969: Military Justice Tested." In *Marines and Military Law in Vietnam.* Washington: History and Museum Division, Headquarters, U.S. Marine Corps, 1989.

Draper, Mahkewa, and McVey, and we watched in fascination as one six-man team of 1st Force Recon Marines, who had just returned from a mission, decided to gross out several U.S. Army soldiers who occupied a nearby table. Well on the road to intoxication, these Marines began to pass around a large chunk of ice from mouth to mouth, demonstrating to all who observed them that they were a "tight" team. They could, and would, share everything, and this included their ice. When the size of the ice cube had diminished after its third pass around the table, one of the team members noticed a huge toad which had positioned itself outside the club's front door. The bright outside lights drew scores of moths and other flying insects, which, in turn, had attracted the big toad with the possibility of dinner. Having nothing more edible to share with one another, one team member captured the toad and brought it back to the table. Opening his mouth wide, he placed the head of the toad inside, and turned to his nearest teammate, challenging him to take the amphibious offering. Without a moment's hesitation, the hind end of the toad disappeared into the other Marine's mouth. The toad, obviously not wanting to play this game any longer, then did what toads normally do when frightened; it emptied its bladder and secreted an acid through its skin. The resulting look of astonishment on the drunken Marine's face when the offended toad filled his mouth with urine and defensive acid resulted in screams of laughter throughout our club. The toad was unceremoniously spit out onto the concrete floor, and the insulted Marine ran from the club, trying in vain to wipe the poison from his lips and vomit the urine from his throat. The hilarious scene was unanimously voted as the best floor show the enlisted club had ever seen, and it answered the question as to why those Vietnamese toads grew to be as large as they did.

TRAINING FOR PATROLS

LATE IN 1969, THE WRITING WAS CLEARLY ON THE wall that operations in I Corps were slowing down for most Marine ground units, but 1st Force Reconnaissance Company's role as the eyes and ears of the Marine Amphibious Force commander had actually called for an increase in our patrolling activity.

First Force Reconnaissance Company had been the recipient of the Meritorious Unit Commendation and, in part, the citation read:

> During November 1969, in the face of numerically superior enemy forces, who were employing aggressive, well-trained counterreconnaissance forces, the First Force Recon Company repeatedly reentered enemy sanctuaries and provided information vital to the subsequent fixing and destruction of these forces. Employing genuine long-range patrols, the enemy supply route was located by patrols forty miles outside the main allied defense perimeter and well in excess of the range of supporting arms. It was determined that the 'Yellow Brick Road' [Route 614], which had been assumed to be the main supply route, was in fact not being used. After further extensive patrolling to within thirteen miles of the Laotian border, the company confirmed that the new route was now Route 610.

During the period of 9 March to 23 November 1969, patrols from 1st Force Reconnaissance Company had sighted 7,747 enemy and captured nine POWs as well as many enemy documents. Activity was heavy enough to recommend the following individual honors during this period: two Navy Crosses, eleven Silver Star Medals, two Legion of Merit Medals, thirty-two Bronze Star

Medals, and forty-three Purple Hearts. The importance of the intelligence-gathering capability of Force Recon Company patrols is reflected in the recommendation for the Meritorious Unit Commendation for this period:

Specific missions of the company ranged from the penetration of deep and long-range reconnaissance patrols into the very heart of enemy-controlled territory to locate enemy troop concentrations, supplies and lines of communications, to the capture of enemy personnel. In the face of numerically superior enemy forces, who were employing aggressive, well-trained counterreconnaissance forces, the company repeatedly reentered enemy sanctuaries, completing assigned missions and providing information vital to the subsequent fixing, interdiction, and destruction of untold numbers of enemy forces. Accomplishing a total of 191 patrols, the information gathered by patrols formed the foundation and impetus for operations and massive air and artillery strikes against enemy base camps, lines of communications, and supply depots. The identity and locations of the newly infiltrated 90th NVA Regiment into Quang Nam Province, the egress of the 21st and 1st NVA Regiments from Quang Nam Province and the subsequent return of these units was established in large measure by information gathered by the company's patrols. Intelligence derived from information by these patrols went on to precipitate highly successful forays, including Operation Durham Peak, by the 1st Marine Division into the Que Son Mountains and Antenna Valley, where extremely complex enemy base camps and large quantities of supplies were uncovered and destroyed. The enemy was denied a vital stepping-stone to Da Nang from the south and An Hoa from the east, and his designs for offensive operations against these areas were effectively preempted. While embarked on operations for the III Marine Amphibious Force, the company was tasked to locate the enemy's Military Region V and Group 44 headquarters, their related installations, and supply and communications routes in the southwestern reaches of Quang Nam Province. Force Recon patrols were able to provide a flow of heretofore unknown and extremely valuable information from the interior of the enemy's base areas. With the repeated interdiction of his newly identified installations and facilities, the enemy was effectively kept off balance and rendered unable to launch a 1969 summer offensive of the magnitude he had intended.

One of the recipients of the two Navy Crosses, which were awarded to Marines of 1st Force Recon for actions during this period, was Sgt. Joseph R. Crockett, Jr.

On Tuesday, 12 March 1970, Marine Maj. Gen. Raymond Davis proudly presented the Navy Cross to Joseph Crockett, who was at that time a student in C Company at the Marine Corps Development and Education Command, Quantico, Virginia. Crockett was decorated with the nation's second-highest award for his extraordinary heroism while leading an eight-man team against forty North Vietnamese soldiers.

Sergeant Crockett was leading a team consisting of an assistant team leader, two radiomen, one M-79 grenade-launcher man, two M-14 riflemen, and an M-16 rifleman. This 1st Force Recon team had been given the mission of observing a suspected enemy supply route for five days. The mission had been extended for an additional day when the team made contact with an NVA unit consisting of approximately forty enemy soldiers at 0640 hours on 23 April.

The team broke contact with the enemy unit, after killing one of them, and began a series of harassing tactics on the North Vietnamese position. This action lasted until almost 1300 hours, when the enemy soldiers came charging at the Marines. With all other Marines wounded, and with one dead from the initial moments of the second contact, Sergeant Crockett seized the M-79 grenade launcher and moved across fifty meters of exposed terrain to deliver heavy fire upon the enemy.

In an interview published in the base newspaper, the *Quantico Sentry*, Sergeant Crockett stated, "I used forty M-79 rounds before I knew what was happening."

He killed one enemy soldier and wounded four others before running out of ammunition.

Using a radio, Sergeant Crockett then called in artillery fire to within fifty meters of his men. Running from one Marine position to another, he hurled all the grenades he could find at the enemy soldiers, causing them to fall back and regroup.

The enemy began lighting fires in an attempt to burn out Sergeant Crockett's position. He tried, but failed, to put the fires out with his jacket. Sergeant Crockett then moved his wounded companions away from the fires, stopping only to render emergency first aid and to fire at the enemy.

When a rescue flight of ten helicopters arrived, Sergeant Crockett tied an air panel to his back and boldly moved into an open clearing. With the colored cloth on his back, he stood in full view of the enemy and marked the landing zone for the evacuation craft.

The flight included four helicopters containing a Marine infantry reaction force and six gunships, which took over the battle. Sergeant Crockett assisted in the evacuation of the wounded, then chose to walk out of the area rather than be evacuated himself.

Around the same time that Sergeant Crockett was being awarded the Navy Cross for his heroic actions, 1st Force Reconnaissance Company had been dropped from the operational control and administrative control (OPCON and ADCON) of the 1st Reconnaissance Battalion, and was tasked with providing reconnaissance support to the commanding general, III MAF.

Starting in December 1969, while 3d Force Recon Company was patrolling deep in the A Shau Valley, 1st Force Recon Company began the long and dangerous mission of area reconnaissance of the Thuong Duc Corridor, commonly referred to as the "Yellow Brick Road." It had become a standard practice for 1st Force Recon to conduct training patrols outside of the company area prior to sending teams in to recon the Thuong Duc Corridor. The first training patrol that I joined had been given a four-day mission of operating along a section of beach located several miles south of Da Nang, and this training patrol immediately opened my eyes to the similarities and differences in how training had been conducted in 3d Force Recon and 1st Force Recon Company.

We had been given three days to prepare for our mission. Our new team was comprised of seven men: a sergeant, named Christopher, who was assigned as the team leader; his radio operator; the assistant team leader (ATL), who was a corporal; three riflemen; and me. One of the three riflemen was picked to carry a secondary radio at the insistence of the ATL.

We began our preparation for the patrol with a team briefing conducted by the new sergeant.

"I know most of you only from having seen you in the company area. This will be my fifth recon patrol as team leader, but we are all being evaluated on this patrol before we go on any missions west of Da Nang. I need some information from each of you. First, I need your rank, last name, the last three digits of your service number, your blood type, and then the number of missions that you have been out on prior to this one."

"Pfc. Adams, 952, B positive, none."

"Lance Corporal Morgan, 442, O negative, eight missions."

"Lance Corporal Holk, 303, B negative, none."

"Pfc. Dickerson, 222, O negative, none."

"Lance Corporal Davis, 787, O, none."

"HM3 Norton, 690, O negative, twenty-two."

"You're the new doc from 3d Force, right?"

"Both Lance Corporal Morgan and I came here from 3rd Force."

"Well, with thirty missions between you, I'm glad that they have assigned the both of you to this team."

The sergeant's remark was meant as a compliment, but to suddenly realize that the majority of this team's members had little or no experience in the bush made Lance Corporal Morgan and me pay particular attention to what was now being discussed.

The sergeant continued his brief, going over the general nature of our mission and his hourly schedule for our training. This included the standard checklist of weapons to be carried; the amount of ammunition to be taken along by each man; the special equipment to be checked out, such as PSIDs, starlight scopes, pyrotechnics; and our rations of food and water. We were told that this mission would be a route recon and that during our four days out we would establish several observation posts, implant and retrieve our sensors, and determine if any of the trails in the area were being used.

We spent the better part of the next day conducting rehearsals of the immediate actions (IA drills) that we would take during an ambush, practicing at being the ones who initiated the ambush, and practicing those actions required by the team to break through an ambush. These actions had to be practiced until they were instinctive. After IA drills were rehearsed, we practiced our hand-and-arm signals to the satisfaction of the team leader and his assistant. Then we practiced exactly how we would move while patrolling. This included the order of march. It was a matter of crawling before walking, and walking before running. The object of our practicing this type of movement was to be assured that *any* member of the team was capable of taking over if the senior man was killed or injured.

Our training in 3d Force Recon was designed to make us tired. As Major Lee had said, "When you are tired you will make mistakes, and those mistakes can cost you your life. It isn't as easy on the fifth day out to climb over two thousand meters as it is the first day out, when you've been rested. Train to be tired, make your mistakes in the rear, and then correct them."

This was a brand-new team, and even though I had confidence in our sergeant team leader and in Lance Corporal Morgan, I had no confidence in the others, nor did I expect them to have any confidence in one another, or in me. The type of confidence that we expected from one another had to be learned and demonstrated in our training and then put to application in the field.

As a team member in 3d Force Recon Company, Lance Corporal Morgan had repeatedly shown his ability to be knowledgeable in the bush, a dependable team member, and cool under fire. He knew how to use his map and compass. He knew first aid, and he knew how to use the radio to call in air support. The same could not be said for the rest of our new team, and that was what made our training all the more serious. Each man's life, and the success of the team and the accomplishment of our mission, was dependent upon our paying strict attention to what was being taught and rehearsed. This was an opportunity for Morgan and me to help in the detailed preparation of this patrol, for what had been second nature to the two of us was a new experience for the four members of this team who had never been in the bush. The sergeant was anxious for our help and was reassured by our level of experience. We shared everything we knew with the team.

We started our cross training of these new men with a checklist, just as we had been trained to do in 3d Force Recon Company. The PRC-77 radio was taken apart and reassembled until every man could do it blindfolded. The method of how to preset radio frequencies was described and practiced, as was the method of properly cleaning all of the radio's battery and handset connections. The importance of the radio could not be overstated. This one piece of equipment was our only link to the outside world and to any type of additional support that we might suddenly need. It was one thing to be considered the eyes and ears of the III MAF commanding general, but if we couldn't communicate our observations, we were worthless to him and a liability, not an asset.

Our personal gear was standardized. Each man carried his equipment the exact same way, and that equipment was packed in our rucksacks in the same place. Each team member knew where my medical equipment was. They knew exactly where I kept my morphine, and they knew how to administer it. They also were taught how to administer the serum albumin (blood volume expander) that I always carried. I knew who carried what specialized equipment and ordnance and how to use it. By cross training one another this way, we improved our chances for survival.

Our team leader's rules for the conduct of the patrol were rou-

tinely repeated. He would allow no talking during the mission.
Because no talking was the rule, hand-and-arm signals were our
only internal means of communication. The rule was that as long
as the signal was understood by every team member, then we
would practice it and use it.

Detailed inspections of us and of our equipment were a daily
event. We trained fully dressed and carrying blank ammunition.
We started our daily routine with a team leader's inspection. Our
patterns of camouflage paint were inspected to make sure that they
covered the backs of our heads and ears. Slings and sling keepers
were removed from our rifles because of the noise that they made.
Nylon parachute cord was used to replace the slings. Each team
member was told to jump up and down; when a metallic sound
was audible, it was located and silenced. Our jungle boots were
thoroughly inspected. If the heels were worn down, the boots were
replaced. The seemingly smallest of things could cause a team
member to be seen or heard in the bush. Dog tags rattling, water
sloshing in a half-emptied canteen, or a smoker's cough could
prove fatal. Because of this, it was considered the duty of each
team member to be overly critical of his teammates.

Even the exact manner in which we would eat and sleep was
rehearsed. The sound of a can being opened could alert the enemy
to our hidden position. The sound of a metal can being carelessly
discarded would do the same. Our team leader would not allow for
any two men to eat at the same time. Meals were to be eaten when
each man was given the go-ahead signal by the team leader and
not before. All emptied cans would be quietly buried. There were
to be no clues that we had ever been in the area left behind.

When it came time to sleep, we would find the thickest vegetation possible in which to hide ourselves. No one would be allowed to smoke once we had moved into our harbor site, and no
one would be allowed to leave the harbor site for any reason other
than to empty their bowels nearby. If any man snored, he was only
allowed that luxury for one short moment. After that he slept with
a gas mask covering his camouflaged face.

All of this attention to detail was agreed upon by every member
of the team. What wasn't covered by the team leader or his assistant was mentioned by either Morgan, or myself. We knew that
much of an experienced team member's time was spent in watching new guys for possible mistakes. Of course mistakes could be
made while training in the rear areas. That was the reason for the
training. There wasn't time to practice patrolling skills when the
mission was under way.

By the end of our third day of numerous rehearsals, IA drills, and hand-and-arm signals, we felt that we had the makings of a pretty fair team. We were at least trained well enough to patrol for four days along a nine-kilometer section of beach and return, together.

We were inserted by a Marine CH-46 helicopter early the following morning, and we wasted no time in moving out of our LZ toward an area of high ground less than one kilometer to our west. Since we saw no signs of the enemy, we felt that our insertion had not been compromised, although there was never any guarantee of that no matter what type of insertion was used.

The terrain within our zone would allow us to observe the flat coastal area to the east and the small rolling hills to the west. Our point man, Lance Corporal Holk, did a very skillful job of using all of the available cover to constantly protect us from possible observation. His movement was slow and steady, and our recon-team leader, Sergeant Christopher, knew where he wanted the team to go in order for us to move in and occupy our first observation point. He had studied his map well, plotted his insertion point and subsequent places that he thought would give us the advantages of elevation and concealment, while we studied the area below us.

We had no trouble in our movement or in setting up the OP. Even the weather was on our side. Despite the constant glare of the hot tropical sun and stifling humidity, no changes in the weather had been predicted for the next forty-eight hours. The news of good weather was always encouraging, because our ability to observe distant terrain through binoculars was lessened by fog, rain, and heavy cloud cover.

Sighting no enemy activity, we reported our position and moved away from our OP to spend our first night in a secure and well-concealed harbor site, less than three hundred meters from our OP. There was even a tactic for moving into the harbor site.

Never being sure if the team had been observed while moving, team leaders usually moved their teams twice before sleeping. The first movement was used as a rallying point, a place that would be familiar to all members of the team by its obvious location. The second movement into the actual harbor site was done just after nautical twilight. The team leader would get the times of sunrise and sunset from the company intelligence chief prior to the team's departure and use these times for movement into and out of the harbor site.

Once we had moved as quietly as possible into our hiding spot,

Sergeant Christopher leaned toward me and whispered, "Doc, I want you and Morgan to take Dickerson and place our PSIDs and claymores around our harbor site. He's never done this before, and you two can show him just how it's done."

I was pleased that our new team leader did not regard me as "only a corpsman," and was quick to realize that I had the ability to not only do the job, but to teach the skill as well. When I pointed to Dickerson and gave him the signal to ditch his pack and follow Morgan and me, he did so without hesitation. I know that he was dying to ask what it was that we were about to do and why he was chosen, but I purposely did not whisper or signal to him.

The implanting of the sensors was not too difficult. Lance Corporal Morgan provided cover for us as we moved into position. The vegetation around us was green and did not make the type of crackling sounds that drew attention during the drier times of the year. The soil was clay and sand, which meant that the reception through our PSID receiver would be better than average. We completed the task in less than an hour. Dickerson was ever so watchful while I set up the PSIDs and claymore mines. He became a good student because he realized that the next time it might be he who was called upon to do the job.

People pay attention when they are handling high explosives, and Dickerson was no exception to this rule. He handed over the claymore mines like they were priceless antiques, and I was glad to see that he took his job so seriously. When we returned to the harbor site, we carried in the wires for four well-concealed claymore mines. Each team member knew exactly which hell box corresponded to which mine and exactly where they could be found in the event of our discovery.

We passed our first night without incident. Our newest team members acclimated themselves to the hundreds of mosquitoes and other bloodsucking insects which kept them awake most of the night. Their failure to reapply insect repellent to their boots, hands, and faces was another lesson learned, one not likely to be repeated.

Our training had paid off. During the night our rotation for radio watch worked well. No one had committed the unpardonable sin of falling asleep while on duty, and there had been no movement detected around us. With only a hand signal from Sergeant Christopher, Morgan and Dickerson and I moved out of the harbor sight and retrieved our sensors and claymores. This time, however, it was Dickerson who did the actual work, while Morgan and I covered his movement. This was a learning experience, and the

more times that a new man was required to participate, the better
it was.

Before we had left the company area for our insertion flight, we
had been reminded that this area was considered relatively secure
and that we should not expect to see any enemy activity. We
would have no artillery in direct support of our mission, but we
would have air support if we requested it. Still, we took this
mission just as seriously as any mission we had been on where
contact with the enemy could be expected. To think for a moment
that any mission would be a cakewalk allowed for mistakes to go
uncorrected, and that would cause the team members to slack off
in their attitude.

We spent our second and third days moving slowly through the
area, taking every opportunity to use this time to teach the new
team members the art of patrolling. Old tracks, made weeks earlier, were pointed out and compared to newer ones. We crossed
small, open areas one man at a time, just as we had practiced in
the rear. The cleaning of our individual weapons, each morning
and each time we stopped to observe a particular area, was routine. All of this was done without conversation, using hand-and-
arm signals.

On our third night out, we received word over our radio that a
Marine CH-53 helicopter would be used to extract our team early
the next morning. Sergeant Christopher had studied his map and
selected a good LZ near the beach, not too far from the harbor site.
Before nautical dawn arrived, each of us had already eaten a cold
breakfast, and we were packed up and on the move toward the
beach.

We had been able to patrol through six of the nine kilometers
that had been our area of operation (AO) and had not seen any
enemy activity. We had been able to observe the other three
kilometers from our observation points. Our radio communications equipment had worked perfectly, and no one had required
any emergency first aid, save for the continuous treatment of
insect and leech bites. Our approach to the selected LZ was cau-
tious and allowed us enough time to study the area before moving in.

At 0540, our primary radio operator handed the handset to our
team leader, who was preparing to give the incoming CH-53 pilot
his requested LZ brief.

The advantage of an early morning helicopter extract was that
the enemy could not observe a helicopter or the actual landing
from any distance. There was just enough light for the escort

gunship pilots and the CH-53 pilot to orient themselves and to clearly make out the exact location of the LZ. If a reconnaissance team did come under observation and subsequent attack near the landing zone, there would be enough time to call in additional air support or a reactionary force. The greatest disadvantage of an early morning extract was that the team being extracted would not have the benefit of oncoming darkness in which to break contact and hide.

"Blue Fox, three six, this is Sandhurst Actual. Over."

"Sandhurst Actual, this is Blue Fox, three six. I'm approximately five mikes out from your third base. Do you have a visual at this time? Over."

"Roger Blue Fox. We are located at your two o'clock, west bound."

"Go ahead, Sandhurst."

"Your LZ is approximately one hundred meters long and sixty meters wide. There are no, repeat, *no* known obstacles in the LZ. Your best approach is from south."

"Roger, copy southerly approach."

"Blue Fox, three six, there is a light wind of five knots coming from the north. Any enemy fire would likely come from the west. There have been no, repeat, *no* sightings of enemy in this immediate area. Your helo is cleared to fire in a westerly direction out to one thousand meters. Your LZ will be marked with a blinking single strobe light at the southern end of the LZ. Over."

"Roger, Sandhurst, standby."

The signal was given for us to get up and be ready to move toward the CH-53 as soon as it landed. It would only be a matter of a few minutes before we would be airborne and on our way back to Da Nang, but this was one of the most critical moments of the patrol. There was now a sense of urgency to get on the helicopter as soon as it landed, but this had to be overcome so that no one let his tactical guard down in the rush to climb aboard. As the huge Jolly Green Giant made its powerful approach toward our position, I motioned to Morgan to put on his gas mask. It had been a long time since he and I had been picked up by a CH-53, but we remembered the power of the helicopter's jet engines to drive sand and dirt outward by the rotor wash. The other team members followed suit, and this prevented them from becoming temporarily blinded by the stinging sand.

The rear gate of the helicopter was already down as we scrambled aboard, each of us taking our preassigned positions inside the helicopter. The thumbs-up signal was given to the pilot by the crew chief, signaling that we were all safely aboard, and within a few seconds, we were out of the zone and headed back to Da Nang and the debriefing session with the company's intelligence chief.

The importance in the quality of our training for reconnaissance patrols cannot be overstated. First Force Recon Company had suffered several casualties in the name of training during 1969 and 1970. The unfortunate death of Sgt. Darrell Ayers was attributed to the many problems associated with taking too many new guys to the bush.

Sergeant Ayers had come to 1st Force Recon Company from 2d Force Recon Company at Camp Lejeune, North Carolina. He was considered by those Marines who knew him well to be an extremely knowledgeable and mature Marine noncommissioned officer, having once left the ranks of the Marine Corps but returned to duty after tasting the mundane world of civilian life. Now assigned as a team leader in 1st Force Recon Company, Sergeant Ayers continued to enjoy the excitement of life in the bush and earned an outstanding reputation as a platoon sergeant, always ready and eager to go to the field. Due to the small number of trained reconnaissance personnel checking into the company, new and untrained Marines had to be "brought up to speed" in order to support the numerous mission requests given to 1st Force Recon. The solution to the problem was to take one or two new guys out on a patrol and then let them learn from the experience.

Sergeant Ayers informed his platoon leader, 1st Lt. J. J. Holly, of his intention to take out a patrol that might have to include five newly joined Marines in the platoon. Though warned against doing this by Lieutenant Holly, who reasoned that no more than two new men should be taken out on the patrol, Sergeant Ayers disregarded the advice, believing that he would be able to handle it. When 1st Lieutenant Holly departed the company for a well-deserved R & R to Australia, Sergeant Ayers went to the field.

Shortly after his team had been inserted into their reconnaissance zone, the team's point man signaled the team to "freeze." Sergeant Ayers went forward and asked the point man why he had stopped the forward progress of the team.

"I think that I hear something up ahead, and the terrain is opening up," he replied.

Seeming annoyed by the Marine's explanation, Sergeant Ayers was reported to have said, "No, there's nothing up there. I'll show you."

Knowing that he had a new man as the point of his team, Sergeant Ayers went forward, carrying the team's primary radio,

Doc Norton at SCUBA School, Subic Bay, PI.

Parachute training at Subic Bay, 1970.

(Left to right) Gunnery Sergeant Bud Fowler, Staff Sergeant Lynch, and First Sergeant Maurice Jacques, 1st Force Recon Company.

Corporal Donald Mahkewa, 1st Force Recon Company, on Hill 510.

Rear view of OV-10 with first jumper (1st-Lieutenant Robnick) in place.

Jumper's view from rear of OV-10 as the aircraft leaves the runway. Note the dogtag inside the laces of the right boot.

Sergeant Robert Crain Phleger, Team Rockmat, 1st Force Recon Company, two days before he was killed and eaten by a Bengal Tiger.

Dead 300-pound Bengal Tiger being carried back to camp by 1st Lt. Lou Daugherty (left) and Sgt. Michael Larkins of 1st Recon Battalion.

First Force Recon
Company Team A
La King being set
down by SPIE Rig
on Hill 510.

Touchdown
on Hill 510.

"Four-deuce" mortar firing at NVA positions from Hill 510.

Doc Norton on Hill 510 the morning after the NVA assaulted the position. Trees were downed by NVA mortar fire. Note the M-16 with grenade launcher, M-60, ammo hanging from tree trunk, and handle of ax.

Hill 510 after NVA assault.

One of dozens of unexploded NVA TNT charges left around the LZ on Hill 510.

Doc Norton commissioned a second lieutenant, United States Marine Corps, College of Charleston, December 1974.
(Left to right) Col. Donald Layne, Capt. C.C. "Bucky" Coffman, 2nd Lt. Bruce H. Norton, Captain Ted Stern, USN (ret), President of the College of Charleston.

to personally observe the dangerous area and listen for any sound of the enemy before allowing his team to move on. While looking over the area, he was taken under heavy fire by two groups of North Vietnamese soldiers waiting in ambush. He was seen to have been hit numerous times by the resulting enemy fire. The team immediately moved away from the open area in order to form a small defensive perimeter and to break away from the contact. The team's secondary radio operator managed to call in the contact, screaming over his handset that the team was defending itself against repeated enemy attacks and needed an emergency extract. Finally, with the assistance provided by another 1st Force Recon team, led by 2d Lt. John Baker, Sergeant Ayers's team was extracted, but only after 2d Lieutenant Baker's team used Marine close air support and a Spooky gunship to suppress the enemy's fire. In an effort to recover Sergeant Ayers's body, several recon teams from 1st Reconnaissance Battalion were sent back into the area several days later, but only his radio, rifle, and equipment were found. His body was never recovered.

Another death occurred in June 1970, when Sgt. Dave Wickander, also a former 2d Force Recon Marine, was leading a patrol. Sergeant Wickander was well liked by all of the Marines in 1st Force. Older than most sergeants, Wickander had gotten out of the Marine Corps, decided that he didn't like what he saw on the outside, and came back on active duty, only to be sent to Vietnam. His technical knowledge and skill as a team leader was superb. While leading his third patrol in an area which was commonly referred to as the "French Plantation," a tremendous thunderstorm began to build, moving closer to the team's position. At the same time, a large group of gibbons, known as "rock apes," began to panic and run through the team's area. When great rolls of thunder began, Sergeant Wickander ordered his team members to remove all of their electrically detonated ordnance and pile it on a nearby slope. Once this was done, he tried to disperse his team to protect them from the possibility of any electrical detonation of their grenades or claymore mines. He then pegged his primary radio to the ground, extended the antenna to its limit and stretched out the radio handset as far as it would go from the PRC-77 radio. None of his well-intended precautions worked. As he remained close to his radio handset a bolt of lightning hit the radio antenna, traveled down the radio and through the handset, and struck Sergeant Wickander in the ear. He, too, was killed instantly.

A MISSION OF MISTAKES

FIRST LIEUTENANT BLOTZ HAD BEEN GIVEN THE MISsion of leading our seven-man reconnaissance team on a four-day patrol through a piece of territory just twelve square kilometers located south of the area known as the Yellow Brick Road. Assigned to our team was Pfc. Adams, who was given the job of point man. He was followed by our Kit Carson scout (KCS), Bong Dinh. Lieutenant Blotz would follow Dinh, with a lance corporal named Davis carrying the primary radio behind him. I would follow the primary operator, with Staff Sergeant Martin following me. Lance Corporal Holk was the last man in our team, our tail-end charlie.

The presence of the KCS, Bong Dinh, bothered me. Dinh had served in the North Vietnamese Army for more than ten years, and he had risen to the rank of captain in the 1st NVA Regiment. His regiment had operated against Marines for years in the Que Son Mountains and in the area which we had now been assigned to patrol. For reasons probably known only to Dinh, he had surrendered to American forces, almost a year before coming to 1st Force Reconnaissance Company, under what was known as the *Chieu Hoi* Program. This was one of several government programs designed to weaken the Viet Cong and the North Vietnamese. *Chieu hoi* meant open arms, and with the promise of amnesty, relocation, and large sums of money, the governments of the United States and South Vietnam tried to induce great numbers of the enemy to surrender. Those Viet Cong and North Vietnamese soldiers who did surrender to U.S. or South Vietnamese Forces were supposedly treated well, reeducated at Open Arms Centers to the ways of the West, and then a few select individuals were allowed to become Kit Carson scouts and ultimately lead U.S. forces against the very men with whom they had recently served.

Bong Dinh's presence in our company area and as a member of our team did not sit well with me, or any other former member of 3d Force Recon Company who had been recently assigned to 1st Force Recon. We had spent the past nine months tracking, finding, and killing the North Vietnamese, and Dinh certainly did not endear himself to any of us, and we thought him a questionable asset. We felt that anyone who was willing to lead Marine Force Recon teams against members of his former unit was simply not to be trusted. I did not like having him assigned to a position of responsibility at the front of the team. But we were told to rely on Dinh's knowledge of the area and his experience in the field and not to worry about his former position as an NVA captain.

The day prior to leaving on our mission, 1st Lieutenant Blotz held a briefing, and as usual, the general nature of our mission was explained to all members of the team. We knew that we were going out for four days to an area that Dinh had operated in with the North Vietnamese Army. We learned that we were being sent there to see if the NVA was still using a series of trails which served as supply routes filtering into the Thuong Duc Corridor. An army Special Forces camp had been repeatedly hit by long-range NVA rocket attacks, and the MAF commanding general wanted to know where these rockets were coming from and how they were being brought into the area. We would not have the luxury of three days of rehearsals, since timely reporting was considered critical, and the plan called for us to be inserted by CH-46 helicopter that following morning.

After having resupplied my Unit-1 bag with new medical gear, I joined the rest of the team as we packed our rucksacks, drew new ammunition, and cleaned our weapons to the satisfaction of our assistant team leader, Staff Sergeant Martin. The night before we left was spent in relative seclusion. It was not unusual for reconnaissance teams to spend this brief period of time prior to departure in isolation. Last-minute letters to home were written, unused gear was packed away in footlockers, and this time of solitude was used to focus our minds on what was about to happen to us.

We had been told that there would be one Marine artillery unit providing fire support to us during this mission. Our maps had been carefully plotted to show our reconnaissance zone, our general route, areas of interest to be checked out such as trail junctions, possible LZs, and preplotted artillery fire concentrations. All of this was done to protect the team in the event that we made contact with the soldiers of the North Vietnamese Army (all former friends of our KCS, Bong Dinh).

On the day of our insertion, we had been brought to the Da Nang military airstrip by truck. We staged our gear outside of one of the helicopter squadron's operations hootches prior to our departure. Inside, we received the latest weather report. The likelihood of thunderstorms, which were common during the spring, the forecasted amount of rain that might impede our progress and affect our ability to communicate via our PRC-77 radios, were all noted.

Our initial departure time was delayed long enough for us to realize that we would not be on the ground near the Yellow Brick Road until late in the afternoon. But when we finally received word to mount up, we wasted no time in getting on board the Marine CH-46 Sea Knight that would be inserting us. On boarding, each member of the team positioned himself next to one of the porthole-type windows which ran down the length of both sides of the helicopter. All the clear Plexiglas windows had been removed from our bird, and though the opened windows caused a significant amount of air turbulence inside the helicopter, their removal provided us with a clear view outside of the aircraft and an open window from which we could return fire if that need arose.

When I had been a team member with 3d Force Reconnaissance Company, the Marine Corps helicopter pilots of northern I Corps had decided not to be a part of our secret operations in the A Shau Valley. Our requests for helicopter support had been quickly answered by the Army helicopter pilots and crew members of the 2d of the 17th Air Cav, stationed at Camp Eagle, and they had done a fantastic job of using their small and highly maneuverable UH-1D Huey helicopters to get us into our reconnaissance zones. Piloted by young and totally fearless Army warrant officers, we were always confident that our insertions would go on time and that any request for an emergency extraction would be answered immediately. Most of the times we had been flown into the A Shau Valley, we had done so without the use of additional helicopter gunship support, either because it simply wasn't available or because the use of additional air support was considered too obvious.

Using Marine CH-46s now meant that our helicopter would fly us into our insertion point accompanied by two or more AH-1G Cobra gunships. In addition to the Cobras, OH-6 Cayuse helicopters had become a part of the insertion package, and all of this firepower and noise would certainly draw the attention of the North Vietnamese soldiers and the Viet Cong to our recon zone.

After spending half an hour flying west, our pilot began to orbit the ground below. This was our signal to prepare ourselves for the moment of insertion. The crew chief began moving up and down the center aisle of the aircraft, while our two door gunners charged their .50 caliber Browning machine guns. When the crew chief finally positioned himself beside the starboard window gunner, we knew we were going in. We unbuckled our seat belts, locked our magazines into our weapons, and every man chambered a round. Our two radios were rechecked, and each team member visually inspected the teammate to his right and to his left. The respiration rate of every man on board increased noticeably, and that strange and wonderful adrenaline started to flow through our veins.

Our CH-46, frequently referred to as a "flying body-bag," suddenly began a downward spiral in an attempt to put us on the ground quickly. Lieutenant Blotz was between the pilot and co-pilot. This was for several reasons. First, he needed to be certain that the LZ we were going into was the same one that had been previously selected. More importantly, he needed to know our true position and the compass direction that we would run in once the helicopter's rear ramp went down.

The whine of the helicopter's engines made it impossible to hear what was being said in the cockpit, but by watching the nodding of heads and the pointing of fingers, it was obvious to us that there were questions being asked of the pilot. Finally, with his map still in hand, Blotz rose from his kneeling position, and gave us the signal to get out of the CH-46 and to turn to our left as we exited the bird. Within seconds of our last man running out the back of the helicopter, the engines changed their pitch as power was applied to the great chopping rotors. Our last link with the outside world dipped its green nose forward and lifted up and out of the LZ, heading back to the relative safety of Da Nang.

Our new point man had moved the team forward toward a grove of banana trees near the base of a small hill, when Lieutenant Blotz signaled the team to halt. Pulling out his map again, he wanted to double-check our location and to make sure that he had good communications with our communications people in the rear. This first stop, so soon after getting away from the deafening noise of the helicopter, was smart because it allowed us the time we needed to regain our lost hearing, clear the smell of aviation fuel from our noses, and observe our area for any possible enemy movement. After waiting ten minutes, the sounds of the jungle— the buzzing of insects, the calls of small birds, and the smooth rustle of the wind—returned to normal. We crept away from the little banana grove in a single, slow-moving column, straining to see, hear, or smell anything unusual.

By 1700, we had moved up and through the heavily vegetated slope of the hill that was intended to be our first observation point. The wind continued to increase. In the distance, long rolls of thunder and brief flashes of lightning announced the coming of heavy rains. Until this time, our small team had performed extremely well. Our movement had been deliberate, and no great mistakes had been made. But little things soon started to occur that changed my opinion of our team leader.

When the signal was passed by the assistant team leader to begin to eat our evening meal, it was our lieutenant who began to tear through his pack to get at a can of fruit. The forbidden noise of metal hitting against metal was obvious to everyone in the team. Oddly, it was Bong Dinh who moved in beside our thoughtless team leader and, covering the lieutenant's hands with his own, glared at him as a signal to stop this unnecessary noise. The lieutenant's look of embarrassment was reflected in the stares of those team members closest to him. He had not trained with us. He was always being committed to something that took him away from being a training member of our team. Now he must have regretted his decision to forego the simple lessons that we had learned. When we had finally finished eating and burying our empty cans, we were given the signal to move out soon. Naturally, we thought that this would be our last move of the evening and that we would start our search for a good harbor site that would conceal us from observation and possibly from the approaching rain. But seeking a place of shelter and safety was not what our team leader had decided upon.

We moved slowly into a flat, open area, and as the gray twilight was overcome by the approaching darkness of the thunderstorm, our movement slowed to a crawl. Great flashes of lightning suddenly revealed a small bamboo hootch, standing less than fifty yards in front of our frozen team. The primary radio operator slowly moved his right arm back toward me, and feeling the muzzle of my rifle, he tugged on it, signaling me to come the few steps forward to him. When my head moved next to his, he whispered, "The TL wants to talk to you."

I moved past Davis and stood behind Lieutenant Blotz, leaning close enough to hear his whisper.

"Doc, can you see that hootch up ahead?"

"What about it, sir?"

"I think we ought to check it out. Do you think you can get close enough to tell if it's old or new?"

I tugged at the lieutenant's sleeve, motioning for him to squat down.

"This is a bad idea, sir. If we can see them, maybe they can see us too. Let's get out of here and OP that hootch tomorrow."

"I want to know if it's been used. Take the point man, and see if you can get close enough to tell. We'll cover you from here."

The idea of taking Bong Dinh in front of me flashed across my mind. But this was the lieutenant's patrol, and the team leader called the shots.

I crept past a silent Dinh and slid up to Adams, who, unlike the lieutenant, had the common sense to have crouched down as soon as the first flash of lightning had exposed the hootch.

Adams leaned back as he heard me move in beside him. He put his head close to mine. He was breathing in fast clipped breaths, like he had just finished a sprint.

"What are we supposed to do now?"

"Adams, that idiot Blotz wants you and me to check out the hootch."

"What? He ain't serious, is he?"

My silence told Adams that he was very serious.

"I'll approach the hootch from the far left side. You cover me, but don't do anything unless they start to shoot first. Clear?"

"Yeah, no problem, man, I'll cover you from here. Be careful."

Once before, in the A Shau Valley, our team, Snakey, had moved in close to an enemy base camp that we had been watching for hours. We had made up a single plan that called for Bishop and me to check out three hootches, while Kegler, Keaveney, Silva, and Furhman covered our movement with M-16s and one M-79 grenade launcher. It had been a step-by-step movement, and when we got close to the first hootch, we could tell by the cobwebs in the doorways and windows and by the lack of tracks around the trees that no one had been using them for several weeks. But checking out three hootches with a well-trained recon team covering us in daylight was much different than what we had been asked to do now. I popped the quick releases on my rucksack, and leaving my pack next to Adams, I moved off slowly to investigate the lone hootch, carrying my rifle at the ready.

I sat and watched the hootch for several minutes, trying to make out any movement inside. I could see none, but as I sat watching, the wind picked up, and the first heavy raindrops began to fall.

This was the best time to move. The noise of the wind, the natural sounds of branches moving, and the increasing volume of rain—all of these things would combine to mask the sounds of my approach. As the flashes of lightning continued, I tried to time my crawl to coincide with the end of each flash. Soon I was beside the hootch and listening to hear any possible sound from within, but there was none. I laid my rifle down beside me and took the gloves off each hand. I began to feel the inner edges of the doorway for possible trip wires. Feeling nothing around the lower portion of the doorway, I felt the earth in front of the hootch, trying to find the edge of a track, but the rain had begun to pound upon the ground, and my gesture was useless. Convinced that the hootch was abandoned, I made my way back to Adams. I had been gone less than fifteen minutes, and when I found Adams, Lieutenant Blotz was sitting next to him.

"Is it clear?"

"I couldn't find any signs. It looks clear to me, sir. Let's get out of here."

"Why?"

"What do you mean, why? We didn't build it. This is bad-guy land. Let's get the hell out of here before the owner returns."

"If Bong Dinh thinks we can be safe in the hootch, we can stay."

"Sir, please. We don't need to take the chance. The team can stay wet for four days, but we can't stay here."

"Get Dinh up here."

Bong Dinh moved effortlessly up to join us. Blotz pointed in the direction of the hootch.

"Is it safe, Dinh?"

"No. Not good. Maybe old hootch, maybe old VC hootch. Maybe they come back soon. Maybe we come back, take look-see next day."

Finally convinced that his idea of spending the night in or near the hootch was poor, Blotz gave Adams a new direction, and moved the team away from the open area. We found a dense stand of bamboo several hundred yards south of the hootch and decided to use it as our harbor site. By the time we had stopped moving in, it was past 2200. The thunderstorm had moved past us, but the rain continued to pour down. We entered our harbor site tired, wet, and concerned about the lieutenant's lack of good sense. With our radio watch set up for the night, we slept in two-hour intervals until the first light of morning.

Our second day was spent moving slowly under a triple canopy

of trees and across several fingers of terrain. We planned to observe a trail junction known to Dinh. The day's weather was
perfect. A cool breeze helped mask our movement, while the
tropical sun tried to reach the jungle floor to dry our wet gear.
Hoping that the previous night's rain would reveal any fresh
tracks, we continued to patrol but crossed no new or old trails and
saw and heard no signs of the NVA. We moved downhill in search
of a better OP and a harbor site.

The sound of rushing water became clear as we neared level
ground. Again using natural sounds to help muffle our movement,
we found a suitable harbor site prior to darkness. We used the
available light to implant three PSIDs. Our position allowed us to
have good radio communications with the people in the rear, and
the night passed slowly into dawn.

After eating a cold breakfast, we spent time cleaning and oiling
our weapons, and after applying a fresh coat of camouflage to our
faces, we waited as Staff Sergeant Martin and Lance Corporal
Holk were sent out to recover our sensors. As soon as they returned, we were given the signal to move out. We moved closer
to the sound of the rushing stream. I began to hear the sound of
boots walking into the water. I was amazed to see that Lieutenant
Blotz had given directions to Adams to continue walking downstream. Hoping to see Adams move to the other side of the stream
and lead the team out of the water, I watched as he turned back
toward our team leader for directions. He was given the signal to
stay in the stream. By now the entire team had entered the calf-
deep water, and spacing ourselves out at ten-foot intervals, we
continued to move downstream in a column.

Twenty yards ahead of our point man, the stream narrowed to
a small channel and made a sharp turn to the left. Moving through
this part of the stream meant that we would lose sight of one
another and that the terrain would split the team each time a
Marine rounded the bend in the stream. I looked back at Staff
Sergeant Martin, hoping to see a facial expression that would
justify my concern for what we were doing. The look was there.
Martin's eyes were searching the banks of the stream for the
slightest movement. He, too, could see that the narrow banks were
getting higher and that we were now channeled and trapped by the
terrain.

When it was my turn to pass through the sharp bend in the
stream, I noticed an increasing number of green and darkened
yellow stakes, pointing upward against both sides of the narrow
bank. As I moved closer, it became apparent that these pointed,

sharpened sticks were punji stakes, strategically positioned to impale anyone who might have to jump into the stream.

The punji had been used for centuries, originally designed to trap wild game, but these various lengths of sharpened bamboo, hardened by fire, were equally effective as mantraps.

The number of these punji stakes increased as we continued to move downstream, and by now I was convinced that at any moment we were about to be on the receiving end of a dozen Chicom grenades. Both sides of the stream had been well prepared for an ambush, but as quickly as the stakes had appeared, they began to dwindle in number. We passed through an area of punji stakes unnoticed and exited the stream at a point twenty yards past the trap. We moved into a small bamboo stand, where we were given the signal to rest.

We had lost our tactical advantage when we descended into the lowlands. Our ability to communicate had been diminished. Finding no trails, and having made no sightings of the North Vietnamese, we completed our patrolling on the third day, and returned to higher ground. By late in the afternoon we were exhausted, having covered more than three kilometers, moving uphill during the heat of the afternoon through a heavily forested jungle. When the signal was given for the team to rest, Adams, Davis, and Dinh fell asleep.

Our third night was spent in a good harbor site that gave us the concealment we desperately sought each time the evening skies grew dark. We set out four PSIDs and placed claymore mines behind each of the green sensors but no unwelcome visitors came our way during the night. When the first rays of morning light came through the jungle's canopy, we were rested and anxious for the final move to our extraction point.

Our extraction by helicopter was scheduled for 0800, which allowed us more than enough time to cover the short distance from our harbor site to the landing zone. The only problem with previously selected landing zones was simply that what might appear to look good from the air or on a map was not necessarily good when seen from the ground. The landing zone that had been selected on the map had seemed relatively flat and open. It was near the base of a large hill, and that should have easily accommodated one CH-46 helicopter. But as we moved closer to the extraction point, we could see that the flat area was actually covered with heavy brush. The ground was solid enough to support the weight of the bird, but tree limbs, vines, and brush would give any pilot concerns about the LZ. We studied our proposed LZ through several sets of 7x50 binoculars for more than half an hour, making sure that the area appeared safe, then we waited for the radio call from the incoming pilot, knowing that he would request a complete landing-zone brief.

As the rest of our team watched and waited from a concealed position just outside the landing zone, Lieutenant Blotz began to move around, anxious for the helicopters to arrive. Not having received any radio communications from the scheduled flight, our team leader decided that the area we were occupying was hampering our ability to talk over the radio. Taking the radio away from Davis, he proceeded to move out into the open, hoping that he would be able to get better reception over the PRC-77. Finally, the voice of our inbound pilot came over the net requesting the LZ brief. Our assistant team leader, hearing the same radio transmission over the secondary radio, gave us the thumbs-up signal that the CH-46 would be arriving soon. But the term "soon" was not good enough for our lieutenant.

Carrying the radio out into the open, he started scanning the sky for our approaching CH-46, not knowing its inbound direction, altitude, or its estimated time of arrival. To make matters worse, he chose that moment to remove a yellow smoke grenade from the shoulder strap of his suspender harness, and pulling the pin, he tossed the smoke grenade into the open as a visual signal of our location to the incoming pilot. We were amazed to hear the sound of the grenade igniting and the hiss of thick yellow smoke. The smoke grenade was alerting the world to our presence.

"Son of a bitch! What the hell is he doing?"

Our assistant team leader was on his feet and beside the lieutenant in a flash. Motioning to where the team was assembled, Martin advised the lieutenant to get back under cover. There was no way to extinguish the burning smoke grenade. The damage had been done. Now it was a matter of having to sit and wait for the arrival of our ride, and praying that the NVA had not seen the telltale yellow smoke. Assuming a posture of one hundred percent alert, we lay waiting, straining to hear the staccato beat of the incoming helicopter, but there was only silence.

We didn't have the option to leave our location for a safer area. The landing-zone brief had already been given, our location had been plotted by the incoming CH-46, and as long as we sat tight, we probably would not be seen. But the thought of us remaining in the area for an unknown period of time was not pleasant. If the NVA had seen the cloud from the smoke grenade, they would do either one of two things: send out a patrol to find out who was in their backyard, or setting up their mortars to ambush the incoming helicopter.

When two Cobra gunships passed overhead, we knew that our CH-46 would not be far behind. Davis had reclaimed the radio from Lieutenant Blotz, and had given the pilot a good description of our location, based on the terrain features in the LZ. He passed along the pilot's warning that he would be on the ground in less than two minutes, and we prepared ourselves to run for the CH-46 as it approached the LZ. The pilot had not been told about the earlier incident with the premature smoke, because if he had, he probably would have aborted the mission or insisted that we move to a new LZ. With both Cobras circling overhead and having drawn no enemy gunfire, our CH-46 came straight into the landing zone with its ramp down.

On signal, we ran from our cover and into the back of the bird. The crew chief knew the number of "paxs" that he was supposed to pick up, and as soon as Holk's boots hit the ramp, the signal was passed to the pilot to get out of the landing zone. As the CH-46 picked up from the valley floor, we waited by the opened portholes with our weapons, but we drew no fire. We rode in silence all the way back to Da Nang, thinking about what might have happened to us.

I sat on the steps of the hootch, emptied the contents of my rucksack on the ground, and was beginning to clean my .45 automatic, when Dave Draper, Stinky Mahkewa, and Gable showed up to ask about the mission. Dave Draper, sensing that something was seriously wrong, asked the question.

"What's wrong with you, Doc? It looks like you ain't in a happy mood."

"I want out of this place."

"We all want out of this place, Doctor. But you'll just have to wait like the rest of us."

"I'm not talking about rotation dates, I just want out of this company."

"Hey, man, this sounds like some serious bullshit. What's wrong with you anyway?"

I told them what had happened on the patrol. After listening to the story, they just stood there and silently shook their heads.

Stinky broke the silence.

"Man, you can bet your ass that I ain't going to the bush with that dude! No way, man! How come he got away with all o' that shit? If he'd a done that type of stuff with my team, we'd a blown his ass away and solved his problem, big time."

Mahkewa was a no-nonsense Hopi Indian. His words were not taken as the mutterings of an offended friend. He meant what he said.

We continued to discuss what could have happened and how we could prevent those idiotic mistakes from being repeated. Soon we were joined by Davis.

"Hey, Doc, Lieutenant Blotz wants to see you, on the double. He's standing out in front of the admin hootch, waiting for you."

Lance Corporal Davis, primary radio operator and loyal lackey to Blotz, had left the hootch shortly after Draper, Mahkewa, and Gable had come to visit. He had listened to me berate his favorite lieutenant and had left immediately to inform Blotz that the team corpsman found him short of demonstrated ability as a reconnaissance team leader and was sharing his opinion with his friends. I had just been summoned to face the music.

All five feet and three inches of 1st Lieutenant Blotz were aglow with rage as I walked up to him.

"Good afternoon, sir."

"Don't get smart with me, Norton. I know that you've been bad-mouthing me to your friends, and I will not tolerate it! Who the hell do you think you are? What gives you the idea that you can criticize me to anyone you choose? You assholes from 3d Force think that you have all the answers because you saw some action in the A Shau Valley. So what? Have you got anything to say for yourself?"

"Yes, I do, sir. I think that entire team was lucky to come back alive. You are dangerous—and I don't mean that as a compliment. I will never go to the bush with you or that lying KCS bastard Dinh ever again. I want out of your team, your platoon, and this company!"

"Oh, is that so?"

"Yes, sir, that is so."

"If you don't keep your mouth shut, Doc, you may end up in front of the company XO, Captain Centers. I don't think that he'd be too happy to hear that he has a problem-child corpsman in this company."

"That's fine with me, Lieutenant Blotz. Let's go see him, right fuckin' now!"

As soon as the words had come out of my mouth, I knew that I was in big trouble. I had respected and admired nearly all of the Marine officers that I had worked with since coming to Vietnam. Blotz just happened to be the second one who had convinced me beyond a reasonable doubt that he should be somewhere else, doing something other than patrolling.

"If that's the way you want it, then come with me."

When 1st Lieutenant Blotz entered the admin hootch, Sergeant Scanlon stood up from behind his desk.

"Yes, sir, what can I do for you?"

"You can do nothing for me, Sergeant. I want to see the XO. Is he in his office?"

"Yes, sir, I believe he is. Can I tell him what this is about?"

Mockingly, Blotz shot back, "No, you may not tell him what this is about. Just tell him that I want to speak to him, *now*!"

Several minutes later Sergeant Scanlon returned and, turning to Lieutenant Blotz, announced, "Captain Centers will see you now, sir."

Looking at me, Blotz only said, "Wait here."

Blotz entered the captain's office and shut the door. As soon as the door shut behind him, Sergeant Scanlon asked, "What's that all about, Doc?"

"I told Lieutenant Blotz that I wouldn't follow him across the street, and he must have taken exception to my comment. I also told him that I wanted out of his platoon and his company. Then I called his bluff on seeing the company executive officer. And here I am."

"Don't worry, Doc, every lieutenant in this company is terrified of the XO. The captain hates lieutenants, and Blotz in particular. I'd bet that Blotz is there right now, telling Capt'n Centers how much he admires him."

The door to the captain's office opened and Blotz came out, started to close the door behind himself, but Captain Centers followed him into the admin office. Ignoring Blotz, the captain walked over to me, extended his hand and surprised me by saying, "Doc, I'm Captain Centers, the company XO. I was asked to look out for you from a mutual friend of ours."

"Who's that, sir?"

"I received a letter yesterday from Capt. Norman Hisler. He's back at Quantico. Ol' Norm and I served in Korea together, and we did three years together on the drill field at Parris Island. So, tell me, what brings you up here to the admin office?"

"Sir, I was told to follow Lieutenant Blotz here to explain to the company XO why I want out of this company."

The look of surprise on the captain's face turned quickly to anger, and all of it was aimed squarely at Lieutenant Blotz.

"Come into my office, and have a seat, Doc. I want you to tell me what you saw out there. Lieutenant Blotz, wait here."

When I had finished telling the captain about the sequence of events that had occurred during our four-day mission, he asked me if there was anything else that he should know. I told him that, yes, there was one thing that had happened which should be addressed.

"Sir, when we returned from this mission, we were brought back into the camp by truck. We went straight from the truck to the S-2 hootch for our team debriefing with the intelligence chief. It was only at the debriefing session that any of us learned that our KCS, Bong Dinh, reported to the S-2 chief that he had seen seven NVA during the mission! He never signaled to anyone that he saw or heard anything while we were in the bush. I don't like him, and I don't trust him."

The captain ended our meeting, thanking me for not being afraid to tell him about what I had seen and how I felt. He said that there would be no reason for me to have to leave the company and that he would make certain that the mistakes made during our mission were discussed and would not be repeated. I walked out of his office and past the lieutenant. The captain's voice bellowed from inside his office.

"Blotz, get your ass in here, now!"

Sergeant Scanlon nodded, winked, and flashed the familiar thumbs-up signal at me as I walked past him and toward the door out of the company's admin hootch. He stopped me, and he handed me a yellow piece of message-book paper that was folded over. Inside it read, "The company 1st Sergeant wants to see you in his office."

Sergeant Scanlon was regarded as one of the better noncommissioned officers within 1st Force Recon Company. He had done his first tour of duty in Vietnam with "Golf 2/9" as an infantryman, had been wounded, and had been a team member in 5th Force Recon Company at Camp Pendleton, California, before beginning his second tour of duty. His wink, thumbs-up gesture, and smile were all signs of assurance that Captain Centers was about to take immediate and corrective action.

1ST SERGEANT
— MAURICE JACQUES —

IN LATE MARCH 1970, 1ST FORCE RECONNAISSANCE Company witnessed the arrival of a new company 1st sergeant, Maurice Jacques. The previous company 1st sergeant, Flores, had been relieved of his duties and removed from the company, pending an investigation for suspected illegal financial dealings with junior Marines. Allegedly, he would "fine" junior Marines for some small infraction of regulations as he made a daily tour through the company area and then pocket their money. The Marines who were "fined" paid him the money because they were dedicated and wanted very much to remain in 1st Force Recon rather than run the risk of possible nonjudicial punishment and having their military records blemished at the hands of a crooked 1st sergeant. With this scheme finally exposed and legal actions taken to prevent its recurrence, the arrival of 1st Sergeant Jacques was a very welcome relief to all the Marines in the company.

During the afternoon that I was in Captain Centers's office explaining my concerns about 1st Lieutenant Blotz, 1st Sergeant Jacques entered the company admin hootch, and after being told about what was happening behind the XO's closed doors, told Sergeant Scanlon that I was to report directly to the company 1st sergeant's office when the XO was finished. I could only imagine the kind of trouble that I had now gotten myself into because of my personal remarks about Blotz, but I was much relieved to find out that was not the case. After repeating my story to 1st Sergeant Jacques, I found that he agreed with me.

I was assigned as 1st Sergeant Jacques's scuba diving partner while I was in 1st Force Recon, and having spent many hours in the water with this Marine, I learned a great deal about him, but a lot more from him. As the senior enlisted Marine in 1st Force Recon, 1st Sergeant Jacques served as the enlisted advisor to the company commander and as the example of Marine noncommissioned officer leadership at its best.

First Sergeant Jacques had enlisted in the Marine Corps in 1948 from the small town of Lawrence, Massachusetts. After boot camp at Parris Island, South Carolina, he saw combat in the Korean war with the 1st Battalion, 5th Marine Regiment, as a demolitions man. After returning from Korea, he taught his demolition skills to the students of the 1st Marine Division who attended Camp Pendleton's division schools. The 1st sergeant's interest in special operations had begun early in his career when he joined 1st Force Reconnaissance Company. The company had become a reality after two years of research, field tests, and exercises, including ground reconnaissance, pathfinder operations, and amphibious reconnaissance operations that allowed a Marine Air-Ground Task Force (MAGTF) commander to use deep surveillance to a distance of up to a hundred miles from a beachline. In March 1957, the commandant of the Marine Corps had directed that the officers and men who had engaged in parachute and reconnaissance work as members of Test Unit #1 be assigned to duty as members of 1st Force Reconnaissance Company. Test Unit #1 had been designed to ''determine the requirements, elements, organization, and equipment of the combat intelligence systems within the Fleet Marine Force.'' The 104 Marine officers and 1,412 enlisted Marines of Test Unit #1, along with seven Naval officers and forty-one Navy enlisted men, were redistributed throughout the 1st Marine Division when Test Unit #1 was replaced by 1st Force Reconnaissance Company.

The opportunity for Jacques to get involved with 1st Force Reconnaissance Company happened only after he had completed the Navy's scuba school at Key West, Florida, jump school at Fort Benning, Georgia, and pathfinder school. While participating in a Marine pathfinder operation in the desert outside of Yuma, Arizona, in 1964, he got the word to pack up and get ready to go.

''When I was on leave, I reported in to Okinawa and went to what was then called the Test Unit to see if they possibly had a job for me. I walked in to talk with them, and at that time I didn't have a CO, so I checked to see if they would give me a tryout. They gave me the physical readiness test right on the spot. I was handed a set of suntan shorts, called 'brownies,' and was told to put on a pair of sneakers to take the test. I was in super good shape. I could do at least thirty 'dead-hang' pull-ups, and I could run pretty fast, too. When they saw that I was physically fit, they said,

'Well, hell, of course we want you.' And that's just how they got me.

"My first tour in Vietnam began in May 1965, when my platoon was given the word to mount out. First Force Recon had six platoons at that time. The 1st, 2d, and 3d Platoons were sent straight to Vietnam. The 4th Platoon was training at Subic Bay, in the Philippines, and 5th and 6th Platoons remained on Okinawa. We weren't sent into Vietnam as a company. We came over one platoon at a time, and when we arrived in country we were called a 'subunit' rather than a platoon. I guess the reasons they did that were political. We didn't want the enemy to know how many platoons of Force Recon were coming into their area. A great Marine, I. V. Long, and I were together then, and we really weren't surprised to learn about our orders for Vietnam. We knew that we'd be going in sooner or later, and when we became Subunit #1 we knew our number had been called.

"When we first arrived in Vietnam, my platoon was given the mission to conduct beach reconnaissance patrols from a place called Vung Tau, north along the coast. We knew that the war was rapidly escalating and that more Marines from the 1st and 3d Marine Divisions were going to be called in. Good landing areas along the beach had to be identified, and we worked from the Navy's LPR 123, the USS *Diachenko*, using our rubber boats to get us ashore to record the beaches. UDT-12 was given the responsibility of checking out the beaches, and we worked in the hinterlands. When we arrived, all we had were our packs. We carried the M3A1 'grease gun' as our primary weapon. We learned a lot in a short period of time, and since then we have tried to teach what we learned to the junior Marines of Force Recon."

One particular significant incident that occurred in December 1965, 1st Sergeant Jacques used as such a training lesson for the enlisted Marines in 1st Force Recon Company. This was the way he described the incident:

"In early December 1965, my platoon was sent down to an Army Special Forces camp, A-107, near the village of Tra Bong, in support of an operation being conducted by the 7th Marine Regiment. The operation was code named Birdwatcher. Tra Bong had been occupied by the Army's Special Forces people since late August. The III MAF commanding officer, General Walt, wanted more information on the large number of enemy forces operating in that area. We joined up with our Force Recon Marines of 2d Platoon, who had been assigned to patrol out of another Army Special Forces camp, A-106, at Ba To. These two villages, Tra

Bong and Ba To, were in the center of Quang Ngai Province. The area was crisscrossed with jungle trails, shallow streams, and rivers—all used by the enemy. When we flew over the area, the ground below gave us the impression of a huge punch bowl, surrounded on all sides by mountains that were home to the Viet Cong and the North Vietnamese.

"When we first showed up at Ba To, we really looked out of place. All of the Special Forces soldiers wore tiger-striped utilities and carried either AR-15 rifles or the older .30 caliber carbines. They told us to turn in our grease guns and to ditch our utilities for their tiger stripes. We were also told that we could help ourselves to whatever weapons we wanted to borrow from their well-stocked armory. The senior Special Forces soldier told me that I could take his M-1 Garand, if I wanted it. When he showed me this brand-new rifle, still packed in Cosmoline grease, I snapped it up. Then I took it to the armory, told the armorer not to touch it, and took a beat-up M-1 in its place. The M-1 was my favorite rifle since Korea, and I figured that if I could get that 'doggie's' M-1 back to S. Sgt. Don Hamblen in Da Nang, he could get it all the way back home to the States for me.

"Shortly after we had settled in at Tra Bong, we were paid a personal visit by General Walt. His division's intelligence section had told him that the Viet Cong and NVA were 'regrouping after a series of firefights against the 7th Marines.' He said that our mission was to find the possible infiltration routes that the North Vietnamese and Viet Cong might use to regain their lost initiative. Additionally, there was supposed to be a huge enemy staging area, an underground enemy hospital, and numerous trails for us to find or to monitor. The teams from the 2d Platoon had already made a number of contacts with the enemy, and the heavy number of North Vietnamese moving through the area meant that we would have to patrol in larger numbers. We got help from the Special Forces, the ARVN [Army of the Republic of Vietnam], and another group called CIDG [Civilian Irregular Defense Group]. Our platoon was assigned the mission of finding the enemy soldiers of the 325th PAVN Division [Peoples' Army of Vietnam] in an area called Vuc Liem. The members of the CIDG were the local militia, who knew the area better than we did. We couldn't speak any Vietnamese, and they didn't speak any English, but it really didn't matter. Our hand-and-arm signals were mutually understood, and that's what counted: our ability to communicate with one another.

"Our first mission required that each of our three teams be composed of four Force Recon Marines accompanied by three

CIDGs. The remainder of the Special Forces soldiers, ARVNs and CIDGs, were formed up to make a PPB [Platoon Patrol Base]. The idea of a PPB was a good one. While one-third of our small force was patrolling, the second third was alert and defending the patrol base, and the third was either resting or sleeping, after returning from their missions.

"Our PPB had remained in the exact same location for three consecutive nights, and the reason that we didn't relocate was because no matter where we would have moved, the enemy would have known about it. Our PPB was the best defendable piece of high ground in the area, and the top of the hill was so small, we thought that it would be impossible to be hit with any indirect-fire weapons like the small mortars that the Viet Cong carried with them.

"We were wrong. Dead wrong. By 1730 on 16 December, all of our Force Recon teams had returned to the PPB from their patrolling missions. We were a little more than eight kilometers away from the Special Forces camp at Ba To. Our platoon patrol base had been set up on a kidney-shaped piece of high ground that had a shallow river running beneath the face of the hill. The opposite side of the small encampment was only approachable over a gradual slope that was covered in knee-deep elephant grass. At each end of the crescent-shaped hill, two long fingers extended to the low ground, and an ARVN two-man listening post had been established on each of these fingers. The command post of the combined force was positioned on the left portion of the hill, with the Force Recon Marines occupying the right side."

Jacques went on to say that as the darkness of evening began to cover the hilltop, hundreds of camouflaged North Vietnamese soldiers began to silently slither through the elephant grass, intent on killing all of the defenders on the tiny hill above them. The enemy's attack began with a downpour of mortar rounds slamming into the CP exactly at 1900 hours. The dubious honor of being the first casualty was posthumously awarded to the young South Vietnamese lieutenant, who had been placed in charge of the operation. Hot chunks of shrapnel had ripped open his back and shredded his lungs, allowing him to die slowly as he gulped in fresh air and exhaled his life's blood through his twisted mouth and nose.

A second barrage of 60mm mortar rounds impacted around the hilltop, wounding one Special Forces soldier and destroying Jacques's radio. The detonation knocked him to the ground and caused him to temporarily lose his hearing. From 1900 to 2100, the Viet Cong dropped an estimated hundred mortar rounds onto the hill. They raked the open ground with a steady volume of heavy, automatic-weapons fire from well-hidden Chinese RPD machine guns. Then the North Vietnamese began their uphill assault, with a force of more than 250 men hurling hand grenades and firing their AK-47 rifles.

"The South Vietnamese force ran like hell in all directions when the firing started. By hitting us at night, the North Vietnamese figured that they would be able to split us up and then attack our small groups with their superior numbers. My interpreter, Truong, kept telling me that the voices he was hearing were shouting in a distinct North Vietnamese dialect. They were directing fire and calling for replacements to continue their assault. Their initial attack was just too well planned. I really believe that one of the CDIGs was a Viet Cong sympathizer and led the attack force past the ARVN listening posts."

Jacques had rallied his small team to form a tight defensive perimeter, but the second mortar attack had caused them to separate.

"Sergeant Akioka, one of my team leaders; Sergeant Baker, another team leader; Corporal Woo; and Lance Corporals Brown and Sission started to take fire from an adjacent hillside. I wanted to knock out that firing with mortars, but our defensive group had not begun to return mortar fire. One of my lance corporals, Moore, left the safety of his dug-in position to look for the ARVN mortar team, who were supposed to be firing countermortar fire. When he got to their firing pit, he discovered that they had all run away. He found one of them hiding in the grass and pulled him, screaming and kicking, back into the mortar pit by his ears. Moore was pissed, but not being able to speak Vietnamese, he could not persuade the bastard to help him fire the damned mortar. When Moore turned away to unwrap some rounds, the little ARVN jumped up and ran away. I saw Moore there all alone and ran to the pit to help him fire our 60mm mortar. When the gooks saw that we were getting ready to fire, they dropped half a dozen rounds in on top of us. Moore was seriously wounded by the incoming shrapnel, but he could still move a little, and he was able to talk. I yelled for our corpsman, Doc Haskins, but I found out that the doc was also badly wounded. I ran to where Doc Haskins was lying and tried to stop his bleeding. He had a hole so big in him that I could look in and see the bone exposed. I wanted to give him a shot of morphine, but I knew that if I doped him up, it might kill his pain, but he wouldn't be able to walk, and I'd end up having to carry him. I refused to give him the morphine for that reason.

"Just when I thought I had a handle on what was happening all around us, Corporal Joy was wounded in the head. Joy and Haskins had been best friends, coming over from the States together, and when Doc saw his best buddy get hit, he went crazy. He crawled over to Joy and tried to stop his bleeding and bandage his head, but there was nothing that Doc Haskins could do for him. Corporal Joy was dying in his buddy's arms.

"I knew that if we stayed where we were, we would all be dead in a few minutes. The gooks had bracketed our position with their mortars and were trying to shift their machine guns to rake us with more accurate fire. I yelled to Truong to join us because it was becoming impossible to tell one gook from the other. They all were wearing black pajamas, and I didn't want our interpreter to get killed in the darkness because he looked like the enemy.

"I decided that our only hope was to get off the hill and hide. I called for all of the Marines in the platoon to join up with our group so that we could cover our movement with fire. The only ones that could join us were Sergeant Baker, Sergeant Akioka, and Corporal Young. As we began to move over the steep side of the hill, one of the ARVNs who had been hiding in the grass jumped on my back. He must have believed that I would get him out of the mess we were in. I threw him away from me and waited for Sergeant Baker to crawl over to me. He and I covered the rest of the platoon as they moved over the crest of the hill and down toward the safety of a banana grove. We were the last two Marines to leave the hilltop. When we joined up with the rest of the team, we knew that we couldn't move into the stream below us. We had seen the muzzle flashes of several enemy machine-gun positions near the water, and that sight kept us from heading in their direction.

"As we hid in the elephant grass, we heard the NVA shouting to one another as they came upon the wounded body of a kid named Brown. They pulled his fighting harness off of his body, and had begun to strip his uniform away when they heard Corporal Joy moaning in pain just a short distance from where they stood. They ran over to where Joy lay dying and shot him to death. Realizing that he would undoubtedly be the next to die, Brown rolled away from the NVA search teams, and ended up just behind where we lay hidden in the grass. We grabbed Brown, and started to move downhill again, where the sky was lit up from the beam of a searchlight mounted on a tripod.

"The North Vietnamese had gained control of the ARVN side

of the hill and had begun a systematic search for escaping and wounded soldiers. Their green tracer rounds flicked out like little tongues of death, and anyone they caught in the illumination of their searchlight was riddled with machine-gun fire.

"We thought that we were making good progress in getting away from them, when their searchlight picked up the tail end of our column. Fortunately, they had to physically shift their guns to get at us. This gave us time to find cover and concealment in the banana grove, though Baker and Young were somehow separated from us. We covered ourselves with banana leaves, and spent the remainder of the night waiting for the North Vietnamese to attack. We just lay in there and prayed that our aerial spotter planes would find us and be able to coordinate an emergency extraction by early morning."

With the first light of morning came the realization that there would be no emergency extraction. A thick blanket of fog covered the ground and made aerial observation impossible, but using natural cover, Jacques decided to move his men from their hiding spot in the banana grove up the ridgeline in an attempt to find one of the trails they had discovered during their patrolling. As they began to move, the NVA suddenly started firing. They froze in place, only to discover that the enemy firing was not directed at them, but at the ARVN survivors, who were still trying to escape. Knowing that the enemy still occupied the hilltop above them, Jacques changed the team's direction once again.

"We had moved about three thousand meters away from our hiding place when I finally thought that it was safe to rest. I had just put the team in a tight little 360-degree defense when I heard the sounds of the nearby brush starting to break. I thought to myself, 'This is it. I've done everything I can to get away, but the NVA won't give up. They're not going to take us alive.' "

Jacques pulled out a fresh clip from his pouch, inserted it in the M-1 Garand that he had decided to carry as his primary weapon, and aimed in the direction of the noise.

"As I took up the slack in the trigger, one of the CIDG soldiers who had run with us placed his hand over my rifle, signaling me not to fire. Together, we sat and waited for the approaching sound to take form. The noise turned out to be two of our friendly Vietnamese soldiers who happened to cross our trail in their attempt to escape. After the three Vietnamese congratulated themselves on surviving the night, we got the team on their feet and moved away from our resting place.

"We came across a trail that was running in the same direction that we wanted to travel, and although we had always practiced never walking on any enemy trail, we wanted to take advantage of what little time we had before the NVA would continue their murderous search for survivors. We hadn't moved more than a couple of hundred yards along the trail before we heard the sounds of movement behind us. We spread out to form a very hasty ambush, when we saw Sergeant Baker and Corporal Young coming up along the trail. I sure was happy—not only to see them and to know that they hadn't been killed but to see that they had brought their weapons with them. To me, the addition of two more Marine riflemen meant the difference between our team getting back alive or not returning at all. Baker and Young were always dependable.

"All I wanted to do was to be able to return to the safety of the Special Forces camp at Ba To without running head-on into the North Vietnamese. I figured that the smartest way to do that was to put our two Vietnamese CIDGs up on point. Since we had resorted to using gook trails to escape on, I reasoned that if the NVA saw two Vietnamese approaching on their trail, it might just give us enough time to break through their ambush.

"All morning long, as we kept moving back toward Ba To, the dense fog continued to cling low to the ground. But by midafternoon, another cold front was beginning to pass through the area, and with the wind steadily increasing, both elements of nature served to mask our movement. But as well as the fog hid us from the NVA, it prevented us from seeing what was close by. It wasn't until the two CIDG point men signaled a freeze that we realized that our trail had become a well-used road, with unmanned fighting holes hidden alongside of it. We were walking through the area that the North Vietnamese had used to stage their men before the attack."

Staff Sergeant Jacques and his group of seven tired and wounded Marines and one corpsman finally arrived at the Special Forces camp at Ba To late in the afternoon.

Undoubtedly, the most incredible return of any Marine survivor of the North Vietnamese ground assault was Corporal Woo, who returned to the Special Forces camp four days after the attack! A Chinese American who'd enlisted in the Marine Corps from the state of Washington, Woo had gotten separated from his team and subsequently wounded during the initial moments of the first mortar barrage on the night of 16 December. As the NVA assault force swarmed over the hill, they discovered Woo's lifeless body, and believing him to be mortally wounded, they stripped him of all of his gear, and left him to bleed to death from the multiple shrapnel wounds he had received to his legs and groin.

After the NVA search teams had moved away from Woo, he recovered enough of his strength to administer first aid to his wounds and to search the ground around him for something to wear. All that he could manage to scrounge were two discarded K-bar knives and one green waterproof equipment bag, commonly referred to as a "Willie Peter" bag. Corporal Woo cut a hole in the bottom of the Willie Peter bag and, inverting the bag, stuck his head through the hole and wore it to keep dry and warm. Not long after regaining his lost consciousness, two enemy soldiers returned to where Woo's body had been discovered. Woo ambushed both of the NVA soldiers and used them as porters to carry him back to the company camp.

Said Jacques, "Corporal Woo was carried into Ba To between two NVA soldiers. He had his arms around their shoulders and the point of a K-bar was at each of their throats. As soon as the company soldiers saw Corporal Woo and his prisoners outside of their wire, they took charge of his two prisoners and called for an emergency evacuation helicopter, which took Woo to the 'B' medical hospital located at Chu Lai. Corporal Woo's emergency arrival and admission to the hospital confused some of the Navy corpsmen. Woo kept asking to speak to any Marine in the hospital, initially leading the corpsmen to believe that he was a Vietnamese soldier who spoke good English. When General Walt learned about what had happened to Corporal Woo, he sent several of his intelligence officers to see Woo, hoping to gain information about his capture and successful methods of escape.

As a result of the NVA night attack, three Marines from 1st Force Reconnaissance Company were dead: Cpl. R. S. Joy, and lance corporals R. P. Sission and W. P. Moore. Staff Sergeant Jacques, Corporal Woo, Lance Corporal Brown, and HM3 Doc Haskins were all wounded and hospitalized. On 21 December 1965, a joint service recovery force was sent back to search the area of the attack, and recovered the bodies of the three Marines, one Special Forces soldier, the South Vietnamese lieutenant, and nine CIDG soldiers.

Now, in April 1970, 1st Sgt. Maurice Jacques was using those past experiences, from his platoon's terrible ordeal in 1965 in training, to teach the young Marines and corpsmen of 1st Force Reconnaissance Company how to prepare for the bush and how to stay alive.

NAVAL SUPPORT
— ACTIVITY DA NANG —

CERTAINLY, NOT ALL OF THE NAVY'S TWENTY THOU-sand hospital corpsmen who served in Vietnam saw duty with Marine ground-combat units. Many were assigned to duty in rear-area field hospitals, some served aboard either of the Navy's hospital ships, USS *Repose* or USS *Sanctuary*, and others spent their tours assigned to small MEDCAP (Medical Combined Action Program) teams, whose job it was to go out into the countryside of South Vietnam and offer their medical skills to those people living in remote villages. But duty for corpsmen assigned to those rear-area hospitals was no less demanding or any easier than for those of us who served alongside the Marines.

One of the largest and better known Naval hospitals in Vietnam was located on the outskirts of the city of Da Nang and was referred to, throughout all of I Corps, as "NSA, Da Nang." The first time that I visited NSA, Da Nang, was in December 1969, when I was a recon team leader with 3d Force Recon Company. It is worth mentioning, if only to give a more complete picture of the duty a corpsman might be assigned.

I had been given permission to go to the hospital's optical shop in search of a pair of glasses to be made for one of our team members, Lance Corporal Paul Keaveney. Keaveney had broken one of his two pairs of glasses, and the unusual optical prescription that allowed Keaveney to see clearly was not able to be reproduced at the Army's small 85th Evacuation Hospital, at Phu Bai. A one-hour helicopter ride to Da Nang provided me the opportunity to land at NSA, and to submit my emergency request for several replacement pairs of glasses for the "Ol' Man." If he lost or broke his last pair of glasses, we would lose him from our recon team until a replacement pair of glasses could be manufactured. His personal pride and the relentless ribbing that he would have to take from his teammates if he could not physically run the bush made it necessary to get these glasses as quickly as possible.

After the Huey landed on one of the helipads in front of the entrance to NSA, I was directed to their armory to check in my .45 Colt automatic and receive a claim check for my pistol. Leaving the armory, I followed the signs to the hospital's optical shop and handed Keaveney's prescription request over to one of the medical technicians on duty. I explained the urgency of the request. He read the prescription several times and looked up, smiling.

"You must be kidding, Doc. I don't think that there's any glass in Vietnam thick enough to reproduce this prescription, and I don't think we can make a pair of glasses like that here. But we can call down to Cam Ranh Bay and see if they can do it for us. What the hell does this guy Keaveney use now, a Seeing Eye dog? If you can come back in a couple of hours, I'll have some information for you, or I'll make up a pair of glasses from some Coke bottles."

Knowing that the Army Huey that had taken me to Da Nang would not return to take us back to Phu Bai until late in the afternoon gave me plenty of time to locate some of the corpsmen with whom I had served at the Naval hospital in Newport, Rhode Island, prior to coming to Vietnam. The office of the hospital's administrative section was clearly marked, and soon I had the location of several wards and several hootches, where I would be able to find some of these old friends who I knew had been sent to NSA.

I was able to find three corpsmen who had been at NSA for as long as I had been in Vietnam and, fortunately, they were off duty. They eagerly agreed to show me around their hospital. HM3s David Harrison, Tom Richter, and Patrick Duffy had each been ward corpsmen at idyllic Newport but now had seen more of sickness, injury, life, and death in nine months of duty at NSA than they had ever imagined possible.

After seeing how well these corpsmen lived on the second floor of their nonair-conditioned, Butler-building barracks, we started our walking tour of the hospital. These three Navy corpsmen were very interested in my service with 3d Force Recon Company. But before I would tell them about life in 3d Force Recon Company, I wanted to see where they worked and what type of duties they had been assigned as permanent personnel of the hospital.

The very first thing they wanted to show me was the hospital's daily menu, which was posted on a bulletin board inside of their sweltering barracks. After having told them some stories about subsisting in the bush on cold C rations for days at a time, they thought that their standard hospital menu might really impress me, and they were right. Fried shrimp, baked ham, and oven-roasted turkey, with assorted vegetables, white and chocolate milk, and even several flavors of ice cream, were offered on the lunch menu. A choice of either steak, chicken, or fish and assorted trimmings was planned for the evening's dinner meal. If this was too formal for some, hamburgers, hot dogs, and pizza were available.

I told them how similar their menu was to what we usually enjoyed when we came out of the bush and returned to Quang Tri. Our mess hall was a plywood hootch and tin roof, with sandbags and wire used to keep it in place. Fly screens were nailed around the outside of the building, providing a view and ventilation. One large floor fan, stolen from 3d Recon Battalion, stood just inside the mess hall's front door, placed to keep the flies out each time the screen door was opened. Two large, galvanized washtubs were positioned on the floor, and each tub contained a ten-pound block of ice, which was delivered daily so that any Marine in the company, officer or enlisted, could have his choice of either a canteen cup full of ice water or one of chlorine tasting Kool-Aid. Our simple menu was much easier to select from than the confusing multiple-choice sampler that the NSA hospital posted each day. We could have C rations heated in boiling water or nothing. When Duffy mentioned that the Naval Support Activity used the services of some of the Vietnamese to help clear and clean the mess hall, I told them that we, too, had streamlined our field mess sanitation process by using the old, but efficient, Marine Corps's system of immersion burners and had only to dip our stainless steel trays into boiling hot, soapy water, and then we let the wind do all the drying. They looked at me as though I had come to them from the Stone Age.

As we continued on my guided tour of NSA, I was allowed to walk through two of the surgical wards where Harrison and Richter were assigned. Each bed on the ward was occupied, mostly by Marines but with a few sailors and soldiers, all waiting to be medically evacuated to some other military hospital far removed from Vietnam. In saving the best part of their tour for last, Duffy escorted us down to his work area, the hospital's triage center. Here I could see how the receiving, sorting, and disposition of large numbers of incoming wounded were managed.

In NSA triage there was no feeling of pandemonium, as was routinely experienced when Marine CH-46s or Hueys loaded with wounded landed on the medevac pad. Instead, I was able to walk through the triage center when it was temporarily empty of patients but fully staffed with doctors, nurses, and hospital corpsmen, waiting for the word that a medevac bird was inbound. Then their day would, again, be turned upside down in their practiced scramble to administer lifesaving assistance to the wounded. It was the looks upon their faces more than their names or physical descriptions that left such a lasting impression. In a place that was relatively free from the filth and dampness that I lived in, and in an area that was well supplied with medicines and a skilled staff, each member of the triage team looked happy. I can only believe that they had seen so much hurt and had to come to grips with their personal feelings so quickly that the last emotion they could muster showed in the daily pleasure of doing what they did best, saving lives.

We left the triage section and went to the mess hall, where there was a gathering of the hospital's medical personnel and ambulatory patients. The patients were dressed in powder blue pajamas and white seersucker robes. The atmosphere was nothing short of entertaining. The patients were enjoying a quality of care, food, and comradeship that they probably had not experienced in months, and the hospital corpsmen were responsible for much of it. I watched and listened in fascination to what was happening around me. I wanted to be able to recount every detail to the Marines of my platoon when I got back to 3d Force Recon Company. They would want to know what life was really like in the so-called civilized setting of NSA, Da Nang.

When we had finished with the noon meal, we returned to the optical shop to find out if it was possible for me to return to Phu Bai with new glasses for Keaveney. I was disappointed to learn that only the Naval medical facility at Cam Ranh Bay could grind the correct lenses for his glasses, and that it would be a week before we could expect to receive two pairs. With several hours to wait before the scheduled return of the northbound Huey, I was taken to the NSA enlisted men's club, the "Sand Box," as the guest of Harrison, Richter, and Duffy.

When I first arrived in Vietnam, the 3d Force Recon "club" at Quang Tri was nothing more than a shipboard connex container, which was used by our company supply officer to store several dozen cases of warm Carling's Black Label beer. When 3d Force Recon moved south to Phu Bai in October 1969, we were allowed to use the enlisted club that was run by the air wing. That club, as dark and as dirty as it was, was considered to be light-years ahead of the ol' connex box, but neither of these Spartan clubs could compare to what was offered at the Sand Box. The Sand Box was air-conditioned, with wall-to-wall carpeting. It featured a state-of-the-art stereo sound system, an electric-light show, and half a dozen slot machines. The management served not only ice-cold beer and sodas for twenty-five cents but offered a variety of mixed drinks at thirty cents each. These were delivered to your table by beautiful young Vietnamese hostesses. The memory of our old connex box, stuffed with warm beer, vanished.

The time spent reminiscing with my three old friends passed too quickly, and by 1630 I had reclaimed my .45 Colt from the armory and was soon on my way back to the reality of Phu Bai. Little did I realize then that it would be five months before I would see any of my corpsmen friends again, or under what circumstances.

Duffy had mentioned that they had started building the hospital back in 1965, and when the doors first opened, it could accommodate only 165 patients.

"Now we have more than six hundred beds," he said. He said that the hospital had treated more than sixty thousand patients, and that a third of that number were combat-related injuries. He warned me not to become a statistic.

THE THUONG DUC RIVER
———— VALLEY ————

IN APRIL 1970, RECONNAISSANCE TEAMS FROM 1ST
Force began to operate in and around the Thuong Duc River
valley, just twenty-five miles west of Da Nang, trying to locate
and destroy a North Vietnamese Army base camp and several
well-concealed enemy rocket firing positions, which were being
used against a U.S. Army Special Forces camp located several
miles east of the Thuong Duc River.

One of the first teams that was sent out into the Thuong Duc
area was code named Misty Cloud, and during that team's first
six-day mission, their ability to observe and to quickly report their
findings accounted for 145 North Vietnamese soldiers being
sighted. They also spotted numerous hootches, campfires, and
electric lights. Misty Cloud's urgent requests for twelve long-
range artillery fire missions were answered, resulting in ten NVA
confirmed killed, an additional ten probable enemy killed, and
fifteen secondary explosions. Then, using Marine fixed-wing air
strikes against the North Vietnamese soldiers, Misty Cloud accounted for an additional five more confirmed enemy killed, ten
more probable kills, and nine secondary explosions. The team
also reported that they had encountered frequent radio jamming
during their six-day patrol. The jamming of their two PRC-77
radios by the North Vietnamese was nothing new, and to stop the
jamming of their radios required only that the two team radio
operators immediately switch their radio frequencies to one of
several alternate frequencies. Radio jamming had happened to
many of the teams of 3d Force Recon Company during the time
that we operated inside of the DMZ, along the Hai Van Pass, and
throughout the A Shau Valley. But this time the enemy's radio
jamming was more extensive than what had previously been encountered. Perhaps most unusual was the fact that the enemy was

now using women not only to repeat the recon team's call sign but to play Vietnamese music over the recon team's radio frequency and try to break up the team's radio transmission by shouting Vietnamese political phrases, slogans, and curses.

Of far greater significance was the observation made by Team Misty Cloud during one of the fire missions they had called in on NVA soldiers operating in the Thuong Duc River valley; the North Vietnamese Army had begun to grow gardens. They had prepared many small, cultivated, and irrigated patches of land close to the banks of two rivers, and they were observed tending these green garden plots on a daily basis. The great importance of these cultivated fields to the enemy was demonstrated to the Force Recon team when one of the fields caught on fire as a result of a fire mission's artillery round exploding nearby. As the secondary brush fire spread toward the cultivated fields, several of the North Vietnamese soldiers ran from the safety of their hidden bunkers in an attempt to put out the brush fire—while the fire mission continued. Because of this significant increase in the amount of observed enemy activity in the Thuong Duc River valley, immediate plans for the establishment of a radio-relay site and an observation post were put into action. Manned by only a handful of Marines from 1st Force Recon Company, our OP on Hill 487 was to become a regular target of the North Vietnamese Army forces, who considered the Thuong Duc River valley to be theirs.

It was then planned that, during the first week of April, fourteen Marines and one corpsman from 1st Force Recon Company would be inserted onto the top of Hill 487 to establish and defend both the observation post and a two-niner-two radio-relay station that would enable us to transmit the radio reports we received from our reconnaissance teams as well as our own observation reports of the enemy activity along the river. Our map studies showed that Hill 487 was a heavily forested, rock-covered pinnacle high above the junction of two wide, but shallow, rivers that slowly flowed eastward through the Thuong Duc Valley toward the city of Da Nang. The high altitude of this small hill would not only make radio communications easier but would also offer a spectacular view of the surrounding valleys and give us limited protection from the watchful eyes of the North Vietnamese soldiers. The area identified on the hill that we were to occupy was no greater than fifty feet wide and one hundred feet long, with a gradual sloping finger running from north to south along the narrow ridgeline of the hill. The number of trees and boulders and the uneven hilltop terrain did not allow for much of a helicopter landing zone. Those of us

who were assigned to duty at the OP and the operational team
members of 1st Force Recon would get onto Hill 487 in only one
of three ways: by a tailgate insertion out of Marine CH-46 helicopters, by using the special patrol insertion/extraction (SPIE) rig,
or by using an external ladder hooked beneath the bottom of a
Marine CH-46 helicopter. This ladder was capable of holding
eight gear-laden Marines.

Later, with the use of several chain saws, some well-placed
plastic explosives, and a few one-quarter-pound charges of dyna-
mite, a partially cleared area of jungle on the hill's southern slope
was open. But this small LZ permitted only the difficult and delicate landing of one Marine CH-46 helicopter at a time.

The priority of our work was established before we ever landed
on Hill 487. The need to quickly set up our ground security,
prepare and clear sectors of fire, and to establish communications
by constructing the two-niner-two radio transmitter meant that the
time of our helicopter insert would be planned to take full advantage of all available daylight. In addition to our standard gear, we
would bring with us a captured, but serviceable, Type 31 Chicom
60mm mortar, with several cases of high explosive rounds (HE)
and illumination rounds, several cases of claymore antipersonnel
mines, and several cases of hand grenades. This was all for defensive purposes.

I had been in the bush with eight of the thirteen Marines who
were sent out to establish the OP on Hill 478. Bud Fowler, with
whom I had made several parachute jumps out of helicopters and
the OV-10 Bronco, was the 1st Force Recon Company communications chief, and he was responsible for the construction of the
two-niner-two radio transmitter once we secured the hill. Staff
Sergeant Martin, our platoon sergeant and a former grunt, provided expertise on the tactical employment of our small ground
security force and the planned emplacement of our claymore
mines. Corporals Mahkewa, Gabel, Draper, Morgan, and Rabbi
had all come from 3d Force Recon Company to 1st Force, and
they, too, had considerable experience, both in the bush and on
the radio-relay site that 3d Force Recon had used in the A Shau
Valley. Three of the remaining Marines who comprised our group
came from Gunny Fowler's communications section. The last two
Marines were new members of the company, assigned to the third
platoon.

Fortunately for me, Staff Sergeant Martin had assigned Cpl.
Donald J. "Stinky" Mahkewa and me to the job of digging out
a two-man fighting hole which would be near the center of the

hilltop. He used a two-man buddy system to insure accountability. Staff Sergeant Martin reasoned that if anyone on the hill should become sick or get wounded, whether it be during the day or night, everyone would know that my position as the corpsman was close to the center of our hill.

Having been briefed as to the purpose of our mission the night before our insert by 1st Lieutenant Holly, the operations officer of 1st Force Recon, we left the company area before dawn and were driven over to the Da Nang airstrip in two six-by trucks to board one of two Marine CH-46 helicopters that were tasked with taking us out to Hill 478 for seven days before any resupply of equipment and ammunition or relief of personnel. As usual, our clandestine helicopter insert became something of a parade. When our two CH-46s departed the MAG 16 strip at Da Nang, two Cobra gunships, which had been waiting for our takeoff, closed in alongside our two "frogs" and flew as our escorts out to the Thuong Duc River valley. While we orbited above and away from the hill, the two Cobras went in low for a closer look, hoping to see if their presence might draw ground fire from the surrounding hills. When no ground fire or enemy movement was observed, our pilots were given the go-ahead signal to get in and get out as quickly as possible. The two Cobra gunships then gained altitude and assumed a "wagon-wheel" firing position, hovering above Hill 478 in a nose-down, guns-down posture that would allow them to spot and fire on any enemy movement in or near our landing zone. Of course, the North Vietnamese soldiers certainly weren't stupid and would wait until the last possible moment to fire at a CH-46 helicopter—particularly if they knew that Cobra escorts were waiting above the LZ for the first sign of trouble. But it was always at this one moment, when the change in the sound of the helicopter's rotors indicated that we were about to land, that the acid taste of bile rose from the gut and settled in the mouths of every man on board. Then came the shout, "Get ready. We're going in."

Staff Sergeant Martin was no stranger to making helicopter inserts, and his loud warning insured that all of us were alert and as ready as possible for things to go wrong. Every Marine on board had been trained what to do when we went into a landing zone. On hearing his warning, we assumed our firing positions next to the open porthole windows of the helicopter. All eyes searched the ground below for the slightest sign of enemy movement, booby traps, or ground fire. As the tail of the helicopter went down and the nose of our frog pitched upward, the rear cargo ramp lowered, and we were given the signal to get out.

As those Marines who had been tasked to provide security moved away from the helicopter and took up firing positions around the LZ, our crew chief and one door gunner came running to the back of the CH-46 and helped push cases of ammunition, food, and water to the lip of the ramp, while the rest of us grabbed for the rope handles of the supply boxes and tossed them away from the back of the CH-46. When all of our supplies had been shoved clear of the CH-46, we watched the tail ramp go up. Our pilot wasted no time in adding power to his engines. He picked up off the ground and dipped the nose of his CH-46 down and got his frog away from of our little hilltop a lot faster than he had landed.

With the screaming whine of the helicopter's twin jet engines still ringing in our ears, we waited for the sounds of the jungle to return to normal, then cautiously made our way up the hundred yards to the top of the hill. The ground around us gave no evidence of having been used by anyone prior to our arrival. We immediately set to work on our defensive plan and radio-relay site. Gunny Fowler took his communications people to the spot where he thought the radio transmitter could best be positioned. Four Marines provided security to him and his team as they began the job of setting up their long-line antenna.

Staff Sergeant Martin selected the best firing position for the Chicom mortar, and two Marines began to dig out a firing pit and clear an area that would protect our short supply of ammunition. Our old mortar had been captured by a Force Recon team months ago, and had been placed in the company's armory more as a war trophy than a reliable weapon. The only differences between this mortar and its U.S. counterpart, the M2, was that its tube was one inch shorter; it had brass parts instead of steel ones; and it didn't have a handle on the traversing handwheel. This made it no less valuable than the "real McCoy." With a range of 1530 meters, and its ability to digest not only our high-explosive, smoke, and illumination rounds but the enemy's as well, we saw this one mortar as our artillery piece and a great asset for both our day and night defense.

By the end of our first day on Hill 478, we had dug a series of two-man fighting holes. We would be required to improve upon these positions each day that we remained on the OP. We had to clear the jungle growth away from our positions and conceal our fighting holes as well as possible. We filled enough sandbags to offer some protection to our ammunition stockpile. The 292 radio transmitter was assembled and working without problems by the time nightfall descended on the Thuong Duc River valley.

As part of our plan to defend the hill we spent the better part of the afternoon setting up our claymore mines, with two of us placing the mines around the hill, while two other Marines provided additional security. This seemingly insignificant task was no easy job because every claymore mine had to be well hidden from possible discovery by the NVA. The position of each claymore was then recorded to Staff Sergeant Martin's satisfaction. He had divided the hill into quarters, like wedges of a large pie, and as each grouping of claymores was hidden within that wedge, the brown electrical wires that were used to detonate each mine were run back up the hill, covered with leaves, and placed within one of four wooden ammunition boxes placed in the center of the hill. Each of these four wooden ammunition boxes had numerous holes drilled into its sides to accommodate the claymore wires. The placement of the ammunition boxes corresponded with the quarter sections of the hill. In the event of an enemy ground attack, any Marine on Hill 478 had only to get to the four wooden ammunition boxes, open the lids, and consult a hand-drawn diagram that showed where each corresponding claymore mine was hidden. One man could detonate all of the claymores simply by squeezing the detonators inside of the wooden ammo boxes. If, for example, a surprise night attack by the North Vietnamese were to be detected starting from the finger on the northern slope of our hill, box #1 contained the six hell boxes connected to the claymore mines hidden on that side of the hill. The other ammunition boxes corresponded with directions east, south, and west. Before evening chow, our first night on the hill, we had to walk the ground from our fighting holes to the place where the ammo boxes containing the hell boxes had been hidden. There were still several gaps noted in our layered defense because of the limited number of claymores we had brought with us. But a resupply of more claymore mines would correct that problem later.

Early in the afternoon, the names of two Marines who were assigned duty to the listening post (LP) during the night were announced. The rest of us knew that we would assume a 100 percent alert status prior to sunset and lasting for at least one hour after the sun had set behind the mountains. Following the first hour of darkness, we would then assume a 50 percent alert status for the remainder of the night. The 100 percent alert status was again assumed before sunrise until the threat of a surprise attack had passed.

The protection of our two-man-fighting-hole system was looked upon by all of us as our best means of survival. I knew, from having been on several reconnaissance missions with Lance Corporal Mahkewa during our time together in 3d Force, that if I drifted off to sleep, he would simply do one of two things: either accept my fatigue and assume my responsibility for our sector of fire while I slept, or kick me awake. We were always grateful for one another's company.

As the sun began to set, we checked our weapons, buried our empty C-ration cans, and went to our fighting holes to study the ground and to remember the view that was directly in front of our position.

We all assumed that the North Vietnamese knew we were on top of Hill 478. Marine CH-46 helicopters don't land without reason. We also believed that sooner or later—and probably sooner—the NVA would come and take a look at how we were set up. We had only to reverse the situation and ask ourselves how, if we were the NVA, we would assault Hill 478. With that in mind, our defensive plan was designed to defeat their schemes.

The job of the listening-post team was to alert the Marines on the hill to the sound of any enemy movement coming from the most likely avenue of approach. The LP would stay hidden in position all night, using one PRC-77 radio as its communications link back to the hilltop. The Marines on LP took with them one starlight scope, enabling them to see through the darkened jungle area around themselves. Each of the two men carried four hand grenades and two CS gas grenades. When the two Marines assigned to the LP had finished applying new coats of camouflage paint to their faces, they quietly picked up their equipment and weapons and crept slowly past us, moved down toward our tiny LZ, and found their nighttime hiding spot along the narrow slope of the hill. As they disappeared from sight, each of us was thankful that we had not been chosen for that dangerous, but necessary, security assignment. It would only be a matter of time before the rest of us were selected to take the place of those who had just gone before us.

"Okay, Stinky, what's it gonna be? You sleep and me awake first? Or are you gonna spot me two hours sleep, while you fight off the NVA?"

"Ya know, Doc, I think we should have cut down more of that brush out in front of us. Look at all o' them stumps and logs. A gook could sneak right up on top of us, and we'd never hear 'em until they tossed their grenades."

"Christ, Mahkewa, you're just full of pleasant thoughts. Why don't I sleep first, while you figure out who's a stump and who's a gook?"

"That's okay with me, man. All I want to do is get this OP duty over with. At least when we were out in the A Shau Valley, sitting on Zulu Relay, we were up eight hundred meters, and the gooks couldn't climb up after us. But out here we're just sitting ducks on three out of four sides of the hill. How can you sleep knowing that? Answer me that, huh?"

"Only because I have you here to push onto any incomin' grenade, Stinky. That's why. Just set your watch, Stinky. We go on 100 percent at 1900, and we both know that it's gonna be a long night. In the meantime we ought to study those stumps out in front of us, so that we know the difference between what's real and what we'll imagine later on."

Our first night out on the OP was uneventful, with the exception of being able to watch the orange lights from small campfires all around the valley come to life and then die slowly over several hours. Our assumption that we were positioned smack in the middle of the North Vietnamese Army was validated by having counted several dozen fires before midnight. As Corporal Mahkewa gazed out into the night looking at the lights, he began to share his thoughts with me.

"You know, they know where we are, Doc. They can take this hill any time they want to. I just hope that it ain't tonight."

"Stinky, why is it that you are such an optimistic bastard. I was planning on livin' a long time, but you are trying your damndest to convince me that it ain't gonna happen. Why don't you go back to sleep, and I'll take part of your watch. Believe me, I'll wake you up if I hear something."

I didn't really want Mahkewa to go back to sleep. I only wanted him to keep quiet, but as he moved around, trying to get comfortable in the bottom of our fighting hole, I knew that it was my turn to once again convince myself that what I was staring at was nothing more than tree stumps and small piles of cut brush. For at least another hour, my imagination was tested, as the tree stumps began to move ever so slightly, and those small piles of brush began to take on the human outlines of silently creeping North Vietnamese soldiers, intent on killing every man on Hill 478.

"Stinky, wake up," I whispered down into the hole.

He had been asleep for two and a half hours, and the faint gray light of early morning was beginning to peer over the mountains.

"Gunny Fowler has already been by here once, and he wants

everybody up and wide-eyed. You've slept long enough, anyway."

"What time is it?"

"I told you. It's time to get up and wait for ol' one eye to rise in the sky and heat things up around here. It's 0430."

"Has the LP come back in yet?"

"No, I asked the gunny if they had heard anything during the night, and he just shook his head, no."

"Well, the first thing that I'm gonna do after we eat is clear those damn piles of brush and get those stumps away from the front of this hole. I know the gooks were up here last night. I could smell 'em."

We spent the next two days on Hill 478, running four-man security patrols outside the perimeter of the hill and improving our home away from home. Our fighting hole became more of a two-man bunker than a fighting hole. Taking a lesson from what we had seen of the construction of NVA bunkers, we placed logs across the top of our enlarged hole, covered the logs with a poncho and cardboard C-ration sleeves, and placed several feet of dirt and sandbags on top of the cardboard. We figured that our hootch could now withstand a hit from any gook 60mm mortar round, and our ventilation systems made it a very cool place to be when either Gunny Fowler or Staff Sergeant Martin gave us a break from the additional work of digging trench lines or filling sandbags under the hot Vietnamese sun.

On the morning of the third day on the OP, Corporal Draper, Mahkewa, and I were walking back from the vicinity of the LZ, when we noticed a single cloud of white smoke rising from the side of a hill less than five kilometers to our north. As the first cloud of smoke began to disappear, another white cloud took its place, followed by the hissing sound of a rocket engine. In the distance, we could hear the rumble of two large explosions. NVA rockets! Corporal Draper took out his lensatic compass and called out the azimuth direction of the telltale smoke.

"Come on, let's get back up on the hill and tell 'em where that gook rocket position is located! Maybe they can get some air support out here."

Our spotting the smoke signature from what we then believed were two Soviet-made 122mm rockets caused a fast-moving chain of events. Our communications team immediately radioed back the time and position of our observations to the intelligence people in Da Nang, and one OV-10 Bronco was launched to come out and observe the target site. While we waited impatiently for the arrival of the observation plane, we set up two M-49 spotting scopes on ammunition boxes and kept an eye on the area from where the rockets had been fired. The Special Forces camp, which was the target of the NVA rocket attack, reported the incoming rounds almost as quickly as we had seen them fired. They also reported that they had suffered no casualties, because both rockets had impacted several hundred meters short of the camp.

Gunnery Sergeant Fowler and Staff Sergeant Martin had recorded as much information as we could provide. We knew that inquiries would be coming from the interested parties in Da Nang. If the aerial observer in the Bronco could see any movement in the vicinity of the launching site, the pilot would then use his white phosphorus rockets to mark the target area below as a reference point for attack aircraft. It was now a waiting game to see how quickly the Bronco would arrive over our position. While we waited on top of Hill 478, Gunny Fowler checked with two of our operational recon teams to see if they had heard or seen the launch of the rockets. Unfortunately, neither of our teams was operating in the vicinity of the enemy position. Both teams were close to the valley floor and under the cover of triple canopy when the firing took place. It was not feasible to request either team to move to higher ground, so we accepted the responsibility of directing the Bronco toward the launch site as soon as it arrived.

The Soviet 122mm rocket was not a highly sophisticated weapons system. It consisted of four major components: the fuse, the high-explosive warhead, the rocket motor, and a folding-fin stabilizing unit. The 6.2-foot rocket, which weighed fifty-five pounds, fitted inside of an 8.1-foot launching tube weighing only fifty-seven pounds. It could be fired either manually or by using a timing device. The rockets had an accurate range of eleven thousand meters, and a maximum effective range of seventeen thousand meters, requiring only a point detonation to explode the warhead. We knew from past experiences that the NVA could fire their 122mm rockets using a field-expedient method. When they didn't have the metal launch mount and sighting device, the enemy would simply place their rocket tube against the muddy walls of a rice paddy and either add or remove the correct amount of dirt beneath the tube, guesstimating the proper angle of fire. It sounded crude, but their ability to shoot and run accurately using this method was documented all over northern I Corps.

More than an hour had passed between the time we radioed in our sighting of the NVA rocket firing and the arrival of the observation plane, and with an hour of lead time to get away from the area, we didn't expect the aerial observer to have any luck in spotting anyone on the ground near the launch site. When the Bronco finally arrived on station, it took only a few minutes for the pilot to get a fix on our position, and then fly straight toward the launch site on the compass heading we gave him. After circling the area, the Bronco pilot let us know that two Marine A-6 Intruders were en route from Da Nang to bomb the suspected firing site. This word was passed around the hilltop. We knew that there was nothing more for us to do other than to find a comfortable place to watch a well-orchestrated ballet between the small, prop-driven observation plane and the jets. The Bronco made a series of low firing passes over the target site and then pulled up into the safety of the sky, as each of the A-6 Intruders came roaring in low to unleash fifteen thousand pounds of high explosives on the jungle below. We could only assume that the OV-10 pilot and his aerial observer had seen something that called for two A-6s to dump their ordnance. But the enemy had one hour to flee the area, and we knew that the likelihood of any damage being done was remote, at best. After three passes over the target and no secondary explosions, the A-6s and the Bronco had expended all of their ordnanace and departed the area for Da Nang.

"Hey, Staff Sergeant Martin, come 'ere and take a look at this!"

Corporal Dave Draper had been keeping his eye pressed to his M-49 spotting scope during the bombing and was closely watching the open areas of ground near the banks of the river below the target position, in the hope of seeing any NVA who might be trying to get out and away from the area. His vigilance had paid off.

"I can see four gooks down by the water, and it looks to me like they're filling up canteens. Do you think we should call for that OV-10 to come back, or just send in a spot report?"

Staff Sergeant Martin replied, "By the time that Bronco refuels and gets rearmed, those gooks will be long gone. Just plot their position, and maybe we can get some direct artillery support to fire into that area if they begin to make a pattern out of going down to the river for more water."

The chance to observe North Vietnamese Army troops in the open was a rarity, and every opportunity was taken to allow those who had never seen the enemy to do so. Seen from afar, their individual movements, uniforms, and their use of cover and concealment were carefully studied so that all of the Marines on our hill learned exactly what the enemy looked like.

Draper spoke as he continued to watch the four NVA.

"If they are taking the chance of coming out in the open in broad daylight to fill up canteens, then they must know that we don't have anything up here that can reach 'em. Maybe they don't know that we're here."

"They know that we're here," said Gunny Fowler. "They just don't give a shit. In fact, they might just be using those four soldiers as bait to see what we'll do."

Gunny Fowler joined the small group of Marines as they took turns watching the enemy soldiers near the stream bed. He went on to explain that, during his first tour in Vietnam, he had seen the same sort of tactics used. The enemy would send out a handful of soldiers, just to test the water and find out if the possibility of an ambush really did exist.

Corporal Draper interrupted the gunny.

"Look, they're moving back toward the hillside. It looks to me like they're carrying about six canteens apiece, and they probably have at least a platoon of their gook buddies waiting for them to return with their canteens. Too bad we don't know exactly where they are."

"We probably know a lot more about them than they think we know."

"How's that, Gunny?" asked Draper.

"Those poor gook bastards have to hump each of those 122mm rockets on their backs all the way from North Vietnam south to wherever they fire them, and all along the way they get shot at, bombed, and strafed. They can't be too happy when they finally get the chance to shoot and then miss their target. We know that they fell short of their target a little while ago. They probably have an NVA spotter hidden near that Special Forces camp. That tells me that they'll have to move to get at least one click closer to their target if they plan to shoot again. If we can get some dedicated Marine artillery from An Hoa to be on call and ready to fire, then we might just have a chance at ruining their day."

What Gunny Fowler said made sense. But our subsequent attempt to coordinate an air attack on a moving NVA target became a lesson in futility.

At 1500, we watched again as two more 122mm rockets hissed out from the cover of the triple-canopied jungle and arched their way smoothly south toward their intended target, the Army Special Forces camp. Again, we requested the services of a Marine OV-10 Bronco observation plane to help mark the location of the firing point for fixed-wing aircraft to bomb. For the second time, we were too little, too late. By the time the OV-10 Bronco arrived, there simply was no target to be found. The luck of the North Vietnamese had improved considerably. We learned that one of the two 122s had impacted close enough to the camp to severely wound several soldiers who had been caught out in the open. The frustration of the day's events had not been a total loss. By late in the afternoon, we learned that plans were now under way for an artillery unit, located close to An Hoa, to be assigned us in direct support of our efforts. This you-call, we'll-shoot arrangement from an extremely accurate artillery battalion was a welcome bit of news.

With nightfall coming on fast, we turned our attention away from the North Vietnamese, who had appeared on the opposite side of the Thuong Duc River and prepared for night.

Corporal Dave Draper and I had been assigned to LP duty for the night. I had known Corporal Draper for more than ten months and could think of no one that I would rather have next to me during the next ten hours than him. We had been on patrols together on the DMZ and in the A Shau Valley, and Dave had proved himself, time and again, to be reliable, honest, and bush smart. Corporal Draper had come from the small rural town of Anniston, Alabama, into the United States Marine Corps. He approached his work in a methodical manner. His mind was constantly at work, trying to be prepared against surprise. He had been a very good friend to Cpl. Ted Bishop and L. Cpl. James Furhman, when we all lived in the same platoon hootch. He realized just how quickly mistakes in the bush could cost lives, and he did not want to end up as a name in a memorial-service-announcement flyer. By the time I had finished eating my evening meal of old C rations, I could see Corporal Draper walking toward my position, carrying his rifle and our PRC-77 radio.

"It's about that time. I put a new battery in the radio, and Gunny Fowler handed me a new battery for the starlight scope. How are you fixed for dental floss?"

"No sweat, I've got an unused roll of it in my Unit-1, and enough bug juice to get through the night. Do we need to take any other extra gear?"

"No, I figure that between the two of us we've got enough shit to make it through the night. I only wish that we hadn't spent all afternoon awake, watching those four 'gooners' down by the river. I could have used the sleep. Let's get out of here and set up while we still have a little light left to help choose a good spot."

The reason for Corporal Draper's concern for my dental floss was because he wanted to use it instead of wire when we set up a booby-trap system that would protect us and alert the Marines on our hilltop to the approach of any probing NVA.

With one short radio check to Gunnery Sergeant Fowler as our last spoken words for the night, Draper and I cautiously walked off Hill 478 and picked our way past a number of fallen trees, heading in the direction of the LZ. Approaching the edge of this open area, we treated it as a danger area. We slowed our pace to a crawl and used the fallen trees for concealment in our movement. It took at least fifteen minutes for us to skirt the edges of an area that was less than fifty feet wide. After moving quietly into the protection of the jungle growth at the sloping edge of the finger, we stopped briefly to listen to the different sounds around us. Crickets had begun to call, the familiar night sounds of birds began to echo, and the relentless humming of countless swarming mosquitoes surrounded us.

Soon, Corporal Draper led on. Within ten minutes we arrived near to where we would spend our night, listening for the sounds of approaching North Vietnamese. As Draper slowly knelt and readied his M-16 rifle, I removed one small green illumination grenade from inside the left half of my utility jacket and placed it on the ground in front of me. Reaching into the right side of my jacket, I found the metal sleeve that would soon hold the illumination grenade, and I placed it beside a small tree. I wrapped the metal sleeve to the base of the tree with several strands of black electric tape and tested its strength, making sure that it could not move. Then I repeated this procedure, having selected another small but sturdy tree growing less than twenty feet from the first one. When both retaining sleeves were in position, I attached one strand of my thick dental floss to the spring-loaded finger on one of the sleeves. Then I attached the opposite end of the strand of dental floss to the second retaining sleeve and tightened the dental floss until both spring-loaded fingers were facing skyward, in the "up" position. Moving back to my original position, I ran my green camouflage stick over the white dental floss, making it appear no less threatening to the human eye than a greenish white jungle vine. It was stretched just eight inches above the floor of the jungle and hard to see, even for me.

Picking up the first illumination grenade, I straightened out the steel cotter pin, and placed the grenade in the retaining sleeve. I slowly freed the pin from the spring-loaded spoon of the grenade. I repeated this procedure at the opposite tree. With the spoons of both illumination grenades wedged tightly against the retaining sleeve fingers, my illumination booby trap was armed for the night.

In the event that the NVA might decide to send a probing force up to Hill 478, any approaching enemy soldier's groping touch might convince him that the dental floss was only a vine, until the constant pressure of his touch caused the spring-loaded fingers to press inward, allowing both spoons to fly simultaneously, turning night into day. But if the searching enemy thought that the dental floss "vine" was a trip wire, and decided to cut it, the same effect would be realized when the tension on spring-loaded fingers snapped outward, allowing the spoons of the two grenades to fly in the same manner. The illumination grenade booby trap was just one of the defensive measures that we used to alert the Marines on the hill to the presence of NVA and to protect ourselves from their silent encroachment. With this system of protection located behind us, we moved slowly down the finger and stopped next to a tree with a trunk large enough to allow us the comfort of propping ourselves in an upright position while we scanned the area to our front and sides, using the starlight scope, and listening for any changes in the sounds of the moonless night. With our PRC-77 radio positioned between us, the amount of movement that we would have to make would be kept to a minimum. Corporal Draper carried with him an M-16 rifle, and I had brought not only my M-16, with its 40mm grenade launching attachment, but my .45 Colt automatic. With four fragmentation grenades apiece and two additional CS gas grenades taped to our harnesses, we settled in for the night.

Sometime close to midnight I noticed Corporal Draper lean forward and heard him draw in the night air deeply through his nose. Then he nudged me and whispered, "Can you smell that?" I smelled the air and concentrated, hoping to detect what had obviously caught his attention. It was the unmistakable smell of food being cooked.

"It smells like cabbage, and the wind is coming up from the base of the hill. Use the radio."

Corporal Draper contacted one of the Marines who had been assigned to radio watch and whispered his report over the handset.

"What did they say?"

"Some smart-ass up on the hill said that as long as the gooks were cookin' chow, they won't be coming up here. Can you believe that shit?"

"I hope that he's out here tomorrow night pullin' LP duty when they come lookin' for us."

The strong smell of food being cooked over a wood fire heightened our level of alertness throughout the night. We heard no unusual noises during the night, but we did see the orange lights from several small campfires on the opposite side of the valley. We reported their positions to the relay site back on the hill. When the first rays of morning sunlight crossed over the mountains, we received the word to leave our illumination grenade booby trap in place and return to the safety of the hilltop. We reported back to Staff Sergeant Martin and gave him a detailed debriefing as to the location of the illum booby trap, the weather conditions, and the time that we first smelled the food. Our report was radioed back to Da Nang as further evidence of the presence of NVA. As part of the radio transmission, we were advised that we could look forward to the midmorning arrival of several Marine CH-46 helicopters. They would be bringing out additional food, water, batteries, and ordnance to our hilltop. News of a large resupply mission told everyone on the hill that we were not going to be leaving the Thuong Duc River valley anytime soon.

THE DEATH OF
SERGEANT ROBERT
—— CRAIN PHLEGER ——

IN OCTOBER OF 1969, JUST AFTER 3D FORCE RECON-
naissance Company had moved south from Quang Tri to Phu Bai,
our company operations officer, 1st Lt. "Bucky" Coffman, called
for all the recon team members to attend a briefing on the history
of our new area of operations, and of particular interest was a
place called the A Shau Valley. Lieutenant Coffman began his
class by saying that Vietnam was an ancient country. There was
one thing that Lieutenant Coffman had learned in his readings
about Vietnam, and he shared it with all of us: the A Shau Valley,
and areas of jungle to the south and west of it, had for centuries
been considered one of the favorite hunting places for those few
wealthy and adventurous Westerners seeking to shoot a Bengal
tiger. Though scarce in numbers and rarely seen, these members
of the great cat family lived throughout the area in which we were
about to operate. Ready to record this information in our green
notebooks, we listened as he began his brief.

"A gentleman by the name of Edward James Corbett made a
big name for himself in India as a 'great white hunter.' He wrote
six books about his life experiences, and it is from his fifth book,
written in 1954, titled *The Temple Tiger*, that I will read a short
excerpt describing the physical strength of just one particular tiger
that he was hunting.

After a combined breakfast and lunch, I set out to try to
find the kill which—if the young man's sketch was correct—
had taken place five miles from where I had fired at the tiger
the previous day. The tiger, I found, had come on a small
herd of cattle grazing on the banks of the stream flowing
down the main valley and, judging from the condition of the
soft ground, had experienced some difficulty in pulling down

151

the victim he had selected. Killing a big and a vigorous animal weighing six or seven hundred pounds is a strenuous job, and a tiger after accomplishing this feat usually takes a breather. On this occasion, however, the tiger had picked up the cow as soon as he had killed it—as the absence of blood indicated—and crossing the stream entered the dense jungle at the foot of the hill.

Yesterday the tiger had covered up his kill, at the spot where he had done his killing, but today it appeared to be his intention to remove his kill to as distant a place as possible from the scene of killing. For two miles or more I followed the drag up the steep face of the densely wooded hill to where the tiger, when he had conveyed his heavy burden to within a few hundred yards of the crest, had got one of the cow's hind legs fixed between two oak saplings. With a mighty jerk up hill, the tiger tore the leg off a little below the hock, and leaving that fixed between the saplings went on with his kill. The crest of the hill at the point where the tiger arrived with his kill was flat and overgrown with oak saplings a foot or two in girth. Under these trees, where there were no bushes or cover of any kind, the tiger left his kill without making any attempt to cover it up.

Lieutenant Coffman paused and looked around at our faces. "The reason that I'm telling you about the nature and great strength of the Bengal tiger is not to simply scare the hell out of you, but to educate all of you to the fact that there are dangers present, far greater than the soldiers of the North Vietnamese Army, which are also patrolling in our new area of operation. It's my responsibility to tell you everything that we know, not only about the NVA, but about the local terrain, weather, insects, and all other elements that you may encounter in the bush. Jim Corbett's descriptions of tigers and leopards are factual, and if anything, understated. The Siberian tiger is the largest cat of all and can attain a length greater than ten feet and weight exceeding nine hundred pounds. Any animal like the Bengal tiger, the Siberian's smaller cousin, who can sneak into a corral undetected and kill a four-hundred-pound water buffalo calf, and then silently scale the pen's nine-foot-high walls, with the dead calf held in its mouth, is certainly a dangerous force to be reckoned with. These animals are out there, gentlemen. Just be aware of the potential danger."

First Lieutenant Coffman's reading and additional comments as to the tiger's abilities left a lasting impression on everyone seated in the classroom. I'm sure that at that moment the likelihood of encountering such a tiger was considered by most of us to be as rare as the illusive cat itself. But less than two months later, several recon teams operating in the A Shau Valley were privileged not only to hear that unmistakable low guttural roaring that only tigers can make but then to cross over the tracks of these great animals as we roamed throughout the valley. It was only due to our good fortune that none of us ever came face-to-face with a Bengal tiger while on patrol. However, in early May 1970, Marine Sgt. Robert Crain Phleger and his Team Rock Mat of 1st Force Reconnaissance Company were not so fortunate.

Sergeant Phleger had come to 1st Force Reconnaissance Company in 1969 as a radio-repair technician (MOS 2641), having previously been assigned to one of the Marines Corps's force service regiments in Da Nang. Sergeant Phleger was an extremely knowledgeable, dependable, and professional Marine noncommissioned officer, and was the kind of Marine who always was looking to assume additional responsibilities. His assignment to 1st Force Recon Company occurred when there was a critical shortage of school-trained radio technicians in the communications platoon of the company, opening the door for his transfer out of FSR.

Sergeant Phleger stood about five feet ten inches tall, wore dark horn-rimmed glasses, and possessed an extremely dry sense of humor, which he kept hidden beneath his gregarious style of character. He kept his brown hair cut very short, as was the traditional style of all Force Recon Marines, and he always carried at least one tin of Copenhagen snuff in his left breast pocket. He had made something of a ritual out of his snuff-dipping habit. When one tin of snuff was almost empty, he would bring his replacement tin to Gunnery Sergeant Fowler at the staff and officers' club, and pay the gunny to buy one "half-shot" of whisky, which he would then delicately pour over the contents of the new tin, to add a "little flavor" to his snuff.

Always approachable and cheerful, Sergeant Phleger had earned his good reputation by looking out for his junior Marines within the communications platoon and by helping them learn their difficult trade. But Sergeant Phleger wanted more out of life than just being another good communications technician. He wanted to run the bush. First Lieutenant Holly, the operations officer of 1st Force Recon, had met with Sergeant Phleger on many occasions while checking out the radios inside the company's operations bunker, and he had also learned through Gunnery Sergeant Fowler, the company communications chief, that Phleger had frequently requested that he be assigned to any of the operational recon teams, if only to carry the team's primary radio. First Lieutenant Holly finally allowed him the opportunity to join one of the teams and was pleased to learn that Phleger had adjusted well to the demands of life in the bush. Soon he was assigned from radio operator to assistant team leader and finally was put in charge of his own team, Rock Mat. On 2 May 1970, Team Rock Mat was given a warning order that, beginning with their helicopter insertion on the fifth, they would begin a five-day mission of reconnaissance patrols in the Phu Loc area northwest of Da Nang. This particular mountainous area was also known by another name, Razorback Ridge, because the elevation exceeded thirty-two hundred feet, with sixty-five-degree slopes on either side of the ridgeline. The seven-man team consisted of Sergeant Phleger; Cpl. Jerry T. Smith; the Kit Carson scout, Bong Dinh; and four other Marines.

(Ironically, Sergeant Phleger had initially not been considered for duty as a Force Recon team member, let alone rise to the status of a team leader, because as a sole surviving son he was exempted by law from duty in combat. He had requested that a waiver to this rule be granted, which then allowed him to go to Vietnam.)

Having just returned to Vietnam from his long-awaited rest and relaxation (R & R) trip to Hawaii, where he had gotten married to his high-school sweetheart, Sergeant Phleger was told by Gunnery Sergeant Fowler that he didn't have to go out with his team. But Sergeant Phleger, professional that he was, immediately stated his concerns about his rightful place as team leader being taken over by someone less qualified than himself. He brought his arguments to Lieutenant Holly, asking the lieutenant to intercede and allow him to go to the bush. Permission was finally granted and, with his Marine dress-blue uniform, which he wore at his wedding, still hanging on the front of his wall locker, Sgt. Robert Phleger joined his Team Rock Mat, and prepared himself for five days in the field.

Early in the morning of 5 May, the team members of Rock Mat went through their final equipment inspection before boarding the truck that would take them to the MAG 16 airstrip in Da Nang. I had gone to scuba school with Corporal Jerry Smith, and happened to have my camera with me as Team Rock Mat made their last-minute preparations. Corporal Smith said that the team collectively considered this mission to be nothing more than a "walk in the sun," and added that now Sergeant Phleger was an "old married man," he could look forward to staying in the rear while he took over as the team leader, assuming that this would probably be Sergeant Phleger's last mission. With a thumbs-up signal, Rock Mat climbed aboard their truck and headed out of camp for the airstrip.

Corporal Smith was absolutely right about his mission being the last one for Sergeant Phleger, but for the wrong reason.

After Rock Mat had been inserted near Razorback Ridge, they began a steady climb uphill to gain the high ground for better observation and communications. There was not much room for the team to maneuver, as the ridgeline was extremely narrow. By 1800, they had completed their day's climb. After finishing their evening meal, they made their final short move to their harbor site, only to discover that the narrow and rocky ridge of the Razorback did not allow them an area large enough to gather into their standard 360-degree defense. Instead, the men had to position themselves for the night by lying down along the narrow ridgeline, stretched out single file, with Sergeant Phleger having placed himself as the last man at the end of the line. To further complicate things, the team had begun to experience communication problems that had become so severe that the Marines in the rear who were assigned to monitor the recon team's radio communications had suspected that, because of the lack of communications, whoever had been assigned to radio watch may have fallen asleep.

At 2000, those members of the team not yet asleep heard a sudden rushing movement in the dense brush, accompanied by several short muffled screams from Sergeant Phleger. They immediately radioed to the rear and said that it sounded like Phleger was "fighting someone" in the bushes. Then, only silence and darkness.

First Lieutenant Holly and Gunnery Sergeant Fowler were on duty in the company's command-and-control (COC) bunker in Da Nang. They radioed back to the team to stay calm and alert, assuming that perhaps the sergeant had experienced a terrible nightmare and, upon awakening and being scared and disoriented, he had run off into the night.

Being twenty miles away from the scene, Lieutenant Holly and Gunnery Fowler had no reason to think otherwise.

Imagine the thoughts now racing through the minds of the team members. It was pitch black, and the last sounds heard within five feet of their position were the high-pitched screams of a man sounding as though he were in a great struggle, fighting for his life.

What could have happened to him?

Was he the intended victim of a well-planned NVA prisoner

snatch? Was he surprised by one NVA soldier, who just happened upon his position? Or had he experienced a nightmare that sent him running off into the night?

Should the team begin to search for him in the darkness and risk exposing themselves to possible ambush? Should they stay put and run the risk of getting picked off, one by one? They knew that they couldn't switch on flashlights and comb the area. They couldn't call out his name and alert the enemy to their position. And they knew that no one was coming out to help them, for they were twenty miles away from the closest friendly faces. Yet there they sat, scared to death, in the middle of the night, on top of a ridgeline where no helicopter could land, even in the bright light of day.

With their fear greatly compounded by being surrounded in total darkness and then confused because of the silence, the team could do nothing but search the immediate area, feeling the ground for Sergeant Phleger. Failing to locate him in the black of night, they assumed a 100 percent alert posture and waited. With their team leader gone, Cpl. Jerry Smith took charge and radioed back a description of only those events that he knew to be true.

The team stayed in place on the ridgeline, weapons at the ready, until the first light of dawn revealed Phleger's sleeping position. There lay his rifle, pack, gas mask, and cartridge belt, as he had placed them on the ground prior to readying himself for sleep. Leading away from his area they found his bush cover and his camouflaged poncho liner, both covered in blood. They radioed back this information, and then said that they had also found drag marks leading away from the harbor site and down the slope of the ridgeline into patches of thicker brush growing alongside the hill. They were told to follow the drag marks.

And as they followed the drag marks, there was still a great deal of doubt in their minds as to what had happened to Sergeant Phleger and what could have possibly taken him out of their harbor site.

The first sight of Sergeant Phleger's body was of his combat boot sticking out from beside a large bush. On seeing the motionless boot, Corporal Smith radioed back to the rear that they had just found the missing sergeant's body. While Smith was passing this information over his radio handset, the entire team was surprised by the tremendous roar of a Bengal tiger, who now stood less than fifteen feet away, having returned to claim his kill. Several Marines fired their weapons at the animal but he ran from the scene without being hit.

Turning their attention to the dead sergeant's body, the team was horrified to discover that, during the night, the tiger had eaten most of the sergeant from the waist up. The terrible scene sickened every one of them.

Believing that the earlier firing of their weapons had scared the tiger into leaving the area, the six remaining team members busied themselves in preparing for their extraction, but they were quick to learn that a hungry tiger does not give up his kill so easily. Suddenly, hearing another tremendous roar, the team members looked up to see that the tiger had returned. It now stood directly between the team and the body of Sergeant Phleger. Responding instantly to the presence of the huge animal, they scrambled to grab their rifles and fired at the fleeing cat. One Marine threw a fragmentation grenade in the direction the animal had taken. Not certain that anyone had even managed to hit the tiger, they radioed back that the animal had returned to claim his unfinished meal but because of their firing he had now fled from the area.

That morning, when the emergency helicopter extraction finally removed the 1st Force recon team from the lower portion of Razorback Ridge, the remains of Sergeant Phleger, wrapped in a poncho, were taken to the graves registration section of 1st Medical Battalion in Da Nang, and Team Rock Mat returned to the company area. It was later determined, through autopsy, that Sergeant Phleger had been asleep, with his poncho liner pulled up over his head, when he was attacked and killed by the tiger breaking his neck.

The members of Team Rock Mat were so psychologically and emotionally shaken by the traumatic events which they had witnessed in the death of their team leader that none of them ever returned to the bush.

Several days after the death of Sergeant Phleger, a reconnaissance team from E Company, 1st Reconnaissance Battalion was given the mission of patrolling in the vicinity of the Elephant Valley area. The team, led by 1st Lt. Lou E. Daugherty, was in a hidden position, awaiting the final moments before their inbound helicopter would extract them from their recon zone. As the CH-46 landed, the team members ran to board the helicopter, while the team's assistant patrol leader, Sgt. Michael Larkins, counted heads to make sure that no one was left behind. As the team members sat inside the helicopter, they noticed a blur of movement behind their ATL sergeant and signaled frantically to him to turn around. When he did, he became wide-eyed in amazement to see a huge Bengal tiger charging straight for him. The sergeant took up a kneeling position, and raising his M-16, he aimed in on the cat's orange and white head and squeezed off one very well aimed round. The impacting bullet helped to change the direction of the tiger's attack, and with additional seconds to flip Larkins's M-16's selector switch into the automatic position, he continued to fire, emptying his remaining rounds into the wounded tiger, killing it less than fifteen feet from where he stood at the rear of the helicopter. The recon team radioed back to the rear what had happened, and when the team's extraction helicopter landed in the 1st Recon Battalion's compound, 1st Lieutenant Daugherty and Sergeant Larkins exited the bird, carrying the dead tiger trussed beneath a large sapling pole.

With two incidents involving Recon Marines and tigers happening so near in time to one another, it was initially thought that the dead tiger was the same one who had killed Sergeant Phleger, but the physical distance between the two events was in fact many miles apart, and a close examination of the dead tiger revealed that the animal that had killed Sergeant Phleger had to have been a much larger animal than the smaller one that had charged Sergeant Larkins.

Sergeant Larkins's killing of the Bengal tiger made him something of a cult hero within the ranks of 1st Recon Battalion. To be able to turn and face a charging tiger and calmly fire a well-aimed round into the attacking cat not only calls for steady nerves but a certain degree of marksmanship, too. Prior to his shooting of the tiger, the best rifle requalification score that Larkins had fired on a rifle range barely qualified him as a marksman.

- THE NEW LIEUTENANT -

IN THE SPRING OF 1970, 1ST LT. STEVE CORBETT REported in to 1st Force Reconnaissance Company for duty. A native of Virginia, 1st Lieutenant Corbett was no stranger to Marine recon operations, having previously been a recon platoon leader in Bravo Company, 1st Reconnaissance Battalion. His platoon had then been attached to work with 1st Force Recon, operating out of An Hoa. Known as Sugar Bear to his friends, he became our platoon leader after we had returned to the company area from our first week's stay out on the OP at Hill 478.

Having spent his previous six months in Vietnam as a recon platoon leader in Bravo Company, 1st Lieutenant Corbett was not considered by anyone to be a NIC (new in country) lieutenant, and it became readily apparent to all of us in the platoon that he knew a great deal about the complexities of reconnaissance work and that he took his responsibilities very seriously. Within several days after taking charge, our new lieutenant had interviewed every member of the platoon, and as a result of these interviews, he began to reorganize the teams of his platoon by initiating a training program based on a combination of his knowledge and experiences, and ours. He had come to our company well trained, highly experienced, and ready to go to the field. We felt lucky to have him.

When we began this team training, we were asked by 1st Lieutenant Corbett to name some of the problems which we had experienced in the field that we thought needed to be discussed and corrected. Teaching the fundamentals of long-range supporting artillery fire to all of the recon team members became an important training mission. We explained to 1st Lieutenant Corbett that those of us in the platoon who had been team members in 3d Force Recon Company were well trained in the use of artillery fire

support. It had been our best means of protection, especially when
we had been sent out onto the DMZ. Knowing that at least one
Marine artillery battery was placed in direct support of our mission
was a big morale booster. But later, when we left the umbrella of
the supporting artillery that had followed us across the DMZ, and
we began to patrol in the A Shau Valley, we usually found ourselves so far removed from any friendly artillery unit that close air
support became our primary means of protection against the large
numbers of NVA that we had found. Now that we would again
have Marine artillery in direct support of our patrols in the Thuong
Duc River valley and for the dozen Marines manning the OP on
Hill 478, the use of artillery fire support was retaught to every
member of our platoon.

Seated on sandbags behind the platoon's area, we listened at-
tentively as our new lieutenant began his class.

"Having been able to use a great deal of artillery support while
I was in Bravo Company, I want to make sure that all of us are up
to speed on how it's done. It's a skill that will help us to be better
jungle fighters than the NVA, and I want our confidence level up
to the degree that everyone in my platoon is more than able to call
in fire-support requests in their sleep. I won't assume that all of us
are experts at it, so we'll start at the beginning and walk our way
along, beginning with the basics.

"It is not enough to simply point the barrel of a gun in the
direction of the enemy and expect to hit your target. The purpose
of this class is to explain the fundamentals of artillery, so that
when you get the opportunity to use close fire support, you'll have
a better understanding of how it all works, especially from the
artillerymen's point of view. The more familiar you are with the
weapons at your disposal, the more dangerous you become.

"The technique of firing an artillery piece straight at the enemy
would work only if the target was extremely close and the forces
of gravity and air resistance did not have time to take effect. If
your target is farther away, the weight of a heavy shell would
make it drop short of the target. The artillery piece has to be
elevated above the line of sight so that there is an angle created
that is sufficient to make the shell reach its target. Does everyone
understand this?"

All heads nodded.

"Okay, then let's keep going. The distance between the artillery battery and your target is called range. To reach a particular
range, each gun has to be set at a different angle because of the
small variations that exist in each gun as they are manufactured.

These small variations affect the diameter of barrel, called caliber; the length of the barrel; the weight and the shape of the round; and the amount and type of propellant used to fire that particular gun. If you had two identical eight-inch guns, positioned side by side, and used the same type of shell and the same type of propellant, the chances of both guns hitting the same target are very remote. If the guns that shoot in support of our calls for fire are old and have worn-out barrels, they could be off course by as much as three percent. That means that we could kill ourselves with our own fire support if we're not paying attention to what goes on when we call in protective fires around ourselves.''

The lieutenant went on to describe what happens when a round is fired from a gun.

"Once the round has left the gun barrel, the trajectory of the shell is affected by the wind, temperature, and air pressure, and these will all vary according to the different heights that the projectile is passing through on its way to the target. I want you to remember the effects of temperature. If a gun barrel is cold, or if the powder is cold, that will affect the range of the gun. And as more rounds pass through the barrel, the increase in heat will add to the range. Just something to tuck away in the back of your minds if you call for fire early in the morning or at night.

"The firing battery has written tables of calculations and allowances for each gun. When we put out a radio call requesting a fire mission, we do not usually have a straight line of sight from the gun battery to the target. We use indirect fire as our method of hitting the target. The firing battery receives their information from us, and they use an aiming point, which is offset either to the left or to the right of the position of their battery and which the gunners can see. The gun barrel is then traversed from the aiming point, in degrees, and we adjust their fire based on where the rounds impact in relation to the target: add range, shorten range, move the impact to the left or right. Computers are now being used to store all of the information about the targets that we give to the battery. That way, they can go back and fire on a previously hit target using recorded data if we need to shift fires from one known target to another.''

First Lieutenant Corbett then went on to explain the many advantages and disadvantages of artillery fire versus mortar fire and the casualty effects caused by both types of weapons.

"The beauty of the mortar is in the fact that the smaller number of components and the relative simplicity of the fire-control system make the mortar fairly easy to handle, and it reduces the time it takes in training. The simple design of the mortar and its sight allow for a quick switch from target to target anywhere within a 360-degree arc. The low pressure created within the mortar tube, combined with the high-explosive content of the shell and the near vertical angle of the projectile's descent, make for great all-around fragmentation. The blast of the mortar round is much more effective against troops in the open than that of an artillery shell, but the disadvantage of the mortar is that it is less accurate than the artillery piece.

"The kill zone of an arty shell is limited by the angle of impact of the shell. Much of the blast goes up high, or is directed downward into the ground. But the mortar's straight-down descent produces a much better pattern of steel when it fragments. And of course, it's a lot cheaper to shoot. The shorter range of the mortar is a great advantage in close-in fighting because the individual firing can actually see the effect of his work and correct his range by rule-of-thumb changes. But with an artillery unit shooting an indirect fire mission, the observer has to radio back his observations, and then that new data has to be computed before the next rounds are fired. All of that takes time, and by then the target has moved. So, as you can see, the low-cost, light-weight mortar has become the weapon of choice by both the NVA and the Viet Cong. They can drop a dozen rounds on your position and pick up and move before we get one round out in returned fire.

"I haven't heard of any recon team carrying a 60mm mortar along on a mission, but when any of our teams from this platoon get to go out to Hill 478, we'll try and use that old gook mortar to teach and to practice our calls for fire."

Another problem that was brought to the lieutenant's attention was based on the fact that the majority of men are right-handed. The inherent problem with a group of right-handed men formed up as a team moving in a single file is that this allows for the entire right side of the team to be exposed to enemy fire. Right-handed men carry their rifles with the muzzle of their weapons pointed to the left. Even if they are given the area of responsibility to their right as they move along through the jungle, they will continue to have their rifles pointed to the left. Reacting to one man's sudden scream of "contact right" meant that individuals were swinging their rifles across the backs of their team members in the frightful rush to begin firing. Realizing that a fraction of a second meant the difference between life or death when it came to seeing the enemy and being able to fire on him in order to break his ambush, the solution to the everyone-being-right-handed problem was not an easy one.

All members of the platoon that were in the company area were assembled, and out of our total strength of twenty-two Marines and one corpsman, only four individuals were found to be south-paws. Their redistribution within the platoon insured that there was now at least one lefty assigned to each of the three teams in the platoon, solving the problem of the unprotected right flank, at least to some degree.

The classes that 1st Lieutenant Corbett wanted taught to the platoon were designed not just to cover new ground but also to allow those of us who had participated in numerous deep recon-naissance missions to teach the basics and the tricks of the trade to the newer and less experienced members of the platoon. Time, or lack of it, was always the critical factor in teaching those quality subjects, such as field communications, observation reporting, and first aid. But within a week of his arrival, 1st Lieutenant Corbett had managed to improve significantly the level of training throughout his platoon. He believed that we were always superior in the bush to the NVA, and his confidence as to our abilities was not only infectious but shared by everyone else in the company.

It was his ultimate goal to be able to go to the field with any one of the recon teams within his platoon and find the level of that team's capabilities and confidence consistent because of the high quality of our repetitive training. As a member of one six-man recon team, handpicked and led by 1st Lieutenant Corbett, I found myself in the good company of Sergeant Sexton and corporals Draper, Mahkewa, and Gable. Between the six of us we had participated in more than seventy reconnaissance patrols during the previous year. Corporal Mahkewa was assigned to walk as the team's point man. First Lieutenant Corbett took the team leader's spot at the number two position, carrying the team's primary radio. I was assigned the number three position in the team, fol-lowed by Corporal Draper. Sergeant Sexton walked fifth and car-ried the secondary radio, with Corporal Gable as our tail-end charlie. Even with such an experienced recon team, nothing was taken for granted. Immediate-action drills were practiced over and over again, and cross training by individual team members was conducted around the company area while we waited for the word of our first mission assignment. That message came in the form of one sentence being spoken when 1st Lieutenant Corbett walked in on one of our training classes and said, ''We've been 'fragged' to go to the bush early tomorrow and take a three-day look at those

cultivated fields that the gooks are protecting in the Thuong Duc
River valley.''

The following morning, Team A La King was packed and ready
to go, waiting in front of the MAG-16 helicopter operations hootch
for the pilots' briefing to finish. We had all been briefed by 1st
Lieutenant Holly and Staff Sergeant Lynch the day before. We
were going to an area north of Hill 478. Nearly everyone in the
platoon who had spent time out on Hill 478 had been able to
observe the area while they were at the OP, but actually walking
the ground would be a different matter than observing it from the
safety of several kilometers' distance. During our premission
briefing, we discussed all of those physical terrain features that we
had observed previously through our spotting scopes and binoculars. We had all focused in on those cultivated fields that grew
along the banks of the Thuong Duc River, and we had secretly
wondered what it would be like to be down there, to hide close by,
and to meet the gardeners who tended them. Our secret desires
were about to be fulfilled.

When the plywood door to the MAG-16 ops hootch swung
open, we were given the thumbs-up signal by our team leader to
mount up and follow him and our pilots out to the flight line. Two
CH-46 helicopters had been assigned to fly us out to our insertion
point, which was a little more than a mile from the edge of one of
the larger cultivated fields. We would move to a position north
of the fields that would provide us with good observation, and
after the first day, we planned to move in closer until we could
take some photographs and some plant samples to determine just
what was being grown and to find out how many of the NVA were
required to protect their area. We would be extracted on the afternoon of our third day in the bush.

Our two CH-46s were met by two escort Cobra gunships shortly
after we cleared the runway in Da Nang, and we headed west
toward Hill 478 as the morning sun was just breaking over the
mountains. In less than an hour's flying time, we were approaching the river valley. We watched out the porthole windows as we
passed over our radio-relay site, still secure on top of Hill 478.
Spotting the tiny LZ near the radio-relay site gave notice to all
hands that we would be going down in a matter of minutes,
waiting only for the Cobra gunships to take a final look at our
intended landing zone.

The first sign of big trouble came as we watched puffs of gray
smoke coming from the sides of the Cobra gunships. They had
seen something on the ground that they obviously didn't like and

were making gun runs at whatever had now become their target. The two door gunners, manning the big air-cooled .50 caliber Browning machine guns located in the forward windows on both sides of our CH-46, cleared their weapons and began to fire into the same area that the Cobras had been hitting. All of us took up positions close to the open portholes, and we could see the muzzle flashes of white and orange popping out against the dark green background of the jungle as the North Vietnamese gunners fired up at us.

"Christ, it's alive with gooks down there!" shouted Corporal Draper, as we all watched and heard the action pick up between the firing helicopters. Rockets from the Cobras began to explode in the jungle, and we could see tan-and-green-uniformed men running for cover.

"The Cobras must have caught them in the open when we came up over that last ridgeline. I wonder if we're still going in?"

First Lieutenant Corbett had positioned himself in the spot reserved for the recon team leader, kneeling behind an instrument console in the cockpit of the CH-46, map in hand, watching where the pilot was headed.

"If the lieutenant comes back here, then we'll know that we're going in," Sergeant Sexton said. He was listening to the pilot's conversation on his radio, and he, too, would be one of the first to know if there was any change in plans. As all eyes remained riveted to the air-to-ground firefight raging below, our CH-46 took three jolting hits, just short of the rear cargo ramp, that ripped three large jagged holes in the interior sides of our bird. No one was hit by the rounds or the resulting flying metal, but the sound of the bullets hitting the belly of the helicopter and the spray of red hydraulic fluid from ruptured lines got the immediate attention of our crew chief. He came running back toward the rear of the bird, carrying a small red fire extinguisher with him.

For some of us, the thought of being shot down again was one thing, but for all of us, the idea of going down and being on fire caused a significant rise in the "pucker factor" to which we thought we had become accustomed during our helicopter insertions into hot LZs. The crew chief remained very calm as he carefully inspected the damage that the NVA ground fire had caused to his bird, and his inaudible reply to our pilot had caused an instant change in our altitude and direction. As soon as our helicopter began to climb and turn, we watched for the signal from 1st Lieutenant Corbett. His gloved right hand went to thumbs-down, and the silent and disappointing message came back loud and clear: we were headed straight back to Da Nang to repair the minor damage that the ground fire had caused. But we knew that we would be back soon to try again. The NVA had now been alerted to the fact that there was more than a little interest being generated about their growing fields, and we could only imagine that they would now be preparing for our return visit.

Two days after being shot out of our intended LZ in the Thuong Duc River valley, Team A La King was inserted into an area farther north of our original recon zone. This time our helicopter insertion was accomplished early in the morning and without tipping our hat to the enemy by letting them know where our proposed LZ was located. Instead of relying on the services of the medium-size CH-46 helicopter, we had been flown out in a smaller Huey helicopter that allowed our pilot to practice the art of flying extremely close to the deck and to use false insertions to confuse the NVA as to our actual drop-off point.

Our second attempt at getting close to the cultivated fields was also scheduled to last only three days, and by late in the afternoon of our first day out, we had moved through enough of the area to find that it was crisscrossed with trails, all heavily used by men wearing boots, not sandals. We had not encountered any of the NVA soldiers using them, but as we moved from our insertion point to a small hilltop that we needed for observation, we had crossed over four different trails, all having recent tracks leading down toward the Thuong Duc River.

Just after leaving the safety of our harbor site, early in the morning of our second day, we heard singsong voices moving quickly along a trail that we knew ran parallel to our direction of movement. Corporal Mahkewa gave the freeze signal to the team when the voices moved across his front, and they continued to be heard for several minutes. Not wanting to miss the opportunity to get a look at who was using the trail, 1st Lieutenant Corbett had Corporal Mahkewa change our direction and move to get us closer to where the trail met the river's edge. Having to move very cautiously through the jungle to get into the best possible observation position took nearly two hours, but knowing that the trails we had seen were heavily traveled, we agreed that it would only be a matter of time before another group of NVA soldiers would emerge from the trail near the water's edge.

We set up in a position that was at least three hundred yards north of where we knew one of the trails came down to the water's edge. Our little OP gave us an unobstructed view of ground on both sides of the river. It wasn't long before 1st Lieutenant Corbett had plotted and checked our position in relationship to the high-speed trail and called in our position to the Marine artillery battery that was tasked to fire in support of our team. All we had to do was sit back and watch and wait for the next group of NVA to emerge at the end of the trail. Then we could decide if we would only watch them, or call in artillery fire on the unsuspecting enemy soldiers.

The first "NVA soldier" to appear at the edge of the trail was an old man dressed in a short-sleeve shirt, dirty tan trousers, Ho Chi Minh sandals, and a tan pith helmet. He was unarmed. His homemade, rubber-tire sandals were our clue that he was probably just a local wood cutter, used by the NVA to make sure that the way was clear for groups of their soldiers to cross the river and not get caught in the process by ambush or booby traps. We had heard of the NVA's contempt and total disregard for the safety of the indigenous people in their areas of operation, and witnessing their use of this old man for this kind of work verified what we had heard.

The old man moved slowly toward the edge of the stream and looked up and down the river for several minutes, studying the ground. Then he returned to the underbrush where he had first appeared and returned carrying four green canteens. He knelt at the water's edge and filled the canteens, one at a time. When he was finished, he pulled a package of cigarettes from his shirt pocket and sat down by the bank, enjoying his smoke. Soon he was joined by another helmeted soldier, but this one looked more like what we were after.

He was younger, clean-shaven, and his uniform appeared to be cleaned and pressed. He carried an AK-47 rifle slung across his back, and it seemed that he didn't like finding the old man seated by the trail. We could see that words were being exchanged between the two men, but while the young man stood over the older one, the old man refused to look up at the young soldier while he spoke. Finally, the old man stood up, picked up his canteens and led the way back in the bush.

"What do you think that was all about?" asked the lieutenant.

"The younger gooner with the AK probably found the old man screwing off and was told to bring him back to wherever the rest of their group is hiding," answered Corporal Mahkewa. "Do you think we should follow them, lieutenant?"

"No, all we have to do is keep track of exactly how long it is before that old gook returns to fill up some more canteens. We can figure that filling up canteens must be some sort of regular duty for him, and if he comes back to the same spot with empty canteens, we can figure out just about where the rest of them are hiding by studying our maps.''

Draper and Gable pulled their maps of our recon zone from their pockets and carefully studied the area around the trail. Now our plan for killing NVA began to take shape.

"We've got something to show you, sir. What we see on our maps as a feeder stream is probably a gook high-speed trail that takes them straight down to the river. We've found them using those tight little stream beds before, and that's where they dig out their bunkers. They know that we can't hit them with our artillery fire when they're dug in between the slopes of two hills, so they built their staging fortifications where we can't get at them.''

"Okay, Sergeant Sexton, what do you think we should do?''

"Well, if it were up to me, sir, I'd wait until tonight before we did anything. We can spend the rest of the afternoon watchin' and countin' as gooks come down to the river to draw their water. They'll use the nighttime to try and cross over to the other side. That's when we'll get them.''

By 1700, we had seen the old man return to fill up his load of canteens four more times, and we had plotted his turnaround time to be forty minutes between trips. We figured the NVA must be fifteen minutes away, at the speed an old man would walk in this terrain. Our maps showed us two feeder streams that joined together in the same location as the trail that the old man used, and we knew that on level, unobstructed ground, fifteen minutes of traveling time would allow a man his age to move no more than six hundred meters away from the edge of the river. An arc was drawn on our maps, delineating the distance, and along that line was where we planned to call in our night fire missions. By 1800, we had moved to a new position, a few hundred yards from our previous OP but closer to the river than we had been. We thought that we would be better able to hear the sound of water splashing from our new position if any of the NVA tried to cross to the other side of the river. We set up to use our starlight scope in hopes of catching them in the middle of the river.

"Take a look at that little dot of orange light down there.''

It was Corporal Mahkewa, whispering to me as he studied the river's edge through his 7x50 binoculars. Taking his binoculars, I could see that the orange light was the telltale glow of a cigarette being smoked at the edge of the trail.

"It looks like the old man is practicing some bad habits. Nudge the lieutenant, and let him know what's up."

Spotting the cigarette was just the sign that Lieutenant Corbett had been waiting for. Without hesitation, he grabbed the radio handset and told the Marine artillery battery to stand by for a fire mission. The darkening of night allowed us the luxury of using the starlight scope. The outline of five NVA soldiers seated next to the old man was all that our team leader needed to begin his call for fire. We had kept our gear close by in anticipation of this moment, and with a margin of several hundred yards between ourselves and the group of NVA, we felt well protected in the event that we might be shoving a stick into a hornets' nest.

"Echo four Zulu, this is A La King. Fire mission, target number Bravo Charlie three three zero five, over. Grid seven seven four two zero zero, Altitude one zero zero, Direction three four eight zero mils magnetic, over. Five NVA in the open. Danger Close, northwest four zero zero. Spotter adjust. Over."

The minutes between the time that our request for artillery fire was made until the words "shot out" were passed over the radio seemed to take forever, but four sets of eyes were glued to our watches as we counted the seconds before the first spotter round came screaming out of the night and exploded not more than two hundred yards behind where the group of five NVA soldiers had been sitting.

"Left one hundred, drop one hundred."

Lieutenant Corbett's adjustment would correct for the first shot being long, and again the wait for the artillery unit's response took precious time.

The sound of the next round of incoming fire caused all eyes to focus in on the intended impact area. As soon as that second round exploded just above the tops of the trees, we could hear the screams of men being wounded.

"Fire for effect" were the three words whispered into the radio, telling the firing battery to place nine more rounds from their eight-inch guns exactly where their second round had impacted. The arty battery's return radio message of "shot out" meant that their rounds were on the way, and all we had to do was observe the accuracy of the incoming artillery fire.

The quiet of the night was again shattered by the thunderous roll of incoming artillery shells, spaced five seconds apart, ripping the jungle to pieces, as huge chunks of earth and vegetation blew skyward under the brilliant flashes of orange and white explosions.

"Anyone see or hear any secondary explosions?"

"No, sir, but those rounds fell right in on top of that little party of gooners."

"Keep your eyes and ears open in case they should decide to cross the river. They sure as hell won't be staying in that area much longer. Good job, men. I only wish we knew just how bad we hurt 'em."

We ended our fire mission by radioing back an end-of-mission message which was always followed by a very brief description of the damage that was done and our estimate as to possible enemy casualties. We spent our second night in the bush unable to sleep. The possibility of encountering more NVA troops moving through our area was high, as we had pushed a very great stick into their nest. But our demonstrated ability to find the enemy and wait for the most opportune time to hit him, while remaining totally undetected, gave us reason to be pleased. It also gave the NVA reason for concern.

The following afternoon, Team A La King was extracted by Huey helicopter from the Thuong Duc River valley, and we returned safely to the company area in Da Nang. At the conclusion of our team's debriefing, we learned that because of the jungle terrain that we were to operate in next, thick triple canopy and steep rocky ridges, we would practice insertion techniques using our special purpose insert/extract (SPIE) rigs.

We were going back to the Thuong Duc River valley to find the main egress routes that were being used by the soldiers of the North Vietnamese Army trying to slip into the city of Da Nang.

– EVENTS IN JUNE 1970 –

ON 4 JUNE 1970, MAJ. WILLIAM H. BOND, JR., RELIN-
quished command of 1st Force Reconnaissance Company to Maj.
Dale D. Dorman, but several days before the actual day of the
change of command, a formal dinner party was held, planned by
the company-grade officers to honor their outgoing commanding
officer. In the hopes of making this dinner a lasting and memorable event, under the strict guidance of the company's executive
officer, Capt. Norman B. Centers, the staff and officers' club was
lavishly decorated for the big night. Steak and chicken, and an
open bar, were arranged, and as a very special surprise for the
major, the company supply officer, a young 1st lieutenant, was
instructed to obtain the only set of twelve crystal wine glasses
known to be in Da Nang. These just so happened to belong to the
personal field mess of the commanding general of the Marine
Amphibious Force.

(The general's aide who had reluctantly agreed to this request
was supposed to be an old and personal friend of Captain Centers.)

Their agreement in allowing for the rare and expensive crystal
glasses to be removed from the general's mess for use at the
formal dinner also stipulated that these twelve crystal glasses
would be "personally signed for and guarded" by the lieutenant,
and would be cleaned, polished, and returned to the general's
mess chest the following morning, with no one being the wiser.

Major Bond had no reputation in our company as a drinking
man, but on this auspicious occasion, he joined in with his fellow
Marine officers as they raised their glasses numerous times in the
somber toasting to the names and memories of their departed
brother officers. At the end of the dinner, the officers clapped and
cheered as Major Bond stood up slowly and delivered his farewell

speech to these officers of 1st Force Reconnaissance Company. And, in true Marine Corps fashion, he finished his lengthy tribute to his men by raising his glass of creme de menthe and offering a toast, "To the finest group of Marine officers in the history of our Corps!" Then, obviously moved by the moment, he gulped down his drink, turned, and threw his empty crystal wine glass into the stone fireplace behind him. Without a moment's hesitation, the rest of the officers stood, and assuming the position of attention, in unison shouted back, "To the finest Marine officers in the history of our Corps!" and they, too, followed suit, smashing their wine glasses onto the cold cement floor.

The supply officer, who was present throughout the dinner and was more than a willing participant during the toasts, was reported to have gone into "a state of instant shock" and began to make strange sounds, "like the whimpering of a hurt infant," at witnessing the general's irreplaceable crystal being smashed to pieces. As the lieutenant was being led away from the club, under the assistance of two fellow officers, the CO noticed the lieutenant's pathetic physical condition and asked Captain Centers if he could explain what might have caused the young officer's collapse.

Truthfully, the company executive officer replied, "I guess he was just overcome by the whole event, sir."

"Gosh, Norm, I didn't know I had that kind of effect on the men."

The following day secret internal plans were directed by the captain to give the general's aide-de-camp "anything he wanted," which would serve to keep him quiet until those who had been involved in the original deal had either rotated out of Vietnam, or until some other officer could get to Hong Kong on an R & R flight to procure new crystal glasses for the general's mess.

The pace of life within our company area varied little during the days prior to and after the scheduled change of command. Our practice at team insertions and extractions using the SPIE rig continued uninterrupted and was completed to the satisfaction of the company training officer within one week. Using the CH-46 helicopters and crews from MAG-16, we felt confident in our equipment and the pilots' ability to get us in and out of difficult areas. The wisdom of having had every 1st Force Recon team member individually fitted for his own SPIE rig harness certainly made a lot of sense because, obviously, someone was paying attention to the fact that the SPIE rig offered a much better alternative for fast extractions and insertions than the use of the ladder or rappelling into our recon zone.

The use of 1st Force Recon teams to locate and plot the egress routes of the NVA continued, and by the third week of June, every recon team in the company had been on at least two missions into the Thuong Duc River valley, and all had spent time in the defense of the OP, still located on top of Hill 487.

Having gotten to spend some time in our small company area at Camp Adnair, it was inevitable that the Marines in the platoon would get to know more about 1st Lieutenant Corbett than he may have wanted us to know. We knew that he was a good athlete, but didn't realize the extent of his competitiveness until the day he challenged another officer in the company to assume football line-man's stance, and on signal to butt heads until one of the two gave up. First Lieutenant Corbett never quit.

Another interesting quirk in the character of our platoon leader was his love for listening to the music of Janis Joplin. Marine officers were not usually known as liberal spirits, and for our platoon leader to openly display his interest in the sounds of Janis Joplin, accompanied by the band Big Brother and the Holding Company, endeared him to us even more. The one person who failed to find any sense of enjoyment in the Texas rock 'n' roller's music was our company executive officer, who was also a native of the great state of Texas, Captain Centers. A former enlisted Marine infantryman and veteran of the Korean War as well as a former drill instructor at Parris Island, South Carolina, Captain Centers had a well-deserved reputation as a no-nonsense professional. Perhaps this is why 1st Lieutenant Corbett found so much amusement in turning his newly acquired stereo system up to its maximum volume in hopes of gaining the attention and subsequent wrath of the XO when he toured the company area. First Lieutenant Corbett would watch for the approach of the captain, run back to his hootch to adjust the volume of the stereo, then wait in hiding.

"Corbett, turn that goddamned communist long-haired hippie music off this instant! Do you hear me, Corbett? Lieutenant Corbett, where the hell are you? Corbett, Corbett . . ."

We were never sure if the company XO was really as angry as he sounded, or if he just wanted to practice his command voice as he moved about the area, but this daily cat-and-mouse game certainly did make for some enjoyable times as we watched the two of them. I could only guess that it was done as much for the enjoyment of the Marines in the company as well as their own.

Knowing that each man was a real professional in his own right, we knew they cared about our morale.

First Lieutenant Corbett often visited his old friends in 1st Reconnaissance Battalion, and upon returning to the 1st Force Recon Company area, he would call for an informal formation of his platoon, and over a couple of beers he would share with us what he had learned from his visits to battalion. One of the more interesting stories that he returned to tell us about was of a recent artillery ambush which had been sprung on the NVA, conducted by one of the battalion's recon teams. Interestingly, the lieutenant who was very much responsible for the success of this nighttime ambush was none other than 1st Lt. Mike Hodgins, the same Marine officer who was in charge of the OP that the Marine general had flown out to visit in the Que Son Mountains earlier in the spring.

"You know that before coming over here to square away all of you Marines in 1st Force Recon, I was a platoon leader in 1st Reconnaissance Battalion. That was where I really learned just how valuable good fire support can be, particularly when you're out in the bush all alone, and the only one who can help you out of a jam is the nearest Marine fire-support coordination center [FSCC]. Our battalion commander, Lieutenant Colonel Drumwright, demanded that every recon Marine sent to the field from his battalion was capable of using artillery fire support any time the opportunity presented itself. That opportunity came one time just last week, and I'll tell you as much as I know about what happened.

"We all know that 1st Recon Battalion is the eyes and ears of the 1st Marine Division commanding general, and as part of his area of interest, the Que Son Mountains are a key piece of terrain. The NVA are very much aware that the 1st Marine Division is leaving Vietnam, and they want to find out just how close they can get to Da Nang before they draw too much attention to themselves and get hurt. To keep the advance of these probing NVA in check, 1st Recon Battalion has given each one of its company an OP to man. These OPs are located along the boundary lines belonging to the division. A couple of weeks ago, one of these little OPs began to notice a pattern being developed by the NVA, and they planned a real surprise for them.

"First Lieutenant Hodgins and his platoon began to see NVA scouts coming out of their hiding positions just about every afternoon at dusk. They were using trails through dry rice paddies as their main routes into the area. The recon Marines at the OP on

Hill 861 began to plot the times and places where these units were seen, and then they plotted a series of landmarks where they registered the big guns from the artillery units at An Hoa. They had eight-inch guns, 155s, and even 175s registered to fire on these preplanned targets. They know that the NVA aren't stupid and that they are trying to reposition their forces all along the edge of the 1st Marine Division's tactical area of responsibility [TAOR].''

Lieutenant Corbett reminded us that the NVA soldiers were also well aware of the range of the Marine artillery fan which they were trying to infiltrate, and to keep from getting caught out in the open, the NVA were observed making running dashes in excess of four hundred meters. The reason for the length of these dashes was that after many years of being under the gun, the NVA knew that it required time for the firing Marine artillery batteries to be granted the proper approval in their tactical chain of command for any new adjustments to be made. During these minutes that the firing artillery was down, the NVA soldiers would sprint like hell to get away from the deadly searching artillery fire.

First Lieutenant Hodgins helped to put a plan together, based on the pattern of the NVA and what he could see happening from his vantage point on the OP. He knew that the NVA were using those rice paddies where the people from the U.S. AID program had constructed a dam. The local farmers grow their rice on a seasonal cycle, and these unused and dried-up rice paddies were the best trail system that the NVA had. He also knew the time of day that the NVA would use these trails—in increasingly larger-size units, moving single file, from one checkpoint to the next. Lieutenant Hodgins's plan called for an artillery forward observer to come out to Hill 861, watch the pattern of the infiltrating NVA soldiers, and then using the coordinated firepower of Marine long-range artillery, along with several flights of Marine all-weather A-6 Intruders, each carrying fifteen thousand pounds of bombs, they would bring this massive destructive power on top of the NVA.

Lieutenant Corbett went on.

''It took several weeks of watching, waiting, plotting, and calling in spot reports by the different OPs that were all a part of the plan. But finally last week, an NVA battalion-size unit began to move out of Laos and through the Que Son Mountains, headed for Da Nang. The trap was set and Lieutenant Hodgins and his artillery FO radioed back their observations to the battalion. The artillery battalion at An Hoa, and several other friendly artillery units in the area, adjusted their guns and waited. At the same time the wing tasked six A-6s to take off from Da Nang and to wait, orbiting away from target until the Marines on the OP called for their help. Somewhere close to 2000 hours, they knew that they had more than six hundred NVA soldiers walking down three trails into the Que Sons. These NVA were uniformed, helmeted, and carrying every type of individual and crew-served weapon that's organic to an NVA infantry battalion. They were well rested from their stay in Laos and headed straight for Da Nang, using the night as their cover. That's when Lieutenant Hodgins called up the guns at An Hoa.''

The 155mm Howitzer has the ability to throw a ninety-five-pound high-explosive shell out to a range of more than eighteen thousand meters. The eight-inch Howitzers can throw their two-hundred-pound shell in excess of twenty thousand meters, and those big 175mm guns can shoot their 150-pound projectile out to a range of thirty-two thousand meters.

The first part of Hodgins's plan was to make the NVA believe that they were out of range of our artillery. The Marines requested that several artillery rounds be fired onto the tops of the hills that made up the valley the enemy was passing through, and when those rounds hit, the NVA started in on their four-hundred-meter sprints. That's when they called for a "time on target" (TOT), and all guns shifted to a new target area ahead of, on top of, and behind the NVA battalion. To add insult to injury, the two flights of Marine A-6s came rolling right in on top of that gook battalion and dropped their ninety thousand pounds of high-explosive bombs on target. The BDA reports and aerial photos taken the following morning determined that one reinforced battalion of North Vietnamese Army soldiers had ceased to exist after 2100 that night.

"The best part of all," said Lieutenant Corbett, "was that it was done without one single Marine casualty."

The lieutenant's excitement in telling us this fascinating story was no less diminished by the reflective look in his eyes, imagining that he, too, would perhaps get the opportunity to deliver such a devastating blow against the NVA.

Little did he—or we—know that such an opportunity was very close at hand.

THUONG DUC RIVER
— VALLEY (REVISITED) —

DURING THE LAST WEEK OF JUNE, OUR RECON TEAM was scheduled to return to the Thuong Duc River valley to be part of the defensive group that would reoccupy those positions that protected the radio-relay site and OP on top of Hill 487. Recon teams from the other platoons in the company had also been rotated out to the OP site, after completing several missions, and had worked hard to steadily improve the positions on our little hill. Now that it was our turn, we hoped that when we landed we would find our original fighting positions would now look something like an impenetrable fortress.

Our flight out to the OP was part of an insertion mission that would place two recon teams from our platoon into their zones close to the Thuong Duc River valley. As a team leader of one of these teams, 1st Lieutenant Corbett planned to join the rest of his platoon at the OP after returning from his four-day mission. There had been no requirement for our team to attend the usual intelligence briefing session for the other two teams prior to our departure, as it was a simple matter for us to flip-flop with those Marines who were more than anxious to get off the hill and return to the safety of the company in Da Nang.

In preparation for our week's stay out at the OP, I was given a new 40mm grenade launcher that attached to the barrel of my M-16 rifle, enabling me to fire not only the standard 40mm high-explosive round but illumination and CS gas rounds out to a distance of three hundred meters. Having acquired several of these new grenade launchers, those of us who carried them to the field would add some additional punch to our limited amount of fire-power.

Our flight out to Thuong Duc left early in the morning, and by 0800, both of our recon teams had been inserted into their zones to spend the next four days searching for trails that the NVA were using as they continued to filter into the river valley. When we landed on Hill 487, we quickly unloaded our additional supplies of food, water, and ammunition from our CH-46 and carried our supplies up to the top of the hill. We were pleased to find that the defensive positions we had left only several weeks before had been greatly improved. A deep ammunition bunker made of logs, earth, and empty ammunition boxes provided much better protection for our limited supply of 60mm mortar rounds as well as several cases of hand grenades, 40mm rounds, claymore mines, and our small-arms ammunition. Fortunately, we had been given one M-60 machine gun, complete with two extra barrels and several cases of linked M-60 rounds. The two-man fighting holes that we had left had now been expanded and reinforced, using the cut sections of trees that had been felled to increase the size of the LZ. Alternate fighting positions had also been dug out, and the ground around the LZ had been cleared, allowing for a much better field of view from the hilltop down toward the LZ.

Shortly after we had unloaded our gear and settled in to our assigned fighting positions, we watched as Staff Sergeant Martin went out with a four-man security patrol to personally walk the ground and note all of the improvements that had been added to the defensive plan for our hilltop. One of the Marines who had met our incoming helicopter on the LZ was Staff Sergeant Beyers. He and four Marines from his platoon had elected to remain with us for the week to help defend the hill, to point out the numerous targets which they had plotted, and to show us where they had observed several groups of North Vietnamese soldiers crossing the Thuong Duc River. Several hours later, when the security patrol returned to the hilltop, Staff Sergeant Martin called for us to join him while Staff Sergeant Beyers gave us an informal brief as to what he and his men had observed during their past week.

"Staff Sergeant Martin and I have just come back from our little tour around the area, and we thought that it would be smart if I passed on to all of you as much information as possible about what we have seen and learned out here during the last couple of weeks. There are sixteen of us up here now, including three communicators and the doc. As you can see, the original positions that some of you helped to construct have been worked on by the other Marines who have done time out here. We feel pretty safe up here. But there's more to this place than meets the eye. I have good news and bad news, so I'll give you the bad news first.

"We know that there's been a lot of talk going around the area about our company standing down, but I hope none of you are foolish enough to believe that we'll be leaving Vietnam any time soon. We'll let the North Vietnamese believe that there's something to that rumor. They know that the 1st Marine Division is pulling its troops out of their TAORs, because our intelligence people report that the NVA have been creeping closer to Da Nang every day. Unfortunately, we are situated between the NVA and Da Nang. That's part of the bad news. We have been watching the NVA trying to cross the river below us, on foot and even using canoes at night. We have a new piece of gear up here with us, called a NOD [night observation device], and it has really helped us in our being able to pinpoint their crossing areas during the night. This oversized starlight scope is something that all of you will get a chance to use, and then you'll see what I'm talking about. With this increase in NVA activity around the fork in the two rivers, we can only assume that it will be only a matter of time before the gooks finally get angry enough to try and get us off this hill. That's the good news.

"We have more than forty claymore mines buried around the north, east, and western sides of our hill, and you'll be shown their locations and the locations of the corresponding hell boxes. Each time that we have sent out a security patrol, we have increased the number of booby traps and detection devices that will alert us to any possible probes that the gooks might try to use on us. We have also set up two M-49 spotting scopes to observe the open areas and the two rivers. We also have a series of preplanned targets that the long-range guns from An Hoa can easily hit. They are just a radio call away. Each day, we run three security patrols around the hill, varying the times that we go out, and we'll put two of you out on a listening post each night, down past the LZ. So far, it's been pretty quiet up here, although the Army's Special Forces camp has been hit twice in the last week by more of the NVA's rockets. We have requested that a 'four-deuce' mortar section from the 'Whisky' battery at An Hoa be brought out here to fire down on the gooks in the river, but there's still no word yet from the folks in the rear as to whether or not our request has been approved. Our radio comm has been really good. We can communicate with our teams in the bush without any problems. It does get hot out here, so stay covered up, drink plenty of water, and take your malaria and salt tablets. That's about it for now. Does anybody have any questions?"

The question foremost on everyone's mind was asked by one Marine.

"How close have the NVA come to the hill, Staff Sergeant Beyers?"

"During the past three days we've seen small groups of uniformed NVA, numbering not more than a dozen men to each group, trying to get across the river around dusk. Their crossing point is not more than three clicks way from us, and they know that we're up here 'cause we've brought in 155 artillery fire on them each time that they've made their move across the river. Our biggest problem is in the amount of time it takes for us to get the rounds out from An Hoa and onto the target. The NVA take their chances, knowing that we can't hit them every time they make a try for it, and that's the reason we want those four-deuce mortars to come out here. If the NVA try to cross the river during the daytime, and we catch them at it, those big mortars can do a lot of damage, but they can only stay out here for a day."

A voice from the rear of our group spoke up. "That sounds pretty good, but what happens to us after those four-deuce mortar guys leave?"

The reply was not exactly what anyone wanted to hear.

"That's what you get paid for, Marine."

Our informal briefing session was dismissed on that note, and we returned to our normal duties of improving the area to our own satisfaction and in getting ourselves prepared for the night. The position that I was to occupy was nothing more than a small man-made cave, large enough for two men and reinforced with several layers of three-inch-diameter logs and wooden ammunition boxes filled with dirt. Whoever had taken the time to construct the little bunker had copied it straight from the NVA handbook on field-fortification design. It was shaded by a large tree and well ventilated, and two rubber ponchos were draped over its top to help make it waterproof. The last human occupant had been thoughtful and wise enough to leave behind one roll of toilet paper, kept dry by having been placed inside a mess-hall coffee can.

My position was located close to the center of the hill, and it was the bunker closest to the LZ. The one M-60 machine gun had been placed on top of my roof because the position faced the longest axis of open area, looking straight down the sloping finger of the hill and past the landing zone. It was not long after I had unpacked my gear before Staff Sergeant Beyers walked over to visit.

"Doc, I heard from Staff Sergeant Martin that you humped the M-60 on a number of missions when you were with 3rd Force.

Any objections to keeping that gun right where it is? You probably have had as much trigger time with the sixty as anybody else up here, and I'd just as soon have someone behind the gun who knows how to use it. A lot of these guys are brand-new, and I want them to get a chance to go out on the daily security patrols, too.''

"It's fine with me, but do you know when the last time was that the machine gun was fired?''

"I know that it hasn't been fired since I've been up here, but there's plenty of ammunition, so why don't you check it out. I'll be back after I've talked to everyone on the hill.''

After taking the machine gun apart, I spent the remainder of the morning cleaning all of the gun's parts and punching the bores of both barrels then oiling and reassembling the weapon. When I had reassembled the machine gun, I walked over to where both staff sergeants were busy watching the riverbanks for any sign of the elusive NVA. I requested permission to test-fire the M-60. I guess that the thought of their resident corpsman asking permission to test-fire the machine gun was amusing because the two staff sergeants smiled and laughed politely when I told them what I wanted to do. My request was granted, and I asked Corporal Mahkewa to pick up his rifle and come with me to the edge of the LZ where I planned to test-fire the gun.

"You know, those two staff sergeants get a real kick out of you, Doc.''

"Why do you say that, Stinky?''

"Because most Marines have learned since boot camp that the average life span of a machine gunner during a firefight is about ten seconds. There ain't no one else on this goddamned hill who wants to get anywhere near that machine gun except you. And now you want to go out and test-fire the damned thing.''

"It would seem pretty stupid if we had to use it and then find out that it didn't work, right? I want to get off of this hill in one week and go to Sydney, Australia, Stinky. If that means having to use this M-60, then I don't mind it at all. What I do want is for you to help me out. You got any problems with that?''

"Hey, relax, man. Why are you so uptight about a little ribbing over that machine gun?''

"Okay, Stinky, you asked, so I'm gonna tell you. You guys think that being out here on this OP with a bunch of new guys is nothin' more than a seven-day, in-country R & R. I don't. First Sergeant Jacques spent all afternoon telling us about what happened to him out at Ba To and why it was so stupid for them to have set up, night after night, on the same hill. It's the same sort of deal out here. This OP has been operational since early April, and the gooks aren't stupid. They know we're here. All we are is a little pain under their saddle to 'em right now, but if we bring out a section of four-deuce mortars, and they shoot the hell out of the NVA, what do you think is going to happen to us when that mortar section flies away after one day of shooting? I'll tell you what; the gooks will come up here and take a look at just how few of us are up here holdin' this hill, and then they'll try to kick our ass right off of it. The problem with all of this is that I don't want to leave this hill in a green rubber sleepin' bag. Do you?''

My question put a stop to Corporal Mahkewa's normally good nature, and he thought about my reasons for concern. That kept him quiet for the few minutes it took to walk down to the LZ. By then, his attitude had changed.

"Okay, Doc, so it's you 'n me until we get off of the hill, right? I'm sharing a two-man hole with Draper, and if the shit hits the fan, then you know where we are, and we know where you'll be."

"Stinky, all I'm asking is for you to stay out here and provide a little security for me on the LZ while I fire about ten rounds through this gun. Don't worry about what I said before. I just want to make sure that we all get out of here when our time is up."

There was no reason to worry that the sound of the M-60 would give our position away to the NVA. The Marines who had previously rotated off the hill had fired numerous 60mm illumination rounds, using the mortar, as was evident by the number of empty wooden ammunition boxes, so the sound of a "starter belt" of machine-gun fire would only alert them to the fact that there was at least one machine gun at our position. The test-firing took only a few seconds, and when we returned to the safety of the hilltop, Corporal Mahkewa busied himself with improving the position that he and Corporal Draper would share during the next week. Late in the afternoon, we were informed that the four-deuce mortar section that had been requested earlier was due to be brought out to our position the following morning. The news of our hilltop becoming an ever more popular place caused every one of us to double-check the construction of our positions one more time.

The hot and humid weather patterns of June were extremely predictable, and powerful afternoon thunderstorms were a part of that pattern. The continual gathering clouds along the eastern side of the Thuong Duc Mountains would swell into great black thunderheads by midday, with the first rumbles of thunder and great flashes of lightning sweeping westward and bringing heavy sheets of warm rain over us by four o'clock in the afternoon. Our first

day on the OP was no exception, and these heavy rains only made
the constant job of having to watch the riverbanks for signs of the
enemy that much more miserable. Fortunately, these afternoon
thunderstorms would pass through the area quickly, and though
the wind and the rain did provide some temporary relief from the
stifling tropical humidity, the temperature returned to normal soon
after the storms passed by. These were the times when those of us
who were not on 50 percent alert would write letters to family and
friends. As the afternoon rain storm began to crawl toward our
position, I went into my little cave to start a letter.

The military postal system allowed us to send our letters home
without having to pay for any postage. We had only to write the
word FREE on the upper right-hand corner of any envelope or
postcard and then drop it into the familiar orange mailbag for
processing and delivery back to the States. Often, clean and dry
stationery and envelopes were not available, but that certainly
didn't stop any of us from using the cardboard side panel from a
used C-ration box or, when available, the cardboard from a six-
pack of beer. As much information as possible was scribbled onto
those cardboard postcards, with the ever popular peace symbol
usually drawn in place of the stamp. Of the several hundred cards
and letters that I sent to my parents, sisters, and friends while I
was in Vietnam, and have since reread, I never wrote about the
possible dangers that either we as a recon team had experienced or
that our team could possibly face in the immediate future. I know
that I was not alone in doing this. I can only believe that this was
because none of us wanted to cause the folks back home to worry
any more than they already did, since no good could come from
it. It was while I was writing one of these C-ration postcards that
Corporal Draper came over to my cave for a visit and a cigarette.

"Staff Sergeant Martin told me to tell you we've got LP duty
tomorrow night. He also said that it looks like there's a storm
headed this way, and it'll get here tomorrow night, too."

"The last time I was out here and we pulled LP duty, we could
smell the gooks cookin' food not too far from where we were
hiding. We radioed back that we could smell it, but nothin' happened. I just can't believe that we've had this OP out here this
long and that the gooks haven't tried to take the hill. It'll be just
our luck to have them try it tomorrow night."

"Hey, don't even kid about somethin' like that. I've only got a
couple of months more left to do before I go home, and the last
thing that I need is to start to worry about the NVA comin' up here
for a big-time firefight. The word is out that the four-deuce mortar

section really is comin' out here tomorrow morning, and we'll
have to set up some LZ security before the helicopters arrive. Staff
Sergeant Martin wants you to bring that M-60 down to the LZ first
thing tomorrow morning, and Mahkewa and I will set up with you
and the gun.

"I think that the rain is almost ended. I'll go and get Mahkewa,
and we can cook our chow together. Thanks for the smoke."

Early that evening, Corporals Draper and Mahkewa and I used
the shallow depression in front of my position to hide the bluish
glow from the heat tabs which we used to cook our evening meal.
By the time we had finished eating our dinner, the sun had reappeared briefly, only to show itself before dipping behind the western mountain range that separated the borders of Vietnam and
Laos. As darkness slowly crept in over our small hilltop, we
assumed 100 percent alert status, every man awake, alert, and
aware of the evening's challenge and the password that was supposed to distinguish a friendly voice from that of the enemy.

We sat motionless and waited only for total darkness before we
secured half of our force on the hill, allowing every other man to
get several hours sleep before the other half would assume the
duties.

Sometime close to midnight, I was still wide awake and lying
wrapped up in my poncho liner, thinking about all of the good
stories that I had heard from those Marines returning from R & Rs
in Sydney. The tales they had told about the sights and sounds in
a section of town called King's Cross and of how all the Australian
girls were friendly, beautiful, and always eager to meet Yanks
were the stuff of which dreams were made, and it would only be
a matter of a few days before I would be there and able to see it
all for myself.

My state of semisleep was cut short by the shrill scream of a
Marine, not more than thirty feet away.

"Jesus Christ," someone called out. "Who the hell was that?"

I threw my poncho liner aside, grabbed for my Unit-1 bag, and
crawled out into the night.

"Draper, did you hear that?"

"Who didn't. I think it came from over by the ammo bunker."

I moved over to the direction of the bunker and was met by a
Marine who grabbed my arm.

"Doc, Dickerson, it's Dickerson. He says that something bit
him in the leg."

"Where is he?"

"He's in this hole. Follow me, and I'll show you."

When I found Lance Corporal Dickerson, he was lying on his back, rocking from side to side, obviously in great pain. I turned on my flashlight and the faint light from the red lens only showed me Dickerson, moaning and rocking back and forth with both of his hands holding tight to a place high up on his inner right thigh. I unscrewed the flashlight and removed the red lens filter for a better look.

"Dickerson, what the hell's wrong?"

"Something bit me, Doc. I don't know what. It could have been a snake or somethin'."

"Take your hands away and let me take a look."

Holding the flashlight under my chin, I took a pair of dressing scissors from my Unit-1 and cut up from the knee of his pants leg toward his hip and then tore his camouflage trousers, opening an area around the bite. A large reddish-blue welt, about the size of a golf ball, had begun to form.

"Dickerson, did you see or feel the snake, or did you just wake up from the pain?"

"All I know is that I was sound asleep, and then I felt the pain of somethin' biting the shit out of my leg. That's when I yelled and woke up everybody. Do you think it's a snakebite, Doc? You don't think that I'm gonna get sick and die from one o' them poisonous gook snakes, do ya?"

"All I can see is that you've got one hell of a bite mark, but I can't tell by the marks if it was really a snake that bit you. I'll stay here and watch you, but you and I both know that they'll only send out an emergency medevac bird if you really turn sick."

"Yeah, I know, but just stay close and see what happens to me, okay?"

I kept a close watch on Dickerson's vital signs for half an hour, and after cleaning the wound with a strong disinfectant and giving him several Benadryl capsules to help reduce the swelling, I watched as he fell into a deep sleep. The incident was radioed back to the company, and they, too, agreed that an emergency medevac for Dickerson was not going to be a priority unless he showed the symptoms from a poisonous snakebite, or if he should go into sudden shock.

Dickerson's sudden scream had caused everyone on the hill to come alive and have to spend a long and restless night, wondering what the reason was for the commotion, but it wasn't until morning, when one of Dickerson's buddies started to rearrange some of the protective wooden ammunition boxes near their hole, that the probable culprit was discovered.

"Jesus, take a look at this!"

Underneath one of the ammunition boxes lay two huge red and yellow centipedes, coiled up in their attempt to stay hidden from the light. One of the Marines who had discovered the centipedes held out his canteen cup with one hand and pushed the two insects into his cup, using his K-bar knife. He slapped a box of C rations over the top of his canteen cup and then called for any of us standing nearby to bring a small piece of C-4 plastic explosive to where he stood. He set fire to the C-4 and inverted the canteen cup, allowing the toxic smoke and fumes from the burning explosive to filter up into his trap. Within several minutes, he lifted the cup away from the now dead centipedes, and we examined each one. They were more than ten inches long.

"Take a look at the ass end of these things."

He took the tip of his K-bar and pointed at the formidable set of black pinchers at the tail end of each centipede.

"Here's what probably bit Dickerson, and I bet if we found these two just by movin' a couple of ammo boxes around, we'd find plenty more of them."

The two centipedes were left out to be displayed for those Marines who had elected earlier to shed their camouflage trousers in place of their cooler, tiger-striped shorts. They needed only to look at the business end of the two centipedes before quickly changing their minds and their uniforms.

As soon as we had finished eating breakfast, Draper, Mahkewa, and I gathered up our gear, weapons, and one PRC-77 radio, and walked down to the far side of the LZ to wait for the arrival of the helicopters that would bring the four-deuce mortars out to the OP. We found a two-man fighting hole that offered us a good place to emplace the M-60 machine gun and started in on our standard routine of improving the old position. Within an hour we had dug our hole deeper, cleared the ground in front, and tied a camouflage poncho liner above our position to provide some relief and shade from the increasing heat and sunshine.

Around 0900 Draper answered a call on our radio, and said, "The guys in the comm bunker say that four CH-46s are inbound with the mortar section, and they'll be here in thirty minutes."

Right on schedule, we watched as four escorting Cobra gunships, leading the CH-46s, came over our hill and started their circling pattern over the two river valleys that ran below our position. Hearing of no indication of recent enemy movement and not having received any enemy ground fire, the way was cleared for three CH-46s to begin landing one at a time to off-load the long-awaited four-deuce mortar section. The fourth CH-46 brought the mortar section's supply of ammunition, externally carried in netting slung beneath its belly. Within minutes, our little hilltop LZ resembled an ant's nest, busy with the activity involved in the delicate off-loading of these men, their heavy mortars and ammunition.

The M-30 4.2-inch mortar was well respected as an infantry crew-served weapon system that packed a tremendous punch. One complete mortar weighed 672 pounds, had a range of more than fifty-six hundred meters, and could fire at an initial rate of eighteen rounds per minute, tapering off to a sustained rate of three rounds per minute for as long as the ammunition lasted. Each high-explosive round weighed twenty-seven pounds, and the mortar was fired by simply dropping the round down the barrel, base end first.

What made the four-deuce mortar unique was that unlike both the 60- and 81mm mortars, which had smoothbore tubes, the 4.2-inch mortar had a rifled barrel consisting of twenty-four spiraling lands and grooves, which provided great stability during the flight of the mortar round. The increased range and accuracy of this weapon over its smaller counterparts made its appearance on the position a welcome sight. We only wished that the mortar section would remain to be a permanent fixture.

When the three mortar tubes were finally in place, a list of our preplotted targets, based on what we had observed in enemy activity, was presented to the officer in charge (OIC) of the mortar section. Then, having only to wait as these well-trained gun crews set up their aiming stakes and established their radio communications system, we watched them prepare their ammunition for firing. With all of their preparations completed, each mortar tube fired out three rounds, "seating" the base plate of each mortar, and then the crews reported back to the OIC that they were ready to commence firing. The visiting mortar section spent the majority of the morning and afternoon firing on every preplotted target that fell within the 4.2 mortar's range fan, but there were no secondary explosions recorded, and no sightings of the enemy during the time that the mortars continued to shoot.

Corporals David Draper and Donald J. Mahkewa and I had spent the day at our position, providing what limited amount of security two Marines and one Navy corpsman, armed with one M-60 machine gun and two M-16 rifles, could muster in defense of our OP on the hill. We knew from our previous experiences with the NVA in the A Shau Valley that when we used supporting arms against the enemy from our radio-relay site and OP, they retaliated instantly with countermortar fire of their own. When this section of Marine four-deuce mortars departed our hilltop, we knew that we would pay the price for having the mortars join us to stir up the hornet's nest in the Thuong Duc River valley. The only question was when, and the answer was not long in coming.

By 1700, the three Marine CH-46s had pulled the mortar section off our hill, only leaving behind several stacks of empty wooden ammunition boxes that we quickly carried back to the hilltop and used to fortify our positions. The mortar section had spent the better part of the day firing at suspected enemy staging areas and crossing points along the river, but we hadn't seen any enemy movement during the entire time that the firing was under way. As the late afternoon clouds continued to grow darker, the sudden change in temperature, wind direction, and the low rumble of thunder served notice that the forecasted storm was closing in around us.

"Hey, Doc, you about ready?"

Corporal Draper stood waiting outside my little cave, rifle in hand, with our PRC-77 radio on his back. His face searched across the band of thunderheads, looking, hopelessly, for some relief.

"I'm all set, but do you think it's gonna be worth it for us to take the starlight scope out to the LP?"

"Yeah, we might as well. This thunderstorm could blow by here in just a couple of hours, and then we'd wish we had it with us. I've already checked out the radio, and it's good."

"Okay, let's go."

We walked past Corporal Draper's position and looked down at Corporal Mahkewa, busy opening a can of C rations.

"Hey, Stinky, try and stay awake tonight. Your bunky tells me that you'll probably eat all of his chow while we're out on the LP."

"I hope you guys don't get scared out there and come runnin' back for me to help."

"Don't worry, Stinky, your turn is coming, and you'll probably pull LP duty with Dickerson. Rumor has it that he's queer and he wants to spend a night in the woods with an Indian."

"Get the hell out of here. I'll have some coffee made for you guys when you come in."

"See ya in the mornin', Stinky. Stay dry."

The short joking conversation with Corporal Mahkewa would be our last spoken words until we returned in the morning.

Corporal Draper led our way down from the hilltop past where the mortar section had set up, and we slowly vanished from sight into the jungle growth beginning at the outer edge of the landing zone. Keeping him in sight, not more than ten feet in front of me, I followed in trace as he weaved effortlessly between trees and scrub growth to a spot several hundred yards from the edge of the LZ. He stopped and pointed toward a small tree, signaling that this would be the place we would use as our LP. We moved in next to the tree, positioned the PRC-77 radio between us, and with M-16 rifles cradled in our laps, we leaned back, ready to spend a long night as the ears for the OP.

A steady rain had begun to fall as we left the hilltop, and along with the rain, the increasing winds made it difficult to distinguish between the sounds of nature and those made by man. But still we strained to listen for that slightest unusual noise that would alert us to the presence of the enemy. The first sounds of the North Vietnamese soldiers started at exactly 2200.

Clap, clap . . .

Corporal Draper nudged my side.

Clap, clap . . . clap, clap . . .

"It sounds like bamboo sticks," I whispered.

Clap, clap, clap . . .

"There's a bunch of them."

Corporal Draper was smart enough to have positioned the radio's handset over his left shoulder so that his only motion to touch the handset key was the movement of his hand. He keyed the radio twice.

"LP, this is OP. Are you Alpha Sierra [all secure] at this time? Over."

Corporal Draper purposely did not return the call to alert the OP that something was very wrong. They got his message.

"LP, this is OP. If you have movement around you, key your handset once."

Corporal Draper keyed once.

"LP, this is OP. Can you see anyone? Give me one for a yes, or two for a no."

He keyed the handset twice.

"LP, this is OP. We are hearing sticks being clapped. Can you hear that sound, too?"

Corporal Draper keyed the handset once.

"LP, this is OP. If they are within fifty feet give me one."

Draper replied with one squeeze of the handset.

"If they are closer than twenty-five feet, give me one."

It was almost impossible to tell just how far away the enemy was, but the sounds had not moved any closer to us, so no reply was sent.

"Roger, LP. Somewhere between twenty-five and fifty feet. Just stay at your position until you are told to pull back. Over."

Corporal Draper keyed the handset twice, acknowledging the message and signaling out.

The NVA had finally decided to pay a visit to us on Hill 487, and as was their custom—and ours—they used every means at their disposal to help screen their advance. Darkness, thunder, and wind made their approach silent, then the rain removed their tracks. They had obviously avoided all contact with our booby-trap trip wires as they moved up the sides of the hill. Their tapping of the bamboo sticks served three purposes: it kept them on line as they crept forward in the dark and alert to each other's positions; it made it impossible for us to know how many of them were out there, four or forty-four; and last, it made our imaginations run wild at not knowing what they would do next.

The Marines back on the hilltop, under the leadership of two staff sergeants, responded to their orders. They were reminded in whispers about their fire discipline, demonstrated by the fact that no one fired out at the sounds of the clapping sticks, which was exactly what the NVA had wanted to test. It became a standoff. The NVA did not move closer but continued to clap their sticks together, and the Marines on the hill remained almost motionless. Almost . . .

Under the direction of Staff Sergeant Martin, two Marines, each armed with half a dozen hand grenades, crept to the edge of the hillside and waited in one of the secondary position holes for the next series of clapping noises to begin. As soon as they heard that *clap, clap, clap* sound, they each threw one grenade, hoping that their aim would place their grenade just short of the sound, allowing gravity and the steep sides of the hill to cause the grenades to continue to roll in beside the hidden enemy soldiers. As soon as they tossed their grenades they moved to the opposite side of the hill and repeated the process. The grenades exploding around the perimeter of our hill must have caused the NVA to reconsider their plans, because their clapping sounds stopped for the rest of the night.

Corporal Draper and I remained in position throughout the rainy night until we received the word from the communications bunker to move back to the OP. Still, we waited until we had enough morning light to allow ourselves to see clearly before we made our move back to the lower edge of the landing zone, and then we stopped to closely scrutinize the open, muddy ground between ourselves and the hilltop.

"Do you think the gooks have left anyone behind?"

"I don't think so, but the only way that we'll know for sure is to stay close to the brush and keep low."

"You lead the way back, and I'll cover you. When you stop, turn and cover me."

"Let's do it."

We covered the short distance back up to the OP using this leapfrogging method for our mutual protection, and when we reported back to Staff Sergeant Martin's position, we were each handed a canteen cup of hot coffee.

"Well, welcome back home, gentlemen. From the looks of you it was a long, wet night. We thought that things might have gotten a little too hairy for just two of you out there. Good job."

"How close do you think they were, Staff Sergeant Martin?"

"Maybe thirty yards from the edge of the hill. We think we might have hit a couple of 'em when we tried a few grenade volleys, but we're not sure. There's no real sign of blood. Did you two see any sign of 'em on the way back in here?"

"No, we just heard 'em banging those sticks together and figured that we were better off where we were than being up here on the hill. They never came past us when they decided to leave, but I wouldn't use the same place for tonight's LP. Who's goin' out on that one, anyway?"

"Corporal Mahkewa and Gable. It's supposed to keep on raining all day and into the night, too."

"Have you told Mahkewa yet?"

"No, I figured that one of you two can break the news to him."

"Thanks. He's supposed to have some more of the coffee waiting for us. We'll break the news to him gently. Anything else?"

"Yeah, there's a resupply bird due in here around 1500 to drop off some batteries and ammunition. Make sure that M-60 is up, and take it down to the LZ by 1430."

MEDEVACED

RETURNING TO MY SUBTERRANEAN, BUT DRY POSItion, I had planned to change from my wet and stinking utilities, clean up my equipment, and then eat a hot breakfast before getting several hours of much-needed sleep, but my plans were interrupted by a visit from Corporal Mahkewa.

"Hey, Doc, you in there, man?"

"Sure, come on in, Stinky."

"Hey, man, Draper just told me that I'm on one of the teams pullin' LP duty tonight. I asked Draper a thousand questions about where you two set up last night and how close those gooners got to ya, but he won't tell me shit 'cause he's mad. I know he's just jerkin' my chain, 'cause I didn't have no coffee ready when you guys came in, but I figured that you'd tell me what happened last night."

"Get lost, Stinky."

"Hey, man, I'm sorry about the coffee deal. I just caught a couple a extra Zs, and missed my mornin' wake-up call. 'Sides, Staff Sergeant Martin already had coffee waitin' on you two dudes when you came back in. Draper already told me about that."

"Okay, Stinky, I'll help out later. Just wait 'till I get a couple of hours sleep, and then come back over here with Draper. We'll show you where we set up."

By noontime the heavy sheets of rain had slackened to a constant warm drizzle, and I had managed to get several hours of sleep. The familiar voice of an anxious Corporal Mahkewa woke me.

"Hey, Doc. Draper's out here with me. You awake, man?"

"Hang on, Stinky. I'll be right out."

Crawling outside to meet them, the fresh air and warm rain suddenly felt good and cleansing as I sat on the roof of my bunker and washed, watching as Corporals Mahkewa and Draper did their map study of the area that was being considered for possible use as the new LP. It was during this map study that Corporal Mahkewa began to talk to us about home. It seemed odd at the time, because unlike so many other Marines who shared their thoughts about their families and where they had come from, Corporal Mahkewa was tight-lipped about his roots as a Hopi Indian and his upbringing near Parker, Arizona.

"Hey, Draper, what's your favorite dinner? I mean, if you could have any meal in the world right now, what would be the one you'd choose?"

"I guess that I'd like to have a Thanksgiving dinner. Ya know, a big roasted turkey with all the trimmings: chestnut stuffing, sweet potatoes, peas, biscuits, gravy, and lots of ice-cold milk."

"Hey, Doc, what about you? What would you have if you had your choice?"

"I guess that I'd like to be at a traditional New England clam-bake. Steamed clams, cherrystones, lobster, corn on the cob, and ice-cold beer. That would be pretty spectacular to me. Okay, Stinky, I know you wanted one of us to ask you, what would you want to eat?"

"That's easy. Fried cabbage."

Draper and I just looked at one another.

"Fried cabbage?"

"Yeah, you guys don't know nothin' about real food. My mother makes the best-tasting fried cabbage in the world."

Corporal Mahkewa went on to explain to us, in great detail, not only how this cabbage was grown, watered, weeded, and harvested but exactly how his mother would boil the cabbage in a particular fashion and then fry it in butter to a shade of golden brown, using a huge cast-iron skillet for the frying. The image of home to Corporal Mahkewa was this mental picture of his mother at work in her kitchen, preparing just for him this simplest of meals: fried cabbage. The way he had described their home, his mother, her humble kitchen, and the meagerness of his imaginary meal made us feel guilty for our having wished for so much, but left us hungry by the thought of it.

"Somethin' botherin' you, Stinky?"

"No, I was just thinkin' about home, that's all. I've got less than three months to go before I can leave the Nam for the World and get back home to Arizona. I was just thinkin' about it, that's all."

Staff Sergeant Beyers interrupted our meeting with orders for

Corporal Draper and me to get our gear on and move the M-60 machine gun closer to the LZ, prior to the afternoon arrival of the CH-46. We would remain at the position until the resupply bird had dropped off its cargo and left the area. Moving down from the hilltop, we picked our way between the clumps of brush, Corporal Draper carrying his rifle and one can of machine-gun ammunition, and me carrying the M-60. As we moved toward our position we cursed the rain, slipping and sliding on the muddy patches of open ground that sloped down toward the LZ.

"Christ, I hope that CH-46 gets in here on time. I've just gotten used to being dry, and now I'm soaked to the skin again. What time is it?"

"It's only 1430, and we'll have to stay out here for at least an hour. But the bright side is that we won't have to be out all night on LP duty, like Stinky."

Those were the last words that I remember Corporal Draper speaking as we stopped, frozen in midstride, listening to the unmistakable *pook, pook, pook* sound made when three mortar rounds are fired out in rapid succession.

"Incoming! Incoming! Quick, get down in the hole, get down in the hole."

As our loud warning shouts of "incoming" were picked up and echoed across the hilltop, Draper and I dove into our half-mud-filled position and flattened ourselves against the watery sides of the pit, waiting for the precious few seconds of remaining flight time before the enemy mortar rounds impacted, either near or on us.

Crunch . . . crunch . . . crunch

The three incoming rounds exploded, landing short of the southern edge of the LZ, sending mud, bushes, and branches high into the air. The noise from the falling debris hadn't quieted before we heard the repeat firing of the mortar.

Pook, pook, pook

"Shit, you know they've got a spotter hidden out there who just made an adjustment. Let's hope they're bad at what they do. Get back down."

This time the three incoming rounds impacted harmlessly away on the southern slope of the hill, but still landing halfway between our gun position and the LZ. Had the NVA mortar crew shifted their aim just a bit more to the left, we would have been in serious trouble. We knew now that when the NVA made corrections from the impact of their last three rounds, we'd stand a better than average chance of getting nailed where we lay, but all we could do was remain flat in our hole and hope like hell that our muddly little pit would provide us with all of the protection for which the two of us silently prayed.

Again came the *pook*, *pook*, *pook* sound and this time the three incoming rounds impacted onto the hilltop behind us, landing just short of my unoccupied bunker.

Crunch . . . crunch . . . crunch

I waited for the inevitable scream of "corpsman up" but heard only silence. Fortunately, there had been no one wounded inside the radius of the exploding mortar rounds, but we could see that the explosions had cut down several large trees and had torn the ground apart, leaving it smoking. It was only a matter of absolute luck and good construction of our bunkers that no greater damage had been done.

The NVA mortar crew had clearly demonstrated their ability to creep their rounds onto our hilltop position, but the question that remained in our minds was when they would fire again. Sixteen pairs of ears strained hard, waiting to catch the warning sound that would send us to ground, but the only noise was the continuous splattering of the rain. The pause meant that the NVA mortar crew had either picked up their weapon to relocate, anticipating our responsive call for supporting artillery, or that they were just toying with us, letting us know what they could do.

As suddenly as the mortar fire had stopped, the ripping sound of machine-gun fire, followed by the cracking sounds of bullets snapping just over our heads and into the surrounding trees, put Draper and me back into our watery hole.

"Shit, now how're we gonna get out of here?"

"Did you see where the firing was comin' from?"

"Yeah. That line of green tracers started from the left side of that far ridgeline. They must be six hundred yards away. Can you get the barrel of the sixty over the edge of the hole?"

"I think so, just keep your eyes on where you think they are, and I'll try to get a bead on them."

I positioned the M-60 machine gun so that I would have a good chance of returning fire at the NVA machine gun without exposing too much of myself. Corporal Draper rolled around to my left side, helping to position the belt of ammunition and then, motionless, we waited for the next time they fired. The wait wasn't long.

A ribbon of green tracers flicked out from the edge of the jungle and cut into the trees above our hole. I shouldered the gun and aimed in on the area where the tracers had emerged, firing a burst of no more than ten rounds. Corporal Draper directed my firing.

"Come up some, and a little to the right."

My next burst of fire sent another ten rounds into the brush along the far ridgeline.

"That's good, hold it right on that spot."

With his direction, I fired several more short bursts onto the target, and then waited to see what happened.

Pook . . . pook . . .

"Did you hear that?"

"Yeah, it's us firing back at the gook machine gun. I hope they know how to shoot that mortar."

We waited, only to hear the sounds of our two mortar rounds impacting somewhere off in the distant jungle, but judging from the sound and not seeing any impact, we knew the rounds had landed several hundred yards over their intended target. Again, two more rounds were fired out from our hilltop, and this time the detonation was much closer to the southern edge of the ridgeline.

"They've dropped their range. Next time they fire, they should be close to that gook machine gun."

Two more rounds were fired out from our mortar in rapid succession, and this time the resulting explosions could be clearly seen as they impacted on the side of the ridgeline. Then five more rounds were sent on their way to cover the area.

"Hey, Doc, Draper, get back up here."

Corporal Mahkewa, sent down from the hilltop to provide some covering fire for us, had hidden himself behind two logs and motioned for us to join him. Corporal Draper looked back toward Mahkewa's position and said, "Go ahead, Doc, I'll fire and you make a break for it."

The M-60 machine gun weighed twenty pounds, and the job of picking up the gun and running over open, muddy ground wasn't too thrilling. But this was not the time to debate who would go first. As soon as I had yanked the M-60 from the edge of our hole, Draper started firing his M-16 in the direction of the far ridgeline. That was my cue to move.

Bent over, trying to stay low, and helped by the weight of the gun, I ran, slipping and sliding, toward Corporal Mahkewa's position. I had no sooner cleared the logs when Corporal Mahkewa began to fire, covering Corporal Draper's sprint back to the safety that the two logs provided us.

"They want you to bring the gun back up to the hill. The CH-46s aren't comin' out 'cause of the rain. Let's get out of here."

We made our way back up to the hilltop without receiving any more fire from the NVA. Our situation had been radioed back to Da Nang, and we were told that because of the persistent rainstorm, the possibility of us seeing any close air support coming out to lend assistance was the same as the visibility: zero.

The only fire support that we could depend on would come from the big guns at An Hoa, but we were told that they, too, were busy firing in support of some action involving a battalion of the 7th Marine Regiment. The most urgent requests for artillery fire went to those who needed it the most, and the needs of fifteen Marines and one corpsman must not have scored too high up on the priority list. We were told to prepare ourselves and our positions for the likelihood of a night attack.

The NVA knew the range from both their mortar position and machine-gun position to the center of our hilltop, but the great unknown was whether or not they would elect to attack us, or to wait for a better target, one that would include using the landing zone for their impact area.

No time was wasted in our preparation for the night. High-explosive and illumination rounds were broken out and prepared for immediate use. Our individual weapons were fieldstripped, cleaned, reassembled, and placed where each Marine and his buddy could instantly get to them. The wooden ammunition boxes that contained the electrical hell box detonators for the claymore mines were opened and each hell box was checked and rechecked for immediate use. Orders were given, reminding all of us about noise-and-light discipline, and areas of responsibility were clearly defined. Each position was physically checked by an NCO. If the NVA were going to assault our hilltop this night, they would first have to pass by two listening posts, move through a series of hand-grenade and illumination booby traps, and then subject themselves to our hidden defensive wall of claymore mines.

With what little daylight remained, one five-man security team was sent out to check our perimeter and look back at our positions to ensure that we were well camouflaged. When the patrol returned, these last-minute corrections were made. Nothing was left to chance.

By 1830, four Marines, including Corporal Mahkewa, had gone out to set up their listening posts. These two teams would be our first line of defense, while the rest of us sat and stared out into the rain, waiting, watching, and listening.

The first indication of the presence of the North Vietnamese began at 2300 with the rhythmic tapping of bamboo sticks.

Clap . . . clap . . . clap . . .

Draper nudged me. "Did you hear that? It sounds like they're all around us. Look at that!"

One of the illumination grenades, hidden near the edge of the landing zone, had ignited and turned a portion of the LZ into a foggy version of daylight.

"Can you see any movement out there?"

"No, but don't stare at the light. When it burns out take a look around with the starlight scope."

The illumination grenade burned itself out in about fifteen seconds, and Corporal Draper scanned the LZ, but there was no sign of any movement.

"I wonder what set it off? Maybe it was just the wind."

Clap . . . clap . . . clap . . .

The sound of someone scurrying toward us in the mud made us both turn back to see Staff Sergeant Beyers kneeling down behind us.

"You two okay?"

"No problem. Any word from Mahkewa on movement?"

"No, they're just sittin' out there waitin'. We're gonna try throwing a couple of grenade volleys down at those guys with the bamboo sticks. Just keep your cool. Everyone's doin' real good."

The clapping of the bamboo sticks continued intermittently, for the rest of the night, and to the credit of the Marines on our hilltop, while the "velvet-hammer" sounds continued, the obvious psychological stress which the North Vietnamese soldiers had hoped for never materialized in the form of anyone firing his weapon or by cracking, waiting for something more to happen. The sounds of the bamboo sticks were temporarily silenced with volleys of three or four grenades being pitched out into the rainy night, but the sounds would only start again from another place. We spent the remainder of the night peering out from our holes, waiting. . . .

"The LPs are comin' back in, Doc."

"What time is it?"

"It's just about 0600. There's enough light to make some coffee before Stinky gets here. That'll really make him feel bad."

"I must have fallen asleep after 0400, that's the last time I heard any grenades go off."

"Don't worry about it. Nothin' happened after they threw that last volley."

Corporal Mahkewa came and joined us after both listening-post teams had debriefed the senior staff NCOs about what they had seen and heard during their long night.

"You guys are lucky that you weren't out there, man. We could hear them gooks crawlin' around on the slope of the hill. They froze every time one of those grenade volleys went off. I wonder if we hit any of 'em?"

"Here ya go, Stinky, just like you promised us, remember? Have some hot coffee."

"Jeez, now I really do feel bad. I thought about that all night long."

"What did they say at the debriefing?"

"The word is that they requested an emergency resupply of 60mm HE and illum rounds and that bird is due in here at 0800."

"Do they want us to lug the M-60 back down to the LZ?"

"No, they said that there'd be enough escort birds to work the area over if the CH-46 took any ground fire."

"Yeah, I've heard that one before, too. As long as it's still rainin' don't count on any help from the wing."

Close to 0900 we began to hear the staccato beat of helicopter blades cutting into the wind and looked up to see two Marine Cobra gunships, the escorting birds for the CH-46, starting their patrol around the river valley. There was still no sign of the inbound frog, and we reasoned that the Cobras wanted to test the water before allowing the CH-46 to land in a potentially hot LZ to off-load mortar ammunition.

"Okay, that 'forty-six will be on the deck in less than five minutes. I want a working party of four men standin' by and ready to carry that ammo off that bird. There ain't gonna be a lot of grab-ass time down at that LZ. Corporal Draper, pick three Marines to help."

Draper didn't have far to go to point out with his finger, saying, "You, you, and you, leave your gear up here and come with me."

Those of us remaining on the hilltop watched as the four Marines in the working party moved closer to the LZ and then stopped, looking up into the sky at the progress of the inbound CH-46. The Cobras had stopped circling above our hilltop and had moved several clicks to the north, looking down for any signs of the enemy. That's when the NVA sprung their trap.

The CH-46 was making its final tail-down approach onto the LZ when that frightening *pook . . . pook . . . pook* sound came from out of the jungle. The Marines near the LZ, engulfed by the sounds of the approaching helicopter, couldn't hear the sound of the firing mortar, but they did hear us yell, "Incoming, incoming!" and hit the deck.

The Marine who had been in communication with the CH-46

pilot told him to abort his landing, but the reaction time to the warning was just too short. The first two rounds hit at the edge of the LZ, the third fell short into the jungle. Their next attempt would certainly hit the helicopter.

I grabbed my Unit-1 and started running down the hill toward the LZ, thinking that I could use the same two logs that Corporal Mahkewa had used for cover the day before, but as I got closer to the hovering CH-46, I, too, could no longer distinguish the sounds made by the distant NVA mortar, and I had no way of knowing then that they'd sent three more rounds on the way.

The last thing that I remember seeing was the helmeted face of the CH-46 pilot as he pitched his bird's nose forward and flew directly over me. Instinctively, I ducked and turned away from the flying dirt, debris, and dust cloud caused by the helicopter's twin-rotor wash. The last thing that I remember hearing was the deafening roar from that first mortar round exploding off to my right side, and then I felt the blast as I was consumed by the concussion wave created by the next two rounds slamming into the ground less than twenty feet away, knocking me backward, over the side of the muddy hill. . . .

"Hey, Doc, you okay?"

I looked up to see Corporal Draper kneeling beside me in the mud, and I asked him, "Draper, are you all right?"

"Yeah, I'm okay, but you got blown over the side of the hill. We're safe, right here."

"How long have I been down here?"

"I'd guess about five minutes. Can you move your legs?"

I realized what had happened, and I then became afraid that I might be badly hurt. I looked at my hands, and my right hand was bleeding, but I could move my fingers. I looked down at my feet and I could move them, too. But I saw a patch of blood coming through my right trouser leg, above my knee. When I tried to push myself up off the ground, I felt a sharp pain in my right elbow and another pain coming from my right leg. My ears were still ringing loudly, and I wanted to vomit.

"I think I'm gonna need your help to get back up on the hilltop, Dave."

"We'll stay right here. Those Cobras are comin' back to fire up the gook mortar and machine-gun positions, and when they get done, we'll get that CH-46 back in here and get you out."

Corporal Draper stayed with me on the hilltop until the CH-46 made its landing, and I was helped on board and laid down on a red bench seat. I could see that my right hand and arm and my leg had been bandaged, and when I looked down at my left breast pocket to see if I still was in possession of the waterproof cigarette box which held five injectable morphine Syrettes, I saw that my utility shirt pocket flap was unbuttoned and two of the empty morphine Syrettes were pinned to my collar. . . .

The CH-46 that carried me off Hill 487 landed at the Naval Support Activity hospital in Da Nang. I was carried from the helicopter on a stretcher, brought into the hospital's triage unit, and placed on a gurney to wait before I was examined, X-rayed, and then treated for the removal of pieces of mortar shrapnel from my face, hands, right elbow, right side, and both of my legs. When I returned to the ward, I was sporting a right-angle cast, designed to immobilize my elbow while holding twelve wire stitches in place, and stitches from where the bits of shrapnel were removed. I knew that I was lucky not to have been killed, and I thanked God for it, but as I lay in the comfort of a clean bed, far removed from the danger in the Thuong Duc River valley, I could not help but wonder what was happening out on Hill 487.

– THE LONG WAY HOME –

I HEARD HER FIRST. SHE WAS FAINTLY WHISPERING notes from a light melody that caused me to turn my head slowly in the direction of her song. But still I kept my eyes shut tight, fearing that if I opened them, she and the music would vanish. Then I smelled her; just a wisp at first, getting closer, stronger, and strangely more familiar; a mixing of scents from starch, bleach, and perfume—those strange smells of cleanliness, medicine, and youthful femininity that only the newer nurses brought with them onto our ward. I cracked opened my eyes, trying to focus them on the white glare of a Navy nurse, dressed in a neatly pressed, heavily starched uniform, standing beside my bed, humming her secret song. She gently patted my shoulder to wake me then leaned toward my ear and whispered, "There are three friends waiting outside the ward to see you. Do you think you could handle a little company?"

"Sure, please ask them to come on in."

Captain Centers, 1st Lieutenant Corbett, and 1st Sergeant Jacques walked over to my bed and stared down at me, each one looking as though he was estimating the cost to repair a wrecked car.

"Doc Palmer told us where you were hiding, Doc, so we thought that we'd come over and check on you, before you left us. We brought you some mail, too."

"I really appreciate that, 1st Sergeant. They're sending me to the Naval hospital in Yokosuka tonight, so I guess that this is good-bye. How are things back at the company area and out on Hill 487?"

First Lieutenant Corbett answered my questions.

"Most of the guys in the platoon are still out on Hill 487. They all wanted to come over and see you before you left, Doc, but the war still goes on. They want you to write back and tell us what life is like on a hospital ward surrounded by sweet-smellin', round-eyed women. We'll really miss ya, Doc. You've done a lot for the platoon, and it won't be easy without you. I hope that after we all get back to the States that we can get together again.''

"Yes, sir, that would be great, and I'll keep in touch."

Captain Centers stuck out his hand to say good-bye.

"Doc, I wrote a long letter and told Captain Norm Hisler about what happened. You may want to drop him a line, 'cause I know that he'd like to hear from you, too. The word is out that the company will probably be standing down in less than a month, and our people are getting excited about the possibility of leaving. We've got all your personal gear being boxed up, and it'll eventually meet up with you in Japan. I just wanted to add my two-cents worth, too, and say thank you for all that you've done. Major Dorman wasn't able to make it over here. He's tied up at division, but he wanted me to relay the same from him. We've always been proud of our company corpsmen, and we'll really miss having you in our company. I hope that we'll cross paths again someday. Good luck to ya, Doc, and let us know how you're doing."

It was as difficult for me to say good-bye to these three Marines as it was for them to be there, and knowing that they were my last link to the other Marines in the platoon, I asked them to carry back my message of gratitude to those Marines still out in the field. I knew that they would do that for me. Then, left alone to think about what had happened to me and about the unknown that was going to happen, I was overcome in trying to deal with my emotions. On one hand, I was lucky to be alive and happy to know that I was leaving Vietnam, once and for all. But I was terribly saddened at the thought of not being able to stay with those Marines I had come to know and respect and to not be able to thank each and every one of them for taking care of me. I tried to stay awake and think about what was going to happen next, but the sleeping medication was beginning to take effect.

"Hey, wake up, man. We heard that you were in here, and had to see it for ourselves."

Docs Harrison, Richter, and Duffy had come visiting, with Duffy as the self-appointed spokesman for the group.

"Hey, Norton, we read your chart. You're lucky that you didn't lose your eye, man. All it takes is just one little piece of steel, and you'd be a pirate. That piece of shrapnel that went in above your elbow must have really felt good. The doctor says that all you'll have are a bunch of scars. But better scars than a prosthesis is what they say around here.''

"You guys are havin' a good time with this, aren't you?''

"Nah, we just wanted to cheer you up a little bit. You aren't gonna be here too much longer, so we thought that we'd just stop by and see if there's anything else that we could do for ya.''

"I really appreciate you guys comin' in here and checkin' up on me, but I don't think that there's really anything I need. The service around here has been great. Maybe someday we'll all get stationed together again back at Newport, and we can laugh about all of this.''

"The ward nurse told us not to stay in here too long, and we've got the P.M. shift in a few minutes. Good luck, Norton, and write to us when you get home. You'll be fine.''

That night, I was transported by bus to the Army's 95th Evacuation Hospital for additional processing that would take me to the Naval hospital located at Yokosuka, Japan. Getting to Yokosuka was not to be as easy as we expected. As part of a group of some thirty-odd stretcher and ambulatory patients, we were taken by bus to the flight line at the Da Nang airport. There, a McDonnell Douglas C-9A aeromedical airlift transport jet, commonly referred to as a "Nightingale Jet," was scheduled to take us to Japan. The transport aircraft was capable of carrying a mixture of thirty to forty litter patients and up to forty ambulatory patients in a specially designed interior having special atmospheric and ventilation controls. With an onboard staff of two Air Force flight nurses, and three medical technicians, all patients would be well cared for.

With the seats having been removed, metal-framed racks now divided the interior to accommodate our stretchers, which were stacked four high and five deep on each side of the plane. When the cargo doors were finally shut and the jet began to taxi into position for takeoff, all conversations aboard the plane suddenly ceased, in anticipation of that magical moment and precise second that every single one of us had waited for since our arrival in Da Nang: when the wheels of the plane taking us away from the war lifted and separated us from the soil of Vietnam. Not a word was said during those thirty-four seconds that our plane required to reach its takeoff speed. But when we felt that exact moment of separation, it happened: our plane was filled with those wonderful sounds of happy, laughing, cheering men, who had counted down the months, weeks, days, and hours, clinging with guarded anticipation to this very moment. But once it had passed, and the cold reality of what was really happening to us crept onto our plane, the loud sounds of joy and relief subsided, and were replaced with the softer noises of crying and sobbing men who had faced death and survived, and were now leaving a greater part of themselves behind with their friends, still on the ground.

Sometime during the night flight, I awoke to be reunited with another feeling long lost to the constant summer heat and high humidity of Vietnam—the cold. I felt like I was beginning to freeze to death from the air-conditioning system provided by the airplane, and I was desperately in need of a blanket. With the interior lights turned out, I waited until I caught the movement of one of the nurses silhouetted by a red night-light and then called out to her.

"Excuse me, please. Can I get a blanket?"

"Why sure, honey, we keep forgetting that you guys start to get cold chills when we climb up above twenty-five thousand feet. I'll be right back."

The nameless flight nurse returned with the wool blanket, and as she covered me with it, she said, "I guess that we're not headed for Japan just yet."

"Where are we headed for?"

"The pilot just said that we're being diverted to Clark Air Base. There's a big typhoon headed this way, and now we've been given new flight instructions to wait out the storm at Clark. Have you ever been there before?"

I laughed. "You wouldn't believe me if I told you."

The nurse's information was correct, and upon landing, those of us who were patients were taken by bus to the Air Force hospital to spend the next two days there, while the crew of our airplane also waited for the typhoon to cross the open waters of the Pacific and crash ashore somewhere along the coast of China. When the all-clear signal was given, the wheels of progress began to turn once again, and we were carried back aboard the C-9 for our next destination, the air base at Yokota, Japan. When our C-9 finally touched down at the Yokota Air Base, its cargo doors were opened out into the night air, and we were greeted by a torrential downpour. Under the protection provided us by a waterproof tarpaulin, our group was quickly divided, the Army's wounded going on to Camp Zama, while the Marines and Navy patients were taken by bus to the Naval hospital at Yokosuka. The trip from Yokota to Yokosuka lasted about an hour, and when our bus finally slowed to a stop, the rear doors were opened and anxious hands gripped stretcher handles as, one by one, we were taken into the hospital, placed on staged gurneys, and wheeled to our final destination, Ward B.

"Well I'll be damned, look what the cat dragged in."

I looked at one of the two corpsmen who had brought me onto the ward, and was happy to see the familiar face of HM3 Chuck Vermette, a ward corpsman whom I had been stationed with at the Naval hospital in Newport, Rhode Island.

"Chuck Vermette! Christ, it's great to see someone I know! When did you get here? Sit down, and talk to me."

HM3 Vermette, a native of Vermont, pulled a chair alongside my bed and briefly told me all about his transfer from Newport to Yokosuka and explained what I could expect during my stay in the hospital. As he walked away, returning to his work, he said, "This place is really great, and they'll take good care of you here. You'll see what I'm talking about in the morning. I'll catch ya later."

Completely exhausted from having been constantly awakened by the flight nurses for vital-sign checks of my temperature, respirations, and blood pressure during our flight to Japan, and from our being loaded and unloaded on and off of buses, I needed very little encouragement to fall asleep.

"Eeeeee, tie, eeeeee tie, oooooooooo, eeeeeee tie . . .

"Ooooooh, ooooooh, eeeee tie, oooooooh, eeeeeee tie . . ."

I thought that I was dreaming, but the sounds of a woman's moaning continued to grow louder. I was wide awake and opened my eyes to confirm to my brain that I was still lying in a bed on a hospital ward. Looking to my left and to my right, I could see that I was not the only patient confused and disturbed by what we were hearing.

Again, the woman's orgasmic moaning sounds were repeated, and now there were the added sounds of the many patients beginning to laugh and cheer at what we were hearing. No one on the ward could possibly remain asleep because of the volume of the woman's moaning.

Then suddenly: "Good morning, gentleman, and welcome to the wonderful world of Ward B. Last night, while many of you slept, we had several late arrivals check in with us, and we want to welcome them here to Yokosuka, Japan. My name is Lieutenant Jensen, and this is my ward. It is Sunday morning, for those of you still in a fog, and what you just listened to was the secretly tape-recorded sounds of my former Japanese girlfriend, Meeko, broadcast over my new Pioneer stereo system. The stereo salesman in Tokyo told me that he sold only a high-quality product, and I guess by your reaction to the tape, he wasn't lying. Well, what do you think?''

A great cheer and round of applause began to circulate throughout the thirty-bed ward. Lieutenant Jensen had just achieved a celebrity status with us.

''I've found it much easier to use my stereo system to pass the word along on the ward. If you guys have any popular requests you want to hear, just ask, but no Frank Zappa and no Lawrence Welk.''

He paused.

''Okay then, gentlemen, those of you who are ambulatory patients come on down here and pick up a fresh set of linen. Take a look first, and if the man to the left of you, as you face your rack, cannot get out of his bed, then get a set of linen for him too, and then help him strip and make his rack with the fresh linen. This ain't no hotel, gentlemen, so turn to and get busy. Once that linen is stripped down and tossed into the hamper, get in and use the head before leaving the ward for breakfast. For you new ambulatory guys, the patient's mess is off the ward and down the hall to the right. New patients who cannot walk will get a printed menu card on their tray when their breakfast rolls in. Make your choices, gentlemen, circle them with a pencil, and make sure you write down your correct ward, B, and print your last name. That is all.''

When the lieutenant had finished his welcome-aboard speech, he walked over to his new stereo system and carefully laid an LP record onto the turntable. The first song of the day, and a testimony to the lieutenant's sense of humor, was none other than Little Anthony and the Imperials singing ''Hurt So Bad.'' We knew that we would enjoy life on this hospital ward.

My stay at the Naval hospital opened my eyes to the high quality of individual patient care which the hospital provided. For many of us, the first example of this quality was demonstrated in the hospital mess hall. Breakfast was a confusing choice of eggs in any style, cereals, pancakes, French toast, bacon, ham, sausage, different types of bread, milk, fruits, and assorted pastries. Lunch could be either a trip through the fast-food line, where cheeseburgers, hamburgers, hot dogs, chili, and French fries were the standard fare, or the regular chow line, where there were different types of fresh salad, three types of soup, vegetables, meats, fish, or chicken, and a variety of puddings, ice cream, cakes, and pies for dessert. The dinner meal was equally great. Those patients who had spent months in the bush had only been able to dream of the types of food that were now laid before them, theirs just for the asking. The dumbfounded stares on the faces of new patients, overwhelmed by what they saw, was a constant source of entertainment for the hospital staff, and it made everyone's stay that much more enjoyable.

After two weeks of occupying a bed on Ward B, my cast and stitches were finally removed, and I began a two-week physical therapy program to exercise and strengthen my arm. During my initial examination, I was diagnosed with also having inflammatory bursitis, causing swelling in my hips and knees. A series of cortisone injections to these affected joints and daily visits to a whirlpool bath were ordered. I also received a complete dental examination and had several lively conversations with the hospital's resident psychologist, convincing him that I was probably sane enough to return home and on to full duty. During the remaining two weeks as a fully ambulatory patient, I was put to work in the hospital's archive section, sorting through reams of patient records, and it was there that I came across Lance Corporal Paul Keaveney's medical charts.

I discovered that Keaveney had also been a patient on Ward B. After two weeks on the ward at Yokosuka, he had been transferred to the Naval hospital closest to his home, Key West, Florida, where he would convalesce after having wire stitches removed from both of his arms, right side, and leg. The Navy doctors had decided not to remove either the AK-47 round that had hit him just above his right knee, or the one that had struck deep into his right arm, giving him two souvenirs from the North Vietnamese Army to last his lifetime.

While I was still a patient, I had written a number of letters to my former teammates still back with the platoon, asking them to please tell me what was happening within the company in Vietnam. I soon collected a stack of letters from several of those 1st Force Recon Marines, which detailed what I believe was the last, and the most violent, action that teams from 1st Force Recon were involved in during the entire course of the Vietnam War. The amazing story that their letters told was one of courage, team work, anger, and finally, relief.

In August, as 1st Force Recon Company was preparing to leave Vietnam and return to the States, the decision was made to put as many of the company's teams as possible into the bush in one last effort to locate the North Vietnamese soldiers as they continued to inch their way closer to the city of Da Nang. On August 1st, six teams, code named Impressive, Allbrook, Auditor, Date Palm,

Hansworth, and A La King, were inserted by Marine CH-46 helicopter in the Thuong Duc River valley.

Team Hansworth consisted of eighteen team members, whose mission was to set up a radio-relay site on Hill 510, just north of our old OP site, and to monitor the radio traffic from the other five Force Recon teams as they patrolled below in the valley. After all of the teams were inserted onto Hill 510, they left the relative safety of the hilltop, and silently slipped away in the direction of their respective reconnaissance zones, leaving Team Hansworth in place to defend the small relay site. Then Team Hansworth divided into two groups, with the first team led by a new second lieutenant named Prins, along with fellow team members Lorens, Bradshaw, Hobbs, Falco, Valez, Ski, Clark, and McAndrews, taking the high ground. The second half of the team, led by Corporal Jim Holzmann, with teammates Balmer, Smith, Arnold, Rodreguiez, Baker, Ramsdell, and Oxford held the landing zone. Two Australian SAS Rangers, who were part of a small unit exchange program, had been assigned to accompany Corporal Holzmann's team.

With 2d Lieutenant Prins's team on top of the hill, Corporal Holzmann's team spread out to occupy as much of the landing zone as possible in order to set up a small defensive perimeter one hundred meters below the military crest of the hilltop. Having been the very first team inserted onto the hill, Holzmann's team members had thoroughly searched the area around the LZ, and quickly found two booby traps that had been set up by the NVA. The gooks had dug several holes and manufactured what we commonly referred to as "tomato can" booby traps. Each hole had a charge placed inside a can in such a manner that whoever happened to step on the surface of the camouflaged booby trap would trip a hidden wire, detonating enough high explosive to blow off a man's leg. Fortunately, the insert helicopter's rotor wash had helped blow away some of the leafy camouflage, making the holes fairly easy to locate, and once the team realized that their LZ had been booby-trapped they decided to rig up booby-trap devices of their own for the patrolling NVA. A series of half a dozen claymore mines were rigged up, with the additional emphasis of a white phosphorus grenade being taped to the rear of each of the claymore mines. A number of small illumination grenades were also hidden around their defensive perimeter. Corporal Holzmann's team had also brought along one M-60 machine gun, several cases of hand grenades and illumination grenades, and the old gook mortar, which we had used on the hilltop several months before. By the end of the first day, the Marines on Hill 510 felt that they were ready for whatever the approaching nightfall might bring with it. Oddly, the only event noted during the first night in the defense came from within the team.

The two Australian reconnaissance Rangers, who had been assigned to Corporal Holzmann's team, began to comment openly that they didn't like what they saw and felt uncomfortable with the way things were going. They told Corporal Holzmann that when they went to the bush, it was their practice not to move at night and to shut off their radios after it got dark. Then they would go to sleep and wait for the sun to come up before they turned their radios back on and began moving. Making matters a little worse for the Marines on the hill, the two Aussies finally stopped bitching and went to sleep, only to make so much noise with their loud snoring that Corporal Holzmann had to kick them awake and order them to put on their gas masks to muffle their unwelcome noise. Corporal Holzmann radioed back to the company operations center and described the problem he was having with these two clowns. Early the next morning a CH-46 flew out to the OP, picked up the two SAS troopers, and took them back to Da Nang.

The second day on the OP was spent by both teams digging in. There wasn't any moonlight on the second night in the field, and with the coming of darkness, the evening wind picked up, and with it began a persistent warm summer rain.

Near midnight, the two-man LP that was positioned outside of the lower perimeter reported hearing movement ''in all directions and getting closer and closer'' to their position. Corporal Holzmann radioed this information up the hill to Lieutenant Prins, and told him he was going to throw a couple of CS gas grenades down in the direction of the approaching noise. Lieutenant Prins quickly checked the wind direction and told Corporal Holzmann to wait before he threw his CS grenades, allowing just enough time for the Marines on top of the hill to get on their gas masks. Then he radioed back to Corporal Holzmann to go ahead with the plan.

Corporal Holzmann pulled the pin on his CS grenade and let the spoon fly, igniting the gas grenade before he threw it down at the approaching noise, but the North Vietnamese soldiers had crept up so close to Corporal Holzmann's position that they actually thought he was one of them and that the popping sound of his CS grenade was the NVA signal to commence with their night attack. When they suddenly stood upright, on line, Corporal Holzmann threw his CS grenade straight at them, and that was when all hell broke loose around Hill 510, as an estimated force of more than fifty North Vietnamese soldiers began their assault.

Lance Corporal Michael Hobbs, assigned as one of the two men on the listening post, remembered, "As I sat in my hole, I heard a *click* that sounded like pliers cutting my claymore wire, so I raised up and saw an NVA soldier crawling not more than five feet away from me. He probably felt a tremendous amount of pain as eighteen rounds from my M-16 formed a nice tight pattern in his upper chest."

The first round that the NVA fired at the Marines was a rocket-propelled grenade (RPG), but the NVA had aimed it over Corporal Holzmann's team and up at the top of the hill. The RPG struck Lance Corporal Clark square in the chest, causing a secondary explosion to occur from the detonation of the fragmentation grenades which Clark had attached to his harness. The secondary explosion showered everyone on the hilltop with blood, shrapnel, and pieces of flesh from Clark's body.

One of the attacking NVA soldiers had snagged a trip wire on a hidden illumination-grenade booby trap, and when it went off, it silhouetted another squad of attacking NVA soldiers running straight at Corporal Holzmann's team from the edge of the landing zone. Other NVA soldiers continued to crawl closer, throwing satchel charges and firing their AK-47s, but still none of Corporal Holzmann's team members had yet fired a single round from their weapons, waiting only for the gooks to get close enough to be killed with hand grenades. The NVA fired several more RPGs onto the hilltop, hitting Lieutenant Prins in the neck with a piece of shrapnel and also wounded Lance Corporal Bradshaw.

Immediately after the assault started, Corporal Holzmann had radioed back the team's situation and requested that a "basketball" flare ship and a Spooky gunship come out from Da Nang to lend a helping hand. While the two teams waited for the aircrafts' arrival, Corporal Holzmann and Cpl. Jerry Smith ran over to the old gook mortar, and while Corporal Smith aimed the mortar, Corporal Holzmann dropped high-explosive rounds down the tube. The impacting mortar rounds slowed the momentum of the NVA ground assault, but the NVA still kept shooting at the defenders on the hilltop.

Finally, when the Spooky gunship showed up on station, the pilot radioed down to Corporal Holzmann that he didn't have a very clear picture of exactly where the two recon teams were located, so Corporal Holzmann told Lance Corporal Oxford to break out his strobe light, put it inside of a C-ration box, and make a fast run out to a nearby two-man fighting hole, so that the approaching pilot could pick up the flashing signal of the strobe light from inside the safety of the fighting hole. When the pilot located the flashing of the strobe light he banked his plane in a continuous pylon turn above the hilltop, and provided both teams with the protective fires so urgently requested.

(Later, at the team's debriefing session, Corporal Holzmann said that the sight was nothing short of magnificent, as the Marines watched those six thousand rounds per minute impact "like a lightning bolt dancing on the ground.")

When the basketball flare ship arrived on station, it managed to drop enough flares during its first pass to turn night into day, and that's when the Marines on Hill 510 finally opened up with their M-16 rifles and their M-60 machine gun on the silhouetted and totally exposed NVA.

Even though the NVA soldiers were caught out in the open, they tried to continue their attack up the steep hillside. It was at this moment that Corporal Holzmann saw one of the charging enemy soldiers stop and pick up an unexploded claymore mine that still had a white phosphorus grenade taped to it. Carrying the mine in front of his chest, the NVA soldier ran straight toward the Marines' trench line. Corporal Holzmann simply mashed down the lever of the green hell box, vaporizing the suicidal soldier and showering his NVA comrades with burning chunks of flaming white phosphorus.

Lance Corporal Hobbs added, "Just after that, Corporal Lorens crawled out to my position to bring me Clark's ammo. I had used up all of my ammo and half of Clark's. When Lorens checked on me, he asked if I had set off all of my claymores, and I remembered that I hadn't, so I told him to get behind a nearby tree, and then I squeezed the two hell boxes I had in each hand. I believe that all of my claymores went off because the explosion was very intense, and the sounds of all enemy movement around us stopped."

That was when the attack ended, and the remaining enemy soldiers turned and ran screaming back down the hill for the safety of the jungle.

With the first light of morning, both team leaders ensured that the remaining ammunition was redistributed and then searched the immediate area to determine just who was still alive and who was dead or wounded. Corporal Mike Lorens, the assistant team leader of Lieutenant Prins's team, had immediately taken charge when his lieutenant had gone into shock from being wounded and managed to keep his team together after two of his team members were wounded and one was killed. It was Corporal Holzmann who had to perform the grisly task of collecting what remained of Lance Corporal Clark: his head, right arm, and the boot containing his right foot. He placed his friend's body parts in an empty wooden grenade box, used as a field-expedient casket.

Sometime after sunup, Corporal Holzmann learned that Lance Corporal Hobbs had spent the better part of the previous day with Clark, as the two of them dug their defensive position. Lance Corporal Hobbs told Holzmann, "Clark and I were told to dig a hole for our listening post, just big enough to hold the two of us, and with each shovel full of dirt, we were complaining that Force Recon Marines didn't dig in, or wear flak jackets and helmets. But that small fighting hole saved my life, without a doubt."

Just before the night attack, around 0100, Lance Corporal Hobbs had told Clark to return to the top of the hill to get some sleep. Left alone in the hole, Hobbs had heard movement closing in around him at about the same time that Corporal Holzmann was preparing to throw his CS grenade down near the LZ. Undoubtedly, Lance Corporal Hobbs had also helped stop the ground assault near his area by also throwing out several CS grenades and many of his fragmentation grenades in the direction of the approaching sounds of the NVA. Lance Corporal Hobbs had remained at his position until morning when he felt that it was safe to move, and that was when he discovered just how close the NVA had come to taking his position out.

"At daylight, the area where Clark had been sleeping was covered with dime-sized specks of blood. The ground around our listening post was littered with pieces of enemy clothing, pools of blood, and numerous drag marks. The NVA paid a heavy price for trying to take us out."

While Team Hansworth was occupying Hill 510, Team A La King was operating in an area not more than three clicks away, but they were still fifteen hundred feet below Hill 510, with a river between them and the OP on the hill.

Soon after they entered their recon zone, they had come across a well-used, high-speed trail, and while moving parallel to the trail, they found an NVA mortar position hidden in the grass. They decided to take the enemy mortar, but wanting to make sure that the NVA knew who they were now dealing with, 1st Lieutenant Corbett took out one of the team's "death cards," and wrote on the back of it, "Your mortar was taken by Team A La King, 1st Force Recon Company, USMC," and then put the card inside a pack of cigarettes, which they left behind in the empty NVA mortar position.

The team had just picked up the enemy mortar, and was starting to move away with it, when they heard the voices of several NVA soldiers returning in the direction of the mortar position. The NVA saw the recon team just about the same time that the team saw the approaching NVA, and the ensuing firefight resulted in the NVA point man being killed, while his two buddies turned around and ran like hell back down their trail. Team A La King then spent the following three days hiding from the NVA search teams, which had been sent out in hope of reclaiming their precious mortar. While hiding, the team also had a ringside seat to watch the NVA night attack on Hill 510.

Corporal Draper, a team member of A La King, said, "We knew that there was no way that the company could send out a reaction force to help the guys up on Hill 510 during their firefight, and there wasn't anything that any of the other teams could have done to help them either. Being so far away from the hilltop, we had enough problems with the gooks out looking for us within our own grid square."

The next morning, all of the recon teams were contacted and told to prepare themselves to be extracted from the Thuong Duc River valley. "It was one of the best radio messages any of the team members had heard in a very long time."

When the Marines on the radio-relay site got the word that the extraction birds were coming in, Corporal Holzmann wanted to be absolutely sure that the LZ was as secure as they could make it. While making his security patrol around the perimeter of the landing zone with Lance Corporal Falco, the two Marines made the first of two unique discoveries: in preparation for their night attack, the North Vietnamese had encircled the entire landing zone and placed one-pound blocks of TNT around the edge of the LZ. The enemy explosive charges required that a match be used to ignite the fuse, and the Marines reasoned that the continuous light rain must have helped to prevent the charges from being ignited. The second discovery was credited to Lance Corporal Falco's keen vision; while he and Corporal Holzmann were checking the perimeter, it was Lance Corporal Falco who spotted an NVA soldier hiding in the brush with an AK-47. Falco killed the NVA soldier before he could get off a shot, turned to Corporal Holzmann and said, "Ya know, those little bastards just don't give up, do they?"

One of the Marine CH-46s that came to extract the two teams

from Hill 510 took one team and the two wounded Marines out to the hospital ship USS *Sanctuary*, while the second bird returned to Da Nang with the remaining team members and Lance Corporal Clark's body. During the 1st week of August 1970, the war in Vietnam was finally over for most of the Marines of 1st Force Recon Company.

I also read several letters about a company party which was thrown for the Marines in the company down at the beach near Camp Viking. The Marines enjoyed unlimited steaks and ice-cold beer, and it was a great success, but when the party was over, the last of the Marines climbed on board a six-by truck for the ride back to the company area, and that's when 1st Lieutenant Blotz started to give Gunnery Sergeant Fowler a ration of crap about his having to "stand too close to an enlisted man." Adding to this insult, Lieutenant Blotz said something to the company gunny about him being "only a gunnery sergeant," while he, who had been a prior enlisted Marine, was now "an officer and a gentleman and shouldn't have to ride in the back of a truck in the company of drunken enlisted men." Gunnery Sergeant Fowler, who all of the Marines swore had had "too much to drink," looked Lieutenant Blotz straight in the eye and said, "Blotz, I've known you since you were a goddamned Pfc. You were a little shitbird then, and you're still a little shitbird now. You're outta here, lieutenant." Then he grabbed Blotz, picked him up over his head, and threw him off the back of the moving truck.

Lieutenant J. J. Holly, who was watching all of this happen from the safety of the front seat of the truck, told the driver to "drive on," and Lieutenant Blotz was left squirming in a sand heap by the side of the road. He limped into the company area half an hour later, hoping to find some witnesses to the assault, but no one knew what the sobbing little lieutenant was talking about. I closed my eyes, wishing I could have been there to see it all happen.

Late in August, I finally left Japan, flying from Yokota Air Base to the Seattle-Tacoma airport. I continued eastward, transferring through Chicago's O'Hare airport, and landed sometime close to midnight in Hartford, Connecticut. I was still a hundred miles away from home, but dressed in my Navy uniform, I rented a car and drove along Route 101, to Scituate, Rhode Island, arriving unannounced at my parents' home close to 2:00 A.M. When I knocked on the back door of the old house, there was no immediate answer, but my continuous knocking woke both my parents, who were soon joined downstairs by my grandmother.

Being able to walk into this old farmhouse and to hug my father, mother, and grandmother after having spent the better part of two years away from them was very unsettling. I wanted so desperately to tell them about everything that I had experienced, and they wanted very much to listen. But it was not the right time for me to tell my war stories. This moment was the fulfillment of hundreds of days of hoping—hoping that I could be fortunate enough to return home to be with these people again. The tears flowed freely between the four of us, as I tried to thank them for their kindnesses in having written to me, encouraging me, and letting me know that they were always proud of me and of my teammates. I thanked them for their thoughtfulness in sending "care packages" and photographs to me while I was in Vietnam, but my words soon failed me, and I was silent. The greater part of my happiness that night was in knowing just how fortunate I was to be able to return home in one piece, while so many other men I had known would not be so fortunate. For that I felt sad and guilty, and it would take much time for me to reconcile my feelings before I dared to talk about what I had experienced. It was a part of the times.

After taking advantage of thirty days of leave, I returned to duty at the Navy's medical clinic in the Fargo Building at the 1st Naval District's headquarters, Boston, Massachusetts. It was while stationed there that my life took a new direction, not because of the Navy, but in spite of it.

In 1971, with President Nixon's popular strategy of disengagement growing, and with the process known as "Vietnamization" allowing our remaining military forces to leave Vietnam while strengthening South Vietnam's armed forces, the war dragged toward its predictable conclusion. Still, I watched in absolute amazement as those Naval officers, who had never heard a shot fired in anger, and particularly those bearded and mustached lawyers, doctors, and supply-types, who had slithered into the United States Navy through the cracks of Admiral Zumwalt's "Human Relations Force," left the Fargo Building each day during their lunch hour and returned later, boasting of having "demonstrated in uniform" with the protesters against the war in Vietnam, which was a routine occurrence on the historic Boston Common.

One day, a Marine captain, John Dunn, who happened to have personal business in the Fargo Building, approached me in the hallway, and seeing that we each wore the gold jump wings, we began to talk about our experiences with Marine reconnaissance units in Vietnam. Captain Dunn mentioned that he knew where

Maj. Alex Lee was stationed, deep within the bowels of Headquarters Marine Corps, in Washington, D.C., and gave me the telephone number where I could reach my former commanding officer. The result of that telephone conversation with Major Lee was the beginning of a professional and personal friendship that has lasted twenty-three years. He encouraged me to return to college and to consider a future as an officer in the Marine Corps. I did.

I left the ranks of the United States Navy on 14 July 1972, after being granted admission to the College of Charleston in South Carolina. Two days after being handed my Certificate of Honorable Discharge from the ranks of the United States Navy, I raised my right hand and was sworn into the United States Marine Corps's Platoon Leader's Course (PLC) program, to be commissioned a 2d lieutenant of Marines, in November 1974, by Col. Donald Q. Layne, USMC. Capt. Clovis C. "Bucky" Coffman, the former operations officer of 3rd Force Reconnaissance Company, and 1st Lt. Craig M. Arnold, USMC, a lifelong friend, helped to pin the brass bars of a second lieutenant on my Marine dress-blue uniform.

I have spent the past eighteen years as a Marine Corps infantry officer, and my experiences during those years shall be the subjects of many books to come.

—————— POSTSCRIPT ——————

THE MARINES THAT I SERVED WITH IN 3D FORCE RECONNAISSANCE COMPANY in 1969 and 1st Force Reconnaissance Company in 1970 rightfully deserve their place in the fascinating history of the United States Marine Corps. These men were dependable, honest, caring, and brave individuals, who went about their work with a degree of spirit and discipline that is difficult to explain to those who have never been in combat, but easily understood by those who have. These were common threads that continue, to this day, to be woven into the fabric that makes up a Force Recon Marine. "Daring greatly," as Lt. Col. Alex Lee observed in his foreword to this book, was, to us, nothing more than just doing our job.

Since the publication of *Inside Force Recon* and *Force Recon Diary, 1969*, many people, now aware of the rigid individual requirements demanded of reconnaissance Marines, have asked, "Where do these types of men come from, and what is the selection process like for those who volunteer for this type of military training?"

The answer to these two questions is in this Marine Corps definition:

Selection of Personnel:

a. Individual qualifications. Since the training program of reconnaissance Marines is geared to the development of combat-ready reconnaissance teams, the effectiveness of the program depends a great deal upon the care exercised in the selection of personnel for initial assignment and upon subsequent formation of reconnaissance teams. Screening is essentially the same as that used for classification and assignment of all Marines: finding the Marine who fits the billet or, failing that, finding the Marine who meets the requirement for training in the billet. Normally the number of Marines answering a request for volunteers from local Fleet Marine Force units should exceed the number of vacancies. This does not necessarily simplify the selection problem since approximately one in fifteen Marines will be able to meet the individual qualifications and will have sufficient obligated service time remaining to warrant formal school training. Maturity, experience, and motivation are the principal qualities which the screening board is looking for, but the primary considerations in selection are the physical and medical qualifications and the mental screening conducted by the recon unit itself.

b. Physical requirements. Physical requirements embrace those strength, endurance, and swimming prerequisites established by the Army for parachute training and by the Department of the Navy for SCUBA diving training. Physical requirements for such duty are rigid and will not be waived.

c. Medical requirements. Medical requirements established by the separate Departments for parachute and SCUBA training are usually rigid, but may be waived by the appropriate Department in certain cases. For example, a Marine who is otherwise qualified, but who just misses meeting the minimum eyesight, weight, or height requirements, may be waived. Medical qualifications for assignments are determined by a medical officer.

d. Mental requirements. Mental suitability is principally a matter of attitude, temperament, and the ability to make sound decisions. No simple test has been developed that is capable of assessing individual performance in a strange environment under arduous circumstances. Careful selection prior to assignment, however, will reduce the number of transfers after assignments due to temperamental unsuitability. Similarly, physical testing can be done to establish a great deal about the motivation of a volunteer, as well as determine his physical condition. During the interview and physical testing process, the principal concern is the maturity, resourcefulness, experience, and motivation of the volunteer.

APPENDIX A

Navy Cross

AYERS, DARRELL E.

Citation: For extraordinary heroism while serving as a Platoon Sergeant with the First Force Reconnaissance Company, First Marine Division in connection with combat operations against the enemy in the Republic of Vietnam. On 19 March 1970, Sergeant Ayers was leading a seven-man patrol on a mission to locate primary enemy infiltration routes in the western section of Quang Nam Province. Two days previously, the aircraft by which the team had been helilifted into the territory had come under intense hostile fire as the Marines were disembarking and, in the intervening period, Sergeant Ayers had skillfully avoided any contact which would compromise his mission. As the Marines approached a small river which was spanned by a bamboo bridge, Sergeant Ayers, realizing the danger of encountering the enemy at this position, moved ahead of the point man and, accompanied by another Marine, reconnoitered the approach to the river. When the two men halted to analyze the surrounding terrain, they suddenly came under a heavy volume of automatic weapons fire from enemy soldiers concealed nearby. In an effort to shield his comrade, Sergeant Ayers placed himself between the fusillade of hostile fire and his companion. Mortally wounded moments thereafter, Sergeant Ayers, by his valiant and selfless efforts, was directly responsible for saving the life of a fellow Marine. His heroic actions were in keeping with the highest traditions of the Marine Corps and of the United States Naval Service.

CROCKETT, JOSEPH R., JR.

Citation: For extraordinary heroism while serving as a team leader with First Force Reconnaissance Company. First Reconnaissance Battalion, First Marine Division, in connection with operations against the enemy in the Republic of Vietnam. On 23 April 1969, Sergeant Crockett's team was clandestinely observing a major North Vietnamese Army supply route west of An Hoa in Quang Nam Province when the Marines came under a ground assault by an estimated hostile platoon supported by a heavy volume of automatic weapons fire, and in the initial moments of the attack sustained several casualties. Sergeant Crockett seized a grenade launcher from one of his wounded men and moved across fifty meters of exposed terrain to deliver fire upon the enemy. As a group of North Vietnamese soldiers approached his team's defensive perimeter, he quickly killed one and wounded four others; then, having exhausted his ammunition, utilized a radio to adjust supporting artillery fire to within fifty meters of his men. He then ran from one Marine position to another gathering grenades, which he hurled at the hostile soldiers, forcing them to regroup and withdraw. As the enemy soldiers retreated they lighted several brush fires that rapidly spread toward the team's emplacement. Unable to extinguish the flames with his jacket, Sergeant Crockett repeatedly assisted in moving his injured Marines to safety, stopping only to render first aid and deliver suppressive fire upon the North Vietnamese force. In order to expedite evacuation of his critically injured men, he tied an air panel to his back and boldly moved into an open clearing where he stood in full view of the enemy to mark the landing zone for the helicopters and gunships as they arrived on station. Although nearly exhausted, Sergeant Crockett refused to be extracted, and assisted in a search of the vicinity. By his courage, aggressive fighting spirit, and selfless devotion to duty in the face of grave personal danger, Sergeant Crockett upheld the highest traditions of the Marine Corps and the United States Naval Service.

Silver Star

HOLZMANN, JAMES C.

Citation: For conspicuous gallantry and intrepidity in action while serving with the First Force Reconnaissance Company, First Marine Division (Rein), in connection with combat operations against the enemy in the Republic of Vietnam. Assigned as Platoon Sergeant, First Lieutenant Holzmann, then a Corporal, was placed in charge of one of two reconnaissance teams located on a prominent hill north of Da Nang. For several days, he assisted the company commander in preparing defensive positions and gathering intelligence since there was mounting evidence of enemy movement and an impending attack on this strategic position. Shortly after midnight on 4 August 1970, the enemy threw a grenade into his trench, killing one Marine and severely wounding the platoon commander. Quickly assessing the situation, First Lieutenant Holzmann took charge of his men and skillfully directed the counterattack. Dispersing his men widely along the densely wooded hilltop, he deceived the encircling enemy as to the size of his unit, which forced them to attack from a more distant location. On one occasion, he bravely exposed himself to intensive automatic rifle fire and rushed forward to kill an enemy sapper and detonate the deadly Claymore mine intended to kill and maim the Marines. Personally directing the team's firepower, and in extreme personal danger from over 15 satchel charges which exploded as he dashed among the defensive outposts, he displayed exemplary leadership in the face of overwhelming odds. The keen abilities he displayed were visible in the decisive victory, when dawn revealed the devastation they had wrought on a numerically superior, well-equipped enemy force. His intrepid fighting spirit inspired all who observed him and contributed significantly to the accomplishment of his unit's mission. By his courage, dynamic leadership, and unwavering devotion to duty at great personal risk, First Lieutenant Holzmann upheld the highest traditions of the Marine Corps and of the United States Naval Service.

Bronze Star

HOBBS, MICHAEL A.

Citation: For meritorious service in connection with combat operations against the enemy in the Republic of Vietnam while serving as a Reconnaissance Scout with the First Force Reconnaissance Company, First Reconnaissance Battalion, First Marine Division from 2 February 1970 to 31 January 1971. Throughout this period, Corporal Hobbs performed his duties in an exemplary and highly professional manner. Displaying exceptional leadership, he expeditiously accomplished all assigned tasks, thus providing his company with outstanding support. Participating in numerous long-range reconnaissance patrols deep within enemy-controlled territory, he repeatedly distinguished himself by his courage and composure under fire as he fearlessly moved to dangerously exposed vantage points to deliver fire at the enemy. Particularly noteworthy were his actions on the night of 4 August 1970 when his team came under a vicious enemy attack while occupying a radio relay site in a remote area of Quang Nam Province. From his listening post well forward of the Marine position, Corporal Hobbs, whose companion had been mortally wounded at the outset of the engagement, waged a lone and vigorous defense of the relay site. For five hours, until the arrival of a reaction force, he valiantly hurled hand grenades and fired his rifle in all directions around his fighting hole in a successful effort to prevent the numerically superior North Vietnamese Army force from overrunning the small Marine unit. Investigation of the area the following morning revealed signs of numerous enemy casualties. Corporal Hobbs's professionalism, aggressive fighting spirit, and steadfast devotion to duty throughout his tour in the Republic of Vietnam contributed significantly to the accomplishment of his command's mission and were in keeping with the highest traditions of the Marine Corps and of the United States Naval Service.

The Combat Distinguishing Device is authorized.

APPENDIX B

Force Recon Association

"Link Forever Those Who Served Together"

Membership Criteria as stated in the Association bylaws

1. TYPES OF MEMBERSHIP

   a. Regular. All officers and enlisted men of the Armed Forces of the United States of America or her Allies who are now serving, or who have served with, any Force Reconnaissance Company, or Deep Reconnaissance Platoon, Regular or Reserve, or personnel who served in Amphibious Reconnaissance units between 1943 and 1957.

   b. Associate. Civilians and veterans of the U.S. Armed Forces and Allies who did not serve with a Force Reconnaissance Company, but who made a significant development in or advancement to operational procedures or techniques inherent in Force Reconnaissance operations, or who made a valuable and unique contribution to a Force Reconnaissance Company or to the Force Recon Association.

Force Recon Association
993 South Santa Fe Avenue, Suite C
Vista, California 92083

(Annual Dues: $15.00)   (619) 439-6888

- -

ALPHA RECON ASSOCIATION
C/O Membership Director
62 Mountain Ave.
Pompton Plains, NJ 07444

(Annual Dues $15.00)   (201) 831-0651

3d Recon Battalion Association
15642 Heywood Way
Apple Valley, MN 55124

APPENDIX C

What are they doing now?

I thought that it might be of interest to the readers' of both "Force Recon Diaries" to briefly mention what some of the individual Marines, whom I was privileged to serve with in both 3d Force and 1st Force Recon Companies, during 1969 and 1970, are doing twenty-one years later. Too often and unfairly, the public's impression of the Vietnam Era veteran is portrayed as some long lost, dirty-looking, bearded soul, wearing a black baseball cap, a dirty field jacket and seated behind an old card table strategically placed in front of the local supermarket, with an empty ammunition can in his lap, looking for a handout, but certainly not for work. Unfortunately, these types of individuals do exist, but, truly, they are not indicative of that type of individual that I knew and respected as members of any Marine Force Reconnaissance Company. The personal pride, integrity, and character of a Force Reconnaissance Marine would not allow for it.

Lieutenant Colonel Alex Lee, USMC (Retired)
Commanding Officer, 3d Force Recon Company, 1969–1970
Entrepreneur and Writer

Lieutenant Colonel C.C. "Bucky" Coffman, Jr., USMC (Retired)
Operations Officer, 3d Force Recon Company, 1969–1970
Educator

Colonel Wayne Morris, USMC
Platoon Leader, 3d Force Recon Company, 1969–1970
Commanding Officer
Force Service Support Schools
Camp Lejeune, North Carolina

Lieutenant Colonel Robert Hinsley, USMC (Retired)
Platoon Leader, 3d Force Recon Company, 1969–1970
6815 Landing Way North
Apt. 202
Memphis, Tenn. 38115

Sergeant Major L. C. Henderson, USMC (Retired)
1st Sergeant, 3d Force Recon Company, 1969–1970
Law Enforcement Officer

Mr. Paul Keaveney
M-79 "Blooper Man," 3d Force Recon Company, 1969–1970
Artist and Vice President, Coronado Paint Corporation

Mr. Guillermo "Hi Ho" Silva
Team member, 3d Force Recon Company, 1969–1970
General Motors Corporation

Wallace J. "Nic" Murray
Team member, 3d Force Recon Company, 1969–1970
Correctional Officer

Gunnery Sergeant Dan P. Williams
Platoon Sergeant, 3d Force Recon Company, 1969–1970
Security Chief

1st Sergeant "Sonny" Cannon
Team leader, 3d Force Recon Company, 1969–1970
U.S. Army
Fort Riley, Kansas

Donald J. Mahkewa
Team leader, 3d Force and 1st Force Recon Company, 1969–1970
Construction Company

Steve Parrish
Hospital Corpsman, 3d Force Recon Company, 1969
Physician's Assistant, U.S. Navy

Master Gunnery Sergeant Jim Tate, USMC (Retired)
Logistics Chief, 3d Force Recon Company, 1969–1970
Morale, Welfare, Recreation Representative
Camp Pendleton, California

1st Sergeant Byron Tapp, USMC
(Retired)
Platoon Sergeant, 3d Force Recon
Company, 1969–1970
Landscaper

Sergeant Major William "Rip" Collins, USMC (Retired)
Gunnery Sergeant, 3d Force Recon
Company, 1969–1970
Security Chief, Boeing Corp.

Mr. Mike "The Big M" Wills
Team member, 3d Force Recon
Company, 1969–1970
Lumberman

Mr. Roger L. "Frogman" Hoak
Team member, 3d Force Recon
Company 1969–1970
General Contractor

Mr. David Draper
Team member, 3d and 1st Force Recon Company, 1969–1970
Tax Board

Mr. Bill Moss
Team leader, 3d Force Recon Company, 1969–1970
Anaheim Police Officer

Mr. Richard A. Jenkins
Team leader, 3d Force Recon Company, 1969–1970
School Administrator

Mr. Orlando "Speedy" Gonzales
Team member, 3d Force Recon
Company, 1969–1970
Police Investigator

Colonel J. J. Holly, USMC
Operations Officer, 1st Force Recon
Company, 1969–1970
G-3 FSSG
Camp Pendleton, California

Sergeant Major M. J. Jacques,
USMC (Retired)
1st Sergeant, 1st Force Recon Company, 1970
Construction Contractor

1st Sergeant Charles O. "Bud"
Fowler, III, USMC (Retired)
Company Gunnery/Communication
Chief, 1st Force Recon, 1969–1970
Vice President Hamburg & Hillborn
Corporation

Mr. Michael C. Hodgins
Team Leader, 1st Recon Battalion,
1969–1970
Senior Investment Broker, A. G.
Edwards & Sons, Inc.

Lieutenant Colonel D. L. Scanlon,
USMC
Team member, 1st Force Recon
Company, 1969–1970
ACS/G-1
MCRD
San Diego, California

Mr. Jim Holzmann
Team leader, 1st Force Recon Company, 1969–1970
Attorney

Mike Hobbs
Team member, 1st Force Recon
Company, 1969–1970
USN Seabee

Colonel Sans Robnick, USMC
Platoon leader, 1st Force Recon
Company, 1969–1970
Commanding Officer Marine Barracks, Subic Bay, R.P.I.

Mr. John Baker
Platoon leader, 1st Force Recon
Company, 1969–1970
Football Coach

ABOUT THE AUTHOR

Bruce H. Norton, raised in North Scituate, Rhode Island, enlisted in the United States Navy in 1968 and served as a hospital corpsman at the Naval Hospital, Newport, Rhode Island, and with both 3d Force and 1st Force Reconnaissance Companies in combat in Vietnam from 1969 to 1970. Following an honorable discharge from the United States Navy in 1972, he attended the College of Charleston in South Carolina and received a B.A. in history. He was commissioned a Marine second lieutenant in 1974. Now a major, he has served as an infantry platoon leader, reconnaissance platoon leader, infantry company commander, battalion executive, and operations officer. In 1986–1988, he was the first operations officer for the Marine Corps' Maritime Prepositioned Shipping Program (MPS) at Blount Island, Florida. Major Norton is currently assigned as an operations officer at the Marine Corps Recruit Depot, San Diego, California.